"When I set out to write this book, my purpose was to communicate my experience to those who might benefit directly, especially people fighting paralysis or other serious health problems. But along the way I realized that I've had the opportunity to work through things that are much bigger than just healing my body. I've been able to tap into a force that is there for everyone, whatever the problem."

"I had to break my neck to learn this, but you don't have to. The lesson is easy: We are not bodies with spirits but spirits with bodies."

—from *My Soul Purpose*

"IN... ...ABLY
LIG... ...nt by
one... ...from
the... ...r pre-
dict... ...han a
'tal... ...read-
er... ...f von
Bel...

...*views*

"A G... ...arish
and... ...erent
boo... ...worst
thing... ...happen to you except death."

—*Entertainment Weekly*

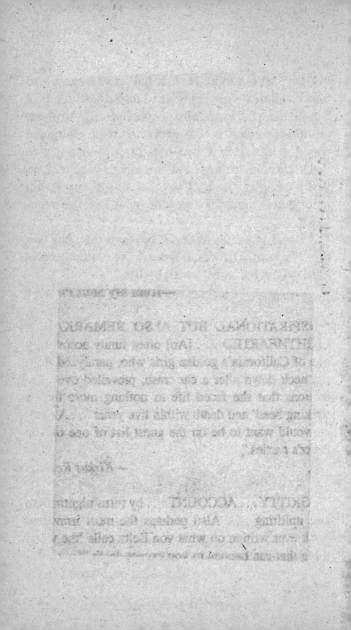

My Soul Purpose

LIVING, LEARNING, AND HEALING

Heidi von Beltz
with Peter Copeland

St. Martin's Paperbacks

First published in the United States by Random House, Inc., New York, and simultaneously in Canada by Random House of Canada Limited, Toronto.

Grateful acknowledgement is made to TIME magazine for permission to reprint an excerpt from "Welcome to Cyberspace" by Phillip Elme-DeWitt. Copyright © 1995 TIME Inc. Reprinted by permission.

MY SOUL PURPOSE

ISBN: 0-312-96431-5

Printed in the United States of America

Random House hardcover edition published 1996
St. Martin's Paperbacks edition/February 1998

St. Martin's Paperbacks are published by St. Martin's Press, 175 Fifth Avenue, New York, NY 10010.

10 9 8 7 6 5 4 3 2 1

To Mom and Brad, who gave me life not once but
twice. To Joanna, who is not only the best friend a
girl could have, but the universe as well. To my
Saint Bernard, Mozart, who taught me the greatest
lesson of all: to listen to my heart.

And to "My Way" . . . without whom this ded-
ication would be meaningless.

"We do not cure the body with the body, we cure the body with the mind."

—PLATO

"If anyone consults a doctor after the age of thirty, he is a fool, since by that time everyone should know how to regulate his life properly."

—TIBERIUS

CONTENTS

INTRODUCTION

I'm the happiest person I know. My life is moving fast in the direction I choose. I have a wonderful family, terrific friends, and a busy schedule. I work hard, I play hard, and I always, always, have a good time.

Some people might find this hard to believe, considering what happened to me on a Hollywood movie set one hot summer day, just a few months before my twenty-fifth birthday. My career as an actress was rocketing along, until the flimsy stunt car I was riding in crashed head-on into a van.

I don't use the word accident. Maybe it's vanity, but I can't believe it was an accident. I had run into obstacles before, and I had changed course, or slowed down or sped up, but this looked like the end of the road. My doctors said that I wouldn't live until Christmas, and that during the few miserable, painful months before I died, I would never move again, not a finger or a toe. That was in 1980.

I never bought into their dismal prognosis, nor did my parents or my friends. I promised everyone I was going to get better and get up, and they never doubted me.

My story is about beating the odds, triumphing over adversity. But that's everyone's story. I have a burden, but so does everyone, whether it's physical or emotional or financial or whatever. I have what people call a "disability," but in some sense everyone does. Frankly, if it had been up to me, I would have picked one a little less extreme, but no one asked. The important thing to remember is you are only as disabled as you think you are.

When I set out to write this book, my purpose was to communicate my experience to those who might benefit directly, especially people fighting paralysis or other serious health problems. But along the way I realized that I've had the opportunity to work through things that are much bigger than just healing my body. I've been able to tap into a force that is there for everyone, whatever the problem.

I discovered the power of spirit. I say "discovered" because it's always been there inside me; all I had to do was accept it. As my mom says, the house is wired for electricity, but everybody's got to plug in their own lamp.

I had to break my neck to learn this, but you don't have to. The lesson is easy: We are not bodies with spirits but spirits with bodies.

I've never accepted my injury as a done deal because I know who's the boss: me. I am in control of my destiny. I've been given a big challenge, but I'm proud to say I'm big enough to handle it. A lot of people have triumphed over things much worse. The way I see it, I got a second chance at life. That's a gift, not a curse.

I've got much more to accomplish on this earth. And you know what? It's a blast.

My Soul Purpose

Chapter 1

CANNONBALL CRASH

A fiery red sun announced the beginning of another hot, clear Nevada day. I started work early, stepping into a state trooper's uniform, strapping on knee pads, and pulling myself into a solid, four-door police cruiser with a very capable engine. The car was equipped with a special five-point safety harness that I carefully fastened, snug but not so tight that I couldn't work the wheel. I felt good, confident, as I rumbled out onto the empty stretch of highway. I was only about twenty-five minutes from Las Vegas, but there was nothing in sight except sun-baked desert, which was getting hotter by the second. Heat waves rippled the road ahead of me, making it look like I was driving out onto a ribbon of black water carved into the sand. There was a walkie-talkie sitting on the empty passenger seat beside me, and I listened to crackly voices barking orders and making last-minute adjustments. I took my position and waited for the signal. A voice came over the walkie-talkie: "Cameras rolling!"

We were shooting *The Cannonball Run* with Burt Reynolds and Farrah Fawcett, whose not-so-secret offscreen romance was much more entertaining than the romance on film. Burt was charming and fun, considerate of everyone and chivalrous to the few women on the set, including me. But his most special charms were reserved for Farrah, who was the perfect match to Burt's tough-guy image: She was sweet, innocent, and delicate, with perfect skin, a perfect smile, perfect teeth, and that famous leonine hair. When I met Burt, he spoke fondly of my dad from their acting days together at Universal Studios. Like most of the people I was meeting in the business, Burt was surprised that the young-looking Brad von Beltz had such a "big girl" for a daughter.

The movie's plot, such as it is, centers on a coast-to-coast auto race called the Cannonball Run. There are no rules, and the object is to cross the finish line first, by whatever means necessary. Basically the movie is a cross-country string of gags mixed with chase scenes and send-ups of other movies. Burt and Dom De Luise play two characters who run the race posing as ambulance drivers. Dean Martin and Sammy Davis, Jr., are a team of racers dressed as priests, and Roger Moore plays Roger Moore, which is supposed to be a spoof of the James Bond movies. He has the Bond car and the Bond look, but he's just plain old Roger Moore, not the suave and daring 007, and none of his secret gadgets work the way they are supposed to.

The best parts of *Cannonball* are the spectacular stunts, and that's where I came in. I was an aspiring actress and director, but I needed some regular work to pay the rent, so I accepted a job on *Cannonball* as a "stuntgirl," doubling for the female stars and doing their driving when it was risky. Few of my scenes were very demanding, and mostly I appeared as a passenger or as part of crowd scenes, but when we moved to a location in Las Vegas, Bobby Bass, the stunt coordinator and my current boyfriend, had good news. He needed a woman to do some high-speed driving, and he wanted me to try. He took me to an isolated stretch of road in the desert, and we practiced until I could do the stunt with my eyes closed. I was nervous about doing it on camera with all my friends on the set watching, especially on location where time is money and every shot has to count, but soon I had the stunt cold and I knew I was ready.

I had done some fancy driving on another picture, *Smokey and the Bandit II*, with the same director and stunt coordinator, so they knew I could drive. In one scene I played a Canadian Mountie trying to cut off the bandit (Burt) in a rocky canyon along the border. We did high-speed chases with long strings of police cars, which was tricky because when the first car was going thirty-five miles per hour, the end car had to go twice as fast to keep up. In another scene I wove a police cruiser in and out of a line of eighteen-wheelers roaring down a highway, doing near misses and cutting back and forth. The driving was a thrill, and the more I learned, the more I enjoyed it.

My claim to fame on *Smokey*, at least among the stuntmen, was for saving a shot that almost went wrong. Legendary stuntman Dick Ziker was supposed to drive full speed off a ramp and soar to a spectacular crash landing on top of a row of cars. I was below the ramp driving one of the waiting cars, engine revving and my hands on the wheel. Looking up through the windshield at Dick flying toward us, I realized he was going too fast and was sailing right over the tops of our cars. While he was still in the air, I threw the tail of my car underneath his trajectory so he smashed into my trunk, crumpling my car and bouncing me like a billiard ball out of the shot. Everyone cheered, and I was hero for a day.

I never thought about what I was doing before I spun the car, or considered that it might be dangerous. I knew we needed to save the shot, and that was what mattered; instinct took over, and I was in pure, perfect control. My body and my mind were one, and there was no time to think, "I've got to do this, and then do that and turn here." It was a glorious and exhilarating feeling, the same kind of rush that pulled me toward professional skiing, running fast, playing serious tennis, and in every way possible, living in motion. I wasn't a daredevil, because I didn't take unnecessary risks, but I worked hard on the stunts and practiced them carefully. To me, this was a highly skilled profession, not a game.

So, on June 25, 1980, when Bobby asked me to do some real driving on *Cannonball*, I was ready. The scene was this: Two female race contestants driving a Lamborghini are lusciously squeezed into skin-tight jumpsuits with zippers down the front. Every time they're stopped by the police for speeding, they lower the zippers a bit to show a few inches of heaving bosom. In this scene, a highway patrol car is racing along from the opposite direction when the trooper spots the Lamborghini, slams on the brakes, fishtails around 180 degrees, and pulls them over. The camera cuts to the women in the car unzipping their suits, planning to wiggle their way out of another ticket. Then the camera cuts to show the face of the approaching police officer: Valerie Perrine, who of course has her own heaving bosom and is unimpressed by theirs. I was going to drive the police car for the spin, and long shots of me driving would be edited with close-ups of Valerie to create the illusion that she was driving the entire time.

The cameras were rolling, the police-car engine was idling fast, and I could feel my heart pounding beneath the safety harness strapped tight across my chest. I stared straight ahead along the empty desert highway, waiting for the signal. The radio squawked, and I heard the voice of director Hal Needham: "Action!"

I punched the accelerator hard down to the floorboard, the powerful engine slammed me back into the seat, and I gripped the shimmying wheel with arms straight. Twenty, thirty, fifty, sixty miles per hour, the heavy car hurtled forward, bearing down on the spot marked on the road where I was going to flip it around 180 degrees. The desert tore by me on either side, but I was focused only on the road ahead of me. I saw it coming, my eyes locked on the target. *Now!* I slammed my left foot onto the parking brake, clicking it all the way down. I felt myself flying forward and straining against the safety harness as the tires screeched and the car began to skid. I jerked the wheel when the back end started to slip out to my right. Hold on. Hold on. I spun the wheel back in the other direction to control the skid, but the car kept sliding like I was driving on ice. Pull it back, pull it back, turn into the skid. The tires bit, the brakes held, and the car swayed to a heavy stop, facing the opposite direction. I sat in silence, my head buzzing and my heart pounding. A voice squawked over the radio: "All right, Heidi! It's a print!"

• • •

I smiled and watched for the sign from Bobby. Cut. I had done my part, and Valerie would finish the scene.

I was proud of myself, and my friends on the set congratulated me, but to the veteran stuntmen it was just another 180. They measure the difficulty of a stunt by the size of the adjustment, meaning the extra pay. This stunt was a small adjustment, but it felt pretty good to me. I was giddy and pumped up when I walked over to the lunch table for a sandwich. I didn't have anything else to do that day, but I didn't want to waste a fine adrenaline rush by going back to the hotel by myself. What I liked to do during down time was to look over the shoulders of the camera crews and the director, trying to learn as much about the business as I could. I studied how they shot scenes and tried to imagine how I would shoot them myself the day I became a director. I saw Bobby talking to some of the crew members and walked over to see if he had any other assignments for me.

I grew up in the movie business, and from the time I was a little girl reciting lines to help my actor dad rehearse, I was intoxicated by Hollywood. I loved the idea of telling stories, expressing so many varied emotions and depicting all the dramas of life. As a child I was a regular on the sets, watching my dad make just about every television western ever produced during the 1950s and '60s, as well as a host of movies. People like James Caan and Steve McQueen weren't "stars"—they were family friends, people who helped me with my homework.

I convinced my dad, Brad, to visit me for a few days while we were shooting *Cannonball* on location, and everyone talked him into doing a scene just for fun. I got such a kick out of watching his reunion with so many old friends and colleagues. The obvious respect they showed Brad made me appreciate even more his years of hard work, something I was beginning to understand better now that I was following in his footsteps.

Brad got a big grin on his face when he spotted Dean Martin on the *Cannonball* set. "Hey, Dean," Brad said. "Did you ever go back to Jericho?"

Dean did a comic double take.

"Remember we had that rough night there," Brad said.

"Brad!" Dean said. "*A Rough Night in Jericho!* Now, that was a forgettable picture! How've you been?"

Brad pulled me over and proudly introduced me to Dean. "Oh, my God!" Dean growled. "Is that a gorgeous thing or what?"

Then Sammy Davis, Jr., chimed in something about my looks, sauntering over to get a better look at Brad's little girl. I towered over Sammy and could only stand there laughing as he leeringly eyed me up and down, mostly up, because he was so short. Brad was happy to show me off, but I'm not sure he would have left me alone in the same room with those two.

I started out on television shows such as *Charlie's Angels*, in which I had costar billing, and did a few movies. When I got *Cannonball* I was considering an offer to go under contract at Universal Studios, which was how my dad had begun a long acting career. Film agents Ron Rifkin and Nicole David wanted to sign me, which was alluring because then I wouldn't be tied to a single studio. Another agent, Nina Blanchard, wanted me to model for her, and that also sounded like a good opportunity. I had modeled since I was a baby, and it was good, easy money. Nina promised I'd have no shortage of work, and she'd already signed my best friend, an up-and-comer named Melanie Griffith.

I always got something at casting calls because I was tall, athletic, and attractive. I was a professional skier as well, which helped me get acting and stunt jobs. In one episode of *The Hardy Boys*, for example, I led a high-speed chase down a mountain. I wasn't content with small parts, though, and I studied acting with the top teachers, including Lee Strasberg, Uta Hagen, and Stella Adler, with every intention of making it to the big time. My parents were proud of me, although they were not thrilled about stunt work. They worried that it would hurt my acting career in caste-conscious Hollywood, and my dad also knew it was dangerous. He had been on the set when a stuntman and great rodeo star named Ross Dollarhide was killed doing a horse stunt, and he never forgot that some people in Hollywood regard stuntpeople as tough but expendable.

"Hey, Bobby," I asked the stunt coordinator. "Don't you have anything for me?"

"Not really," he said. "I've just got this one little thing to do, and then we're done for the day. You had a good day. Why don't you just go back to the hotel and take it easy, go sit by the pool or hang out. I can get an extra to do this."

"Nah," I said. "Lemme do it. I just want to do something. I'd rather get the adjustment than some extra. How much is it?"

"A couple hundred bucks."

"It's mine," I said, always preferring to do something rather than nothing.

"Okay," he said. "Stick around here for a while, and I'll come by and pick you up when we're ready. We've got to get the car ready, but it won't take long."

Lunch was at a crowded table next to the trailers housing the dressing rooms and equipment, the hub of a gypsy camp set up each day in the desert for the filming. People were lounging in the sun, talking and playing cards. Typically on location there are long periods of waiting broken up by frantic action to complete shots while the light is good. *Cannonball* was no exception. The closer the sun came to setting, the more frustrated and tense everyone became and the more we heard shouts of, "Let's go, people! We're losing our light! We're burning daylight!"

I always got up before the sun to exercise. I had been teaching aerobics and was in such good shape that it was hard not to work out; my body craved it. After running and exercising, I did my scenes and then went to work on what I considered to be my true job: a movie apprenticeship. I loved the idea of attending a real-life film school. I already had helped produce one film, and I expected to do many more.

The film was with Noel Marshall, who had produced *The Exorcist* and many other excellent films. Noel, who was married to

Melanie's mom, Tippi Hedren, started my education about directing and film editing when he named me second assistant director on *Roar*, a movie about African lions threatened by poachers. The film was a family affair, starring Noel's three sons, Tippi, and Melanie. Tippi had become a star in Alfred Hitchcock's *The Birds*. Hitchcock was crazy about Tippi, and his obsession with his blond ice goddess made for some bizarre moments for Melanie, who was only about eight years old when her mom was shooting *The Birds*. Melanie told me that for her birthday that year Hitchcock sent her a little doll shaped like her mother—in a coffin.

Melanie and I had shared a beach house in Malibu. Having grown up in show business, we both found it exciting but could keep it in perspective. Melanie was pretty in a coltish sort of way, with long legs that stretched on forever and perfect breasts, but it would be several years before she became a star. The principal drama in her life at that time involved men, and one in particular. Don Johnson was a sweet, down-to-earth guy who talked slowly and played the guitar. He had dark hair that he wore slicked back. He was handsome then, but this was long before the blow-dried, silk-suit glory of *Miami Vice*, and Donnie, as everyone called him, was a good ol' boy who worked hard and only dreamed of being a star.

Working on *Cannonball* was another part of my learning process, and it was a blast. I couldn't believe someone was paying me to do this! I was busy every second of every day, and I could not have been happier. This was my Hollywood, and I was working hard, learning fast, and pushing myself to do more. I've never believed in sitting if I could be standing, and if I'm standing, I might as well be running.

Cannonball wasn't a particularly difficult movie to shoot because many of the scenes consisted entirely of cars whizzing by a camera, but the stunts were the showcase and they were tricky. In Hollywood the men and the few women who do stunts form a close and slightly strange fraternity. They not only have to be willing to put themselves in physical danger, they also need the technical skills to choreograph people, machines, and cameras in the most intricate ballets. The end result of weeks of work might be just a few seconds on film, but those seconds have to be flawless.

The trick is to create the illusion of danger without exposing the stuntpeople to real danger, and most of the time it works. Hal Needham, the director of *Smokey* and *The Cannonball Run*, had started in the business as a stuntman, and he helped turn what was once regarded in Hollywood as a rough job with low prestige into a glamorous profession. Hal and the stuntmen consider the car crashes, the burning buildings, and the falling bodies to be the most important parts of their films; the actors are hired to carry the plot along to the next stunt.

Hal himself had been injured enough over the years to know that stunt work can be dangerous. On the first day of shooting *Cannonball*, Hal gathered all of us—the actors, the crew, and the technicians—for a solemn ceremony. We stood holding hands in a large circle, with the cameras and the trucks and all the equipment in the middle, while Hal led us in a prayer, asking God to bless the set and the people working there and to keep us safe and sound. Just in case something goes wrong on location, every picture has a nurse assigned. Ours was a fine, strong woman named Dorothy Vitale, whom everyone affectionately knew as Nurse Ratched, after the character who torments Jack Nicholson in *One Flew Over the Cuckoo's Nest*.

When Bobby came back for me at the lunch table, he pulled up in a van and I jumped in eagerly. "Thanks for thinking of me," I said, giving him a kiss. We had been dating for a few months, but Bobby was more serious than I was about our relationship. He was ready to settle down, but I was only twenty-four and had a lifetime ahead of me. I knew I would marry the right man eventually and have lots of kids, but that was far down the road.

We drove out onto the highway where the next shot was being readied. Five cars were facing us one behind the other in a line on the road. The sixth car, an extremely expensive Aston Martin sports car, was secure in a place of honor on a flatbed truck. The commercial version of this sleek two-door car was pricey enough, but this one had been specially designed for the James Bond movies and boasted lots of neat gadgets.

Bobby explained that the scene had Roger Moore and a leggy blond companion speeding down the highway, trying to elude the bad guys on their tail. Roger tells the girl to flip switches on the dashboard to activate the 007 oil slick and smoke screen, but instead of the smoke pouring out the back of the car to blind the bad guys, it fills the inside of the car, choking Roger and the blonde and making the car swerve all over the road.

The plan was to shoot a few close-ups of Roger and the woman in the real Aston Martin, then cut those with long shots of the stunt-people weaving in and out of traffic in the smoke-filled car. We would be driving a mock-up that resembled Bond's Aston Martin. For the same calculated reason that there are doubles to stand in for actors, there are stunt cars to stand in for one-of-a-kind cars: If something goes wrong, it's easier to replace the double than the real thing. The mock-up was just a cheap shell fitted on a chassis that had been converted from the American version (with the steering wheel on the left) to the British version (with the wheel on the right).

Bobby called everybody over, and we hunkered down on the ground around him. Bobby told us that stuntman Jimmy Nickerson would double for Roger Moore and would drive the mock-up. A special-effects expert named Cliff Wenger would lie in the back to operate the smoke machine, and I would double for the blonde riding in the passenger seat. I also was to hold the hose that released the smoke. Bobby arranged little model cars in the dirt, showing us how he envisioned the scene. He wanted the five oncoming cars to keep well spread apart and to maintain a steady speed. Jimmy would drive us in the mock-up toward them, moving in and out of the oncoming cars. He wouldn't have to pass very close to the oncoming cars, Hal said, because the camera would be angled to create the illusion of near misses. Nor did he have to drive very fast because the speed of the film could be altered to make the action more exciting.

Then Bobby walked us through the stunt. He arranged us on the narrow strip of asphalt that formed the two-lane desert highway, and we pretended we were sitting in our respective cars. Jimmy stood facing the stuntmen from the other cars, the drivers all holding up their hands as if they were gripping steering wheels. When Bobby shouted "Action," Jimmy walked toward the oncoming "cars," weaving in and out of the other drivers until he reached the end of the line. This looked kind of silly, but we took it seriously because everyone wanted to get the shot right. The practice run reminded me of getting ready for a ski race. I always liked to walk down the mountain through the course, checking each gate to see how to make the turn.

We didn't have much time to practice the scene because it was afternoon already and we needed to finish before we lost the light. There was some precision required to do the stunt, but as Bobby had told me, it wasn't too demanding and the adjustment was small. Even though I wasn't going to be driving, I paid close attention because I wanted to be able to back up Jimmy if he needed me.

"Let's move, everybody," Hal said. "Let's get this done."

We trotted over to our car and climbed in. Cliff went first. A big, thick man, he struggled to wedge himself onto the rear floor next to the smoke machine lodged behind the front seats. Jimmy got into the driver's seat and tried the wheel. He had complained a few days before about the steering being wobbly, and Hal had sent the car out for repairs. I'm not a small person, either; at six feet, I had to scrunch up to get into the sports car. I sat in the front passenger seat on the left and turned to face Cliff, who reached up to hand me the end of a rubber hose coming out of the smoke machine. He showed me how to work the little button that controlled the flow of smoke. In the cramped space that Cliff was nestled into, he couldn't see where we were going, so he told me to decide on my own how much smoke to release. While we were getting ready, the walkie-talkie wedged between Jimmy and me squawked with incessant commands: "Come on, people! We're losing our light."

I adjusted my knee pads and swiveled in the seat to face backward. There were no safety harnesses in the mock-up. There weren't even regular seat belts, which made it easier for me to face

Cliff in the back. Since the shot was long, I wouldn't be recognizable, so no one worried too much about my wardrobe. I was dressed in my regular uniform: jeans, a T-shirt, and a brand-new pair of Nike tennis shoes that I had just picked up on one of the crews' regular forays to the local shopping center in search of diversion. My one concession to style was a pair of diamond earrings, about two carats each, that I wore all the time. (A girl's got to look good, even for a car chase.) I had my hair in a French braid and tucked up under a blond wig, which was the only effort to make me look like Roger Moore's girlfriend.

"Everybody in?" Hal asked over the radio, more and more urgency sounding in his voice as the big, hot afternoon sun was cooling and rolling toward the western horizon.

"Let's do it," Jimmy said, mostly to himself, drumming his fingers on the wheel. He didn't bother to speak into the radio, not wanting to tie up the frequency and knowing that it was just a question of waiting for the signal. Cliff was ready in the back; I had my thumb on the smoke button. "Let's go," Jimmy said. "Let's do it."

"Okay, cameras rolling," Hal said over the radio. "All right, background. Come on you guys, come up now, and . . . Action!"

Jimmy drove the car toward the oncoming cars. I pressed the button to let the smoke escape out the window and counted, one . . . two . . . three . . . four . . . five, and released the button, cutting off the flow. White smoke trailed the car as Jimmy drove us around the oncoming cars, just as we had rehearsed. The shot was over before we knew it. We pulled off the road, piled out of the car, and ran back to the camera to see how we had done.

Bobby met us halfway, and I could tell from his face that he wasn't happy. "Hal wants to do it again," he said. "He wants more speed, more smoke, and more side-to-side action."

Jimmy didn't say anything, but I could tell he was mad. "You did great, Jimmy," I told him, running back to the car. "Don't worry about it. We'll do it again, and it'll be fine. No sweat."

We all thought the stunt had gone perfectly, but it wasn't unusual to shoot a scene several times, sometimes just to get another angle. Precious minutes had elapsed, though, and the desert air was cooling and the sun was getting lower. We hurried back to the car and took our positions again. We knew where we had to be and what we had to do. Jimmy drove us into position on the road facing the other cars. "Let's do it," Jimmy said, his hands on the wheel and his foot on the gas.

"You guys ready?" Hal asked.

Jimmy picked up the radio. "Ten-four," he said, and tossed the walkie-talkie between our seats.

"Cameras rolling . . . Action!"

The car went forward slowly. I had my thumb on the smoke control button. I squirmed around to face Cliff behind me, pushing my right leg against the floorboard and stretching out my left arm to brace myself against the dash. As our car slowly headed toward the oncoming cars, I released the smoke: one . . . two . . . three. Jimmy floored the accelerator, and the little car strained to pick up speed. "Come on, come on," Jimmy said angrily. "This thing's not going!" He pushed down hard on the gas, but I knew we weren't going very fast. I kept my finger on the smoke button . . . six . . . seven . . . Jimmy rocked back and forth in the driver's seat, cursing and willing the car to go faster.

A voice crackled from the radio on the floor: "Come on, come on!"

"I'm doin' it!" Jimmy shouted, as if Hal could hear him. "I'm doin' it!"

We were going faster now, and Jimmy struggled to drive between the first two cars. I kept pressure on the release button, and the smoke was thick around the car. Jimmy turned the wheel right to pull us back into our lane, but our car kept going forward, straight toward the next car in line, a van. Jimmy cursed and cranked the wheel to the left to try to escape the oncoming traffic any way he could. The van was coming at us as relentlessly as if it were on a treadmill. Jimmy swore again and pulled on the wheel. The front of the van loomed closer, hurtling toward us until it filled the windshield and hit us almost head on.

Glass burst and metal crumpled. The impact slammed the mock-up's engine toward us with the force of a freight train. Jimmy, Cliff, and I kept moving forward until we were stopped abruptly by pieces of the fragmenting car. A jagged shard of glass or metal tore free and sliced into Jimmy's head, scalping him and splashing us both with hot blood. Cliff shot stiffly out of the back as if fired from a cannon, and he rolled across the ground to a stop, scraped and banged but not badly harmed.

The force continued through the dashboard and into the hand I had braced there, driving my straight left arm like a pool cue into the vertebrae in my neck. When the top of the long humerus bone struck my spine, two vertebrae shattered like china cups and my shoulder jerked viciously out of its socket. The impact traveled up my leg and snapped the heavy bone in my thigh, popping the femur through the skin and soaking my jeans with blood. My head, with the supporting neck bones suddenly shattered, flopped heavily onto my back like a sack of potatoes carried over my shoulder. My entire body shut down instantly, as if the master switch had been thrown, and I lost consciousness.

The crew swarmed over the crushed remains of the car, shouting, "Get them out! Get them out!" The tiny doors wouldn't budge, and there was no way to pull me or Jimmy through the crushed windows. Jimmy's door opened finally, and they pulled him free, dragging him across the sand to safety. My friends in the crew tore at the fake sunroof cut into the top of the car. They reached me at last and pulled me out the top, frantic because gasoline was leaking but afraid of worsening my injuries by moving me too roughly. "Be careful with her," someone said. "Easy!" Finally, Bobby pulled me through the hole and dragged me away from the wreckage. The car whooshed into flames.

Nurse Dorothy Vitale shoved everyone aside and checked my neck for a pulse. Nothing. She saw a giant raspberry swelling on my neck and knew that I should only be moved extremely carefully if at all. But my vital signs already were too weak to read, and she knew I would die if I didn't get to a hospital fast.

I don't remember any of this, but friends told me later that they loaded me into a car and sped toward the nearest clinic. I stopped breathing on the way, and Dorothy performed mouth-to-mouth resuscitation. When that failed, she punched a hole in my throat to allow me to breathe. Three times Dorothy thought she had lost me, but each time I came back to life. George Furth, a dear friend and a Christian Scientist who was acting in the movie, rode with me and prayed with a tremendous force. A helicopter was waiting at the clinic and sped me, blood-soaked and unconscious, to a hospital in Las Vegas.

Remembering this story now, I just realized something: I never got my stunt adjustment; somebody owes me two hundred bucks.

Chapter 2

HOLLYWOOD CHILD

If my life passed before my eyes on the way to the hospital, I honestly don't remember it. But now, trying to recall what was important in my young life to this point, I realize that everything that came before the crash helped prepare me for what was to come. There was an order and a logic to those events that only now is clear. My past experiences and the things I had learned, mostly from my parents, formed a foundation that proved solid enough to withstand the terrible storm that still was gathering strength around me and my family. The crash, too, had its own logic. I don't believe in accidents: Everything happens for a reason. Sometimes the reasons come into focus only slowly, if at all, and that is when we suffer.

I was blessed with a wonderful childhood and never wanted for anything, especially love. Mine was a busy life in motion, with hot California summers at the beach, girlhood dreams of stardom, sleek horses, a house full of friends, and loving parents. I was born in Hollywood. My mother gave birth at Hollywood Presbyterian Hospital, and I entered the world in a small company town where the sole industry was beautiful illusion, glamour, and the spinning of dreams.

In the 1950s, Hollywood was a place where all the women were beautiful, all the men were brave, and all the endings were happy.

A few years before I was born, my mom went to Hollywood with almost no money and a kid under each arm and settled into a cramped apartment across from Universal Studios. My brother, Jeff, was four, and my sister, Christy, was three. To survive, my mother and her sister, Joanna, opened a little restaurant around Cahuenga Boulevard between Santa Monica and Sunset Boulevard. Technicolor and Paramount and some of the other big studios also were in the neighborhood, and the restaurant's customers included Sammy Davis, Jr., radio actor Byron Kane, and director Hal Ashby. In those days, Sammy couldn't even live in the nicest parts of Los Angeles because of the color of his skin. Another of the young actors was Brad von Beltz, rugged-looking, thick-shouldered, and strong as a bull. He came from Arizona, and he looked like he had just roped fifty head of cattle, whipped the bad guys, and saved the girl, and that's usually how he was cast.

Brad was working at Technicolor, and one day in 1953 he stopped into the restaurant for a cup of coffee. Brad had met my mother at a Christmas party for Sammy Davis at the home of actor Jeff Chandler. My mother greeted Brad warmly, poured him a cup, and another. She was so beautiful that there was no reason for him to leave. He told her that he dreamed of becoming an artist and that he had studied at the prestigious Art Institute in San Francisco. My mother was duly impressed and put him to work painting the restaurant, decorating the walls with happy clowns. Together they named the restaurant Clown Corner, Brad became the artist in residence, and they were joyously married.

On the day I was born, September 25, 1955, my mother wrote in her journal: "I doubt whether Miss Heidi would ever have emerged if it hadn't been for Jonathan Winters. He was so excruciatingly funny on some show that I was watching I was laughing and rolling around and my water broke. Joanna and Brad sprang into action, relieved that finally—after herding me up and down Hollywood Boulevard nightly trying to induce labor—it was happening. Even though it was midnight, they were happy to get me into the hospital and begin the final journey." A few days later she added, "This little Heidi is something else. She's so far over term that she thinks she is a month old. She has a very precocious way about her and huge china blue eyes."

We lived in a Nordic-style house shaped like an upside-down boat, with wooden walls and shingles, decks on every side, and tall windows overlooking Hollywood. Laurel Canyon was Hollywood's original artist colony, dating back to the days of Caruso and Harry Houdini, and our neighbors included the successful and the glamorous. Fern Mosk was a popular novelist who had just published a best-seller called *Press On Regardless.* The singer Billy Daniels lived across the canyon, and there was Jack Cole, who had choreographed *How to Marry a Millionaire* among other films and was the fifties answer to Busby Berkeley. My sister and I loved Cole's raucous parties, which could be seen easily from our house, because the pool was always filled with frolicking naked men.

Our house was a favorite gathering place for struggling actors and artists, such as Richard Carradine, who was a classically trained actor, and his wife, Jacqueline. Many of my parents' friends were New York exiles from Sanford Meisner's Neighborhood Playhouse, and people were always dropping by to visit. My mom remembers coming home one night to find a nice-looking young man dressed in black leather sitting in the living room, a matching leather cap in his big hands. He was quiet and proper—my mother says "adorable"—and he was Marlon Brando. My brother and sister were asleep in another room, but Brando insisted on seeing them. My parents were embarrassed because the kids had been at the beach all day and the room looked like a sandbox, but Brando marched in to bounce them on the beds. He was a celebrity already and was shooting *The Wild One* at the time, but Christy and Jeff had no idea who he was, other than a neat guy wearing funny clothes.

One of my dad's best friends was Steve McQueen. Although they both were actors, the real love they shared was cars, the faster the better. Steve had a street D-type Jaguar, Brad had a Mark VII Saloon, and their friend Carlisle had a racing D-type Jag. None of them was content with a factory model, and they spent weeks on end with grease up to their elbows, rebuilding the engines to squeeze out more performance. My mother remembers Steve as a dear, gentle, unassuming person, who wilted under her playful teasing.

"Is this Brad's old lady?" he asked cockily the first time he called the house.

My mom snapped back at him, "Old lady? Whatd'ya mean old lady? What's your story?"

She was joking, but Steve got all flustered. "Oh, no. I didn't mean that. I'm sorry, really I am. It's a musician's term." After that bungled introduction, he was unfailingly polite to her.

Steve was starring in *Wanted Dead or Alive* and was on his way to becoming a star, but he still was more interested in cars than in acting. My mother says that deep down he was a regular, working-class guy trapped into a phony glamour image that he wasn't equipped to handle and didn't have the patience for. He had everything going for him, but for some reason he was obsessed with illness, especially cancer. "I think I've got stomach cancer," he would announce at the slightest hint of indigestion. My mother always scolded him and warned him that he was going to talk himself into a real illness. Eventually, he did get cancer, and that's how he died.

My career in Hollywood began when I was "discovered," tanned and topless, on a warm sunny day. I was only a few months old, and my mother had taken me, wearing only a diaper, to our little country store. She was struggling out of the car with me on her hip when a gleaming silver XK120 Jaguar pulled into the dirt parking lot. The door opened, and out stepped an elegant man with silver hair and an Oxford gray suit. He was staring at the two of us as he hurriedly closed the car door. He rushed over to my mother and gushed, "I've got to photograph this baby! This is the most beautiful baby I've ever seen!" When he caught his breath, he introduced himself as the photographer Carlisle Blackwell, Jr., the son of the silent film star. The younger Carlisle was married to the daughter of Jules Cabenet, a big director in early films. (Everyone famous in Hollywood is the son or daughter of someone famous.)

Of course, this version of Carlisle's ecstatic reaction at seeing me is my mother's unbiased recollection of what happened that day. She wrote in her journal, "Heidi was with her dimples going, giggling and dimpling at him. He has an impressive reputation as glamour photographer, in the league with Hurrel, Paul Hesse and Philip Stern and a few others big in the glamour industry. He's photographed Garbo and Elizabeth Taylor, Marlene Dietrich, Sophia Lauren, and now he's going to photograph our little Heidi."

My mother raced home and asked my dad if they should allow Blackwell to do some test shots. My dad agreed, but he drew the line at getting me an agent. No baby of his was going to have an agent, even if it would mean more work. I started doing calendars, in the warm, homey fifties style with the cherub-faced baby and the beaming mother. By ten months of age, I was cast as that most wholesome of infants, the Ivory Soap baby. My brother, Jeff, got into the act, too, and on one shoot at Lake Malibu they dressed him like Huck Finn and launched him in a rowboat with a little spaniel character dog (Yes, there are character dogs, like character actors). My sister, Christy, was a beautiful little girl and a natural ham, and pretty soon nearly the whole family was appearing together in calendars and advertising.

My mother attributes my steady work to the fact that I was never shy and had no reservations in front of the camera. The lights seemed to animate me rather than scare me. My only bad habit, she says, was trying to drink the baby oil used as a prop. Eventually, I was working so much that my parents finally put a stop to it, deciding that it wasn't healthy for me or good for their own busy work schedules and social lives.

My mom's best pal was Bette Powelson-Howard, who was the kind of beauty my mother calls "drop-dead, show-stopping fantastic-looking." Bette had a twenty-inch waist, a long dark braid, and a dainty nose, and was so petite that even Sammy Davis, Jr., called her

"Little Bits" because she was the only girl in town shorter than he was. Bette was married to Bob Howard, a.k.a. Huckleberry Horwitz, who had just finished being a Broadway press agent for Walter Winchell. Bette had a natural jazz voice and was forever being offered screen tests, which she steadfastly refused. She could have been another Judy Garland, but she always told my mom that the world wasn't ready for another Judy Garland.

Bette was taking an acting workshop with the dynamic Richard Boone, who had a TV series called *Medic* and later *Have Gun Will Travel*. Bette was so enthusiastic about it that she convinced my dad to join her. My dad's real interest then was painting, and he regarded acting mostly as a way to make a living. He was a staff artist at the ad agency Foster & Kleiser, and his idol was the western painter Charlie Russell. He had fallen into show business by accident as an art student working nights at the Orpheum Theater circuit in San Francisco. When the theaters were featuring a world-premiere movie, the owners brought in actors like Stanley Kramer, Jerry Lewis, and Dean Martin as hosts. My dad was good with a crowd and looked smashing in a tuxedo, so he became master of ceremonies. One of the actors he met was Jeff Chandler, who introduced Brad to the agent Meyer Mishkin, and Brad joined Meyer's stable, which included Charles Bronson, James Coburn, Chuck Connors, Lee Marvin, and Aaron Spelling, who later became the prolific producer.

By the time I celebrated my first Christmas, my dad was a regular member of Boone's theater workshop, which included Natalie Wood, Leslie Nielsen, and Bob Fuller, one of my dad's best buddies who was doing a western TV series for Universal called *Laramie*. They were joined by a crazy bunch of stuntmen, led by Hal Needham, and a chorus line full of cute young women. "An interesting, if motley, group," as my mother described the workshop in her journal.

Under Richard Boone's guidance, my dad reluctantly put away his paintbrushes and started acting full time, reasoning that while Charlie Russell had the real West to portray, his own canvases would be movie screens showing the larger-than-life West created by Hollywood. He went under contract with Universal and did just about every TV show they had: *Maverick, Cheyenne, Hawaiian Eye, 77 Sunset Strip*. Eventually he also did *Have Gun Will Travel, Gunsmoke, Surfside Six, Bonanza, The Rifleman,* and *Wanted Dead or Alive,* among others. The contract actors were owned body and soul, and the studios had a voracious appetite for programming to fill up airtime on the new medium of television.

I vividly remember one of those shows, an Alfred Hitchcock piece about the Civil War, which aired when I was about five years old. My mom and us kids gathered around the set to watch my dad playing a Confederate soldier returning home from the war tired, dusty, and defeated. All he wants is to see the loving wife he had left behind and to eat a bowl of her famous peaches. The camera shows my dad as he walks into the farmhouse. Cue up music: "Glory, Glory Hallelujah." The camera cuts to a jar of peaches, smashed on the floor. Pan to the wife's lifeless body. Cut to the soldier's horrified stare. He breaks down weeping. Angrily he searches the house for the nasty Northerner who done it, they struggle, a shot is fired. The Confederate soldier—my dad—goes down, dead. Like the South itself, never to rise again. Cue up music: "Glory, Glory Hallelujah."

My dad could really die, too. He grew up hunting and fishing in the country, and he knew what happens to an animal hit with a bullet. When he was shot in a period piece, he never clutched his chest and fell forward because he knew the old weapons were big calibers with slow-moving bullets that packed a huge wallop. Instead, he coiled his muscles and braced himself with one foot planted forward. When the director fired the "shot," Brad launched himself backward into the air and collapsed expertly into a pile of lifeless flesh.

As the credits were rolling over Brad's dead body, I started crying, screaming, shrieking. "Baba's dead! Baba's dead! Baba's dead! Baba! Baba!" I was enormously confused. My mother tried to explain it to me, but there was no telling me anything at that point.

After that, I found any excuse to avoid watching him on television. I always looked for something to keep me busy or went outside to play. If there was no way to avoid one of his programs, I made myself fall asleep while he was still "alive." Anything to avoid seeing him killed again.

My mother says that as a girl I never stayed in one place very long, and I never walked if I could run. I'd run along the beach, plunge into the water, run back to my mom, splash in the waves, run to the towel, collapse, and fall into a deep restful sleep. Then I'd jump up again, run back to the water, along the shoreline, up the beach, until it was time to drag me home. We had an Austin-Healey convertible, and my Aunt Joanna had one too, and whenever we could we loaded them up with provisions and gear, so much stuff that it was more like a wagon train going west than a trip to the beach. Anywhere we stopped, the barest beach or the roughest campsite, my dad created a luxury hotel, complete with little bundles of firewood, whittled to the correct size and neatly bound in rope.

When we outgrew our home in Laurel Canyon, we moved to Encino, into an old Mediterranean-style Spanish mansion with thick stone walls. Down the street, at the old Encino Post Office, Clark Gable, Edward Everett Horton, and Al Jolson gathered every morning for coffee. Encino was more popular with executives than with actors, and most of our neighbors worked in radio, television, and the studios. My dad had regular television work, and my mom sold the restaurant and stayed home to be a 1960s housewife, taking care of me and sending my brother and sister off to school each day.

Along with Bette, my mom's other best friend was young James Caan, who practically lived at our house. Jimmy and my mother shared what they regarded as a serious affliction: naturally curly hair, the kind my mother calls King Kong hair. She and Jimmy spent long smelly evenings gobbing on chemical hair straighteners, but their woolly locks never remained straight for very long, and Jimmy eventually ended up without much hair at all, curly or otherwise. He was full of energy and proposals for extravagant outings. Jimmy's idea of fun was to save up for an expensive meal at a fancy restaurant like Mateo's, but my parents preferred the more downscale DuPar's, which they could afford more often.

My best friend was Pam Gannon, and we spent many days riding horses together. Pam and I were not wild by any means, but we did have our share of adventures. One night when we were twelve or thirteen, Pam's parents dropped us off at the movies. My mother was supposed to pick us up after the show, but she fell asleep in front of the television. The uncle of one of our schoolmates offered us a ride home, and we gladly accepted. Right away I knew something was wrong—it must have been something he said or the way he looked at us—and when he headed for the freeway instead of our neighborhood, I reached over, popped open Pam's door, and pushed her out. We ran all the way to an ice cream store, from which we called our parents.

With Pam and all my friends, I always took the lead. If we were playing a game, I was in the center. If we went on a hike, I went first. I didn't have a whole lot of patience, either, so if I was playing first base and I was worried about the second baseman, I'd slide over and back him up just to be sure. I'd play the whole team if that's what it took to win. In basketball I always was picked to be a forward so I could move around and maximize the potential of the whole team. I was very keen on winning—I hope not to the point of being a poor sport. The fact that I was naturally athletic helped my confidence, and I swam, did gymnastics, and played all kinds of organized sports.

I remember myself as a barefoot girl, dressed in faded jeans and a T-shirt. I was lean and tan, and my hair was long. I always had a closet full of "in" clothes, and went through the phase of miniskirts with white patent-leather go-go boots like everyone else my age, but I spent most of my time outside and by myself. Our house in Encino was a five-acre ranch (once owned by the cinematographer Merritt Gerstad), and I had chickens named Henny Penny and Chicken Little and a ratty little monkey named

Thelonius Monk, who pooped all over my room. My room was very mod, decorated with posters and Peter Max wallpaper with matching pillows and a fluffy white bedspread. My special place was a tree house that my dad built for me in an avocado tree. This was not just some boards nailed to the limbs, but three tiers of ladders leading to an A-frame structure with a little balcony, all painted green, and equipped with a telephone and ice chest. For entertainment I watched squirrels bomb my German shepherd, Rex, with half-eaten avocados.

Despite my almost boundless self-confidence, I do remember being preoccupied with one physical defect: my feet. They were huge. All my friends were these darling little creatures who looked adorable in frilly white dresses and had tiny, size-four feet. But everything about me was giantesque. My feet were size eight, and they looked like they belonged to someone else, to my dad maybe. I insisted on having, at the most, size seven shoes, even though I could barely stuff my feet into them and couldn't run, just because the eights looked so enormous. My clown-sized feet were connected to legs that were growing like trees, and I was so tall that at school when we swung hand-to-hand on the rings, my knees dragged on the ground. I can laugh about it now, but as a young girl it was awful being different, and for a while it was more fun to play alone.

My faithful companion and trustworthy confidante was a buckskin horse named Duchess. We were well known in the neighborhood, since I was among the few people who still rode a horse down the streets of Encino. I must have been about twelve years old when a man in a beauty parlor saw me riding by, and he ran out to ask a bizarre favor.

"Can I borrow your horse?" he asked.

"What do you mean?" I said. "What are you talking about?"

"Well, I just want it for a minute. My wife works in here, and I just want to, you know, play a joke on her."

The guy was kind of cute, and I was incredibly stupid, so I said, "Sure."

He took the bridle and led Duchess clopping through the front door of a hair salon called the Syndicate. He nodded his head at the horse and announced to everyone inside, "She's getting ready for the prom and can't do a thing with her mane. Can you help?"

Everybody cracked up, laughing and clapping and cheering. Duchess became excited by the commotion, and when the guy tried to lead her back across the tiled floor, all four legs shot out from under her as if she were a cartoon horse. She scrambled to get her footing, but her hooves slipped on the glassy floor. I was paralyzed with fear and could only stare at her terrified eyes, bulging, all white around the edges. She began to make a strange, plaintive noise I had never heard before, a wheezing sound, and my heart raced. Duchess kicked and rolled and thumped the chairs with her powerful legs, and people ran to escape her thrashing. Oh my God! I thought. Oh my God. What am I gonna do?

"Please, Duchess, calm down," I told her. "Please be still. Everything will be okay, I promise. I'll get you out of here."

Sitting in one of the chairs was a stuntwoman named Patty Heist, who was the only person in the place who didn't run for cover. Duchess was now in complete panic and drifting into shock. Sprawled on the floor, she suddenly stopped moving altogether, which scared me even more than her frenzied thrashing. She's gonna die, I thought. She's gonna die. Somebody do something! Patty calmly approached Duchess and stroked her head. She asked for wet towels, which she wrapped around the horse's hooves to give her enough traction to stand. With Patty's help, Duchess struggled up, and my horse and I—both drenched in sweat and our hearts pounding—inched out the door.

When we got outside, it felt like absolution. I thanked Patty profusely and never forgot her coolness and skill. "I will never do it again, I swear to God," I whispered to myself. Walking Duchess down the road toward home, I prayed out loud, "I promise, God, I will never, ever do anything so stupid again. I will always go to church, I will do anything." All the way home, I repeated this to myself and to the Lord, adding as an aside that there was no need for God to mention anything about this to my parents.

God must have heard my prayers because my dad didn't find out right away. When he did, he realized that I had punished myself enough, and he never said anything about it. He usually found out everything I did, partly because I was such a bad liar but also because he has a way of cutting through what is false or unimportant and seeing things clearly.

Besides Duchess, my main mode of transportation was a purple stingray bike called a Slick Chick, extremely cool. My dad was always after me to protect the bike from being stolen, and every time I rode into town he said, "Lock your bike." I was a busy girl, often too busy to lock my bike. One late afternoon I was playing in the park when I noticed my dad's big gold Cadillac parked across the street. I had left my bike there a few hours before, unlocked, so I dashed across the street to chain the bike before my dad noticed. When I got there, the bike was gone.

My dad came out of the post office with the mail, saw me and said, "Hi. What's going on?"

"Oh, not much," I said, trying to see if I could spot my bike over his shoulder.

"All right," he said. "It's going to be getting dark soon, and it's time to go home. Get your bike and let's go. I'll throw it in the trunk and give you a ride."

"Uh, no. That's okay," I said, looking at the ground and rearranging the rocks at my feet. "Uh, Pam took my bike for a spin, and so I'll just, you know, wait for her, and then I'll meet you down at the house."

"No, no, that's all right. I'll wait and give you a lift."

I stuck to my guns. I didn't have any choice because I was in too deep already. We stood there for a while, looking around, my dad looking at me and me pretending to be looking for Pam, who was supposed to be riding into view any second.

After a few minutes of this, my dad asked, "Where do you think she is?"

"I don't know," I tried. "Maybe she went home already. It's going to get dark soon, you know. Maybe we should just go home and then I can call her from there."

My dad walked over to the car and, without a word, popped open the trunk. I looked in and saw my bike. My shame at having lied to my father far outweighed my relief at learning the bike was safe.

"I'm your best friend," my dad said as we drove home together. "I'm the last one you should lie to. Don't establish that kind of relationship with me, because I'm the one that's here to help you with whatever you need. I'm here to bail you out if you need bailing. When all your friends are gone, I'll be there."

My dad always taught us with object lessons rather than lectures or punishment. He rarely yelled at us or even told us what to do, preferring that we learn by example. He told us that the very word *teach* is a misnomer because every human being is born with all the knowledge there ever was—past, present, and future. People don't learn anything, he told us, and don't wait for someone to teach you. Instead, you become aware of the world around you. Take math, he said. In school, you are becoming aware of the laws of mathematics. You become aware that two and two is four. No one actually teaches you that two and two is four, they just point it out.

The other lesson he wanted us to learn was that attitude is the most important ingredient in any task, that the power of thought is greater than any force on earth.

My least favorite among my many girlhood chores, the thing I hated most, was making my bed. It was an early water bed, really just a big plastic bag filled with water. Every time I pushed one side, the other side bulged out, so it was impossible for me to neatly tuck in the sheets and blankets. On a typical morning I was shoving the water around, yelling at the bed, kicking it and complaining the whole time. My dad walked by my room, stopped in the doorway to watch me and said, "What'sa matter, honey? What are you doing?"

"I'm trying to make the bed!"

"I can see that, but is it that awful?"

"I don't see why I have to do this," I whined. "It's a complete pain."

"If you treat it like a complete pain," he said, "it will always be a complete pain, but if you put a smile on your face and you just do it, it won't be so bad . . ." While he was saying this, he was on one side of the bed and I was on the other, and we were straightening the sheets and pulling up the bedspread.

". . . and boom, it's done," he said. "See? Now you can go play."

My dad was not your typical 1950s, Ward Cleaver–type dad. For one thing, he's always had long hair, and he is big and strong and has a chiseled face. If he were an animal, he'd probably be a hawk or an eagle. He wears jeans and western clothing and looks so young that when I was a teenager, people often assumed he was my boyfriend. As soon as I could pronounce his name I called my dad Brad, not Daddy or Father. When other kids first heard me call him by his name, they teased me, and I came home from school in tears.

"Everybody says you're not my real dad," I cried.

"What are you talking about?" he said. "That's crazy. Of course I'm your real dad."

"Well, they say, 'If he's your real dad, then why do you call him Brad?' "

"You can call me Dad if you want to."

"I can?"

"Yeah, sure. But if you call me Dad, I'm going to call you Daughter."

"Whatd'ya mean?"

"I am your father, but my name is Brad. Father is my title. Just like you are my daughter but your name is Heidi. So if you want to call me Dad, that's fine, but then I should call you Daughter."

"Oh, okay," I said, thinking about it for a minute. That made sense to me, and I never questioned it again.

Just to test these newly cleared waters, I strolled into the kitchen and said to my mom, "Hi, Patty."

She chased me across the room with a spatula, shouting, "Don't call me Patty! I'm your mother!"

I spent every young moment doing something. The world outside was my playground, my classroom, and the source of my greatest discoveries. One afternoon during a long ride, Duchess and I stumbled upon something truly wondrous. We stopped in front of a whirling machine, as big as a house, that had a system of enormous rollers wrapped with a wide loop of heavy carpet. The entire machine tilted, so the carpet became a sloped treadmill, and people were whooshing down on Teflon-coated skis. My mouth hanging open, I sat atop my equally amazed horse and couldn't wait to climb onto that thing and try it myself. I already knew how to water-ski, and when I stood on the revolving carpet for the first time, I felt like I had been doing it all my life. I knew this sport was for me, and I convinced the owner to let me help out in exchange for ski time and free lessons.

Eventually I became good enough that I was giving lessons myself. Normally skiing is practiced on pristine snowy mountains, so there is a trick to teaching people the sport on a revolving carpet in a parking lot, with cars whizzing by and horns honking. For some reason I had a gift for being able to watch people ski only once, then clearly explain what they were doing and help them do it better. I got such a thrill when my students did well that I soon had plenty of customers.

The owner of Ski World was Phil Gerard, who rightly is known as the father of freestyle skiing. He is flamboyant, entertaining, and talented, a gourmet cook and a world-class skier. He learned to move as a dancer on Broadway, and he simply transferred the steps from the stage to the slopes. He could drop off the edge of a mountain and flip his way down as gracefully as he once had dazzled theater audiences. Phil appreciated my teaching talents, but what really endeared me to him was that, like him, I could sell anything. I was so excited about skiing that nobody got away from me without buying something: lessons, equipment, or a package deal. I loved the selling as much as the skiing, and Phil taught me to do both very well.

I had been "skiing" for about a year before I ever tried it on snow. Everyone who saw me on the machine just assumed I had grown up on the slopes, and I never did anything to dissuade them from thinking so. Unfortunately, this misunderstanding started to loom so large, at least in my mind, that I couldn't tell anyone that I actually had never been on real snow. The moment of truth came when a big group of friends invited me to the mountains. I couldn't say, "Oh, I don't really ski, I just teach it," so I jumped into the car, kept my ears open and my mouth shut. When we arrived after a long drive, everyone took out money for lift tickets, and I followed along like I had been doing it all my life.

When I first stepped off the chairlift onto the packed snow, I was thrilled to the bone: The air was crisp and clean, deep green trees bordered the long white runs, and there wasn't any traffic. I watched my friends ski down ahead of me, and it didn't look that hard. I held my breath and pushed off with my poles. On a silicone-coated carpet I really had to push my legs to get an edge, so I was amazed at how much the snow gave under my weight. My edges bit with almost no effort, and the bottoms of my skis felt hard and slick underneath my boots. There was no limit here, no asphalt below me, just endless blankets of snow. It was so easy! First I felt relief, then joy when I moved down the hill, and finally exhilaration as I picked up speed, carved long turns, and slipped over moguls, my knees pumping like pistons shooting sprays of cool snow.

Rather than trying to hide the fact that I had been carpet skiing long before I ever tried real snow, I used my experience to help my students. If I could learn snow skiing on carpet, I insisted, so could they. This wasn't just a theory anymore; it was fact proved by my experience.

After experiencing the real thing, skiing only on carpet would have bored me, but my friends and I were never content to simply go straight down. We did flips and spins, went backward and on one leg, performed crossovers and royals. The first time I tried a back flip on the slopes, I worried I wouldn't be able to get the longer snow skis all the way around. I cranked so hard that I went around once, and then halfway again, landing with a thunk on my butt. I opened and closed my eyes a few times, trying to figure out what had happened. "Am I still here?" The next time, I eased off a little, didn't thrust quite so hard, and landed flat on my skis. The feeling of weightless flight was magic. A group of us traveled from slope to slope, performing tricks and competing, and Phil bragged that I was the best woman skier he had ever coached.

My idyllic life of sunny days, long summers at the beach, horseback riding in the hills, and freestyle skiing competitions was suddenly and deeply darkened by the war in Vietnam. Even though my brother is nine years older than I am, I always considered him a best buddy. He's the one who taught me to ride, even before I had Duchess. He would wake me early in the summer, fix my breakfast, and take me to the Burbank Riding Stables. I grew up watching him surf, and if I was lucky, he let me tag along on nights when he and his friends were drinking beer and cruising Encino.

I was oblivious to the world of politics and current events, but my parents and the adults around me were consumed by the war. My parents didn't like it, but they assumed the government knew what it was doing. Christy disagreed. She vigorously opposed the war, wearing black armbands to high school and leading student protests.

Jeff was ambivalent. When he was a senior in high school, my mother desperately wanted him to apply to Princeton, which would get him a good education and keep him out of Vietnam. He agreed halfheartedly to go to college, but he didn't want to leave California and enrolled at the University of California at Northridge. He soon dropped out, though, and to my mother's horror, he went into the army. He didn't have to go, but he declined to take his student deferment. My dad has always been philosophically opposed to war in general, believing that wars don't solve anything, but as with everything else when we were growing up, he let Jeff decide whether to go to Vietnam. Brad himself had been a paratrooper in an elite army regiment, so he couldn't help but understand and feel proud of his son's decision to serve.

Jeff, Christy, and I were raised to do our best, always, and that's what Jeff did in Vietnam. Even if we didn't like what we were supposed to be doing or found ourselves someplace we didn't want to be, we were taught to try our hardest, that the energy spent on whining should be channeled into making the situation better. Jeff saw his comrades falling and dying around him, and he did the only thing he knew: He tried to save them. On one mission he helped rescue a stranded team of Green Berets. He jumped out of a helicopter amid withering enemy fire, hoisted them aboard one by one, and got them out without a scratch. His bravery was recognized by his commanders, and he earned a chest full of medals, including a Silver Star and a Bronze Star.

While Jeff was in Vietnam, my mother suffered horribly. She followed every engagement of every campaign and learned the names of the most obscure Vietnamese hamlets. She was so worried that she tried to distract herself by taking the most stressful, all-consuming job she could find: booking musicians on movies, television, and concerts. My dad was serene as always, serving as a healthy balance for my mother. "Jeff will be fine. This too will pass," he told her again and again. Together my mom and Brad survived the nightmare of knowing their child was in mortal danger and being powerless to protect him.

When Jeff went away to Vietnam, I was still a tomboy, full of energy and relatively mature for thirteen but still a kid. I have a letter he sent me on March 19, 1969, that says, "Hi Turd. I really love hearing from you but you shouldn't write letters from the library. You should be studying and getting good grades. How's all your animals? I hope they're doing fine. I was very sorry to hear about guinea. Although he did eat and scream too much. Thank you for the 'Love Beads' but the drill sergeant found them in my locker. . . ."

When Jeff returned home after eighteen months, I had grown into my gangly height and blossomed into a young woman. I remember the surprised look on his face when he saw me for the first time. He smiled all over and said, "You're unbelievable." He had changed, too, but that didn't matter to me; I was just glad he was home where he belonged.

By the time I was in high school, I was acting regularly in all kinds of television programs, movies, and special events. I even worked as a "card girl" in a Bob Hope special that featured a mock fight scene with Muhammad Ali. I wore an evening gown and carried a numbered card around the ring, announcing the next round after each bell. I was cast as a water-skier in the Disney movie *Superdad*, which was fun because they put us up in hotels in Newport and blocked off an entire strip of the beach for the shooting.

My first substantial part, with costar billing, was in an episode of *Charlie's Angels*. Our heroines, the Angels, were on a mission to build up the self-esteem of a girl on a women's football team. I played the female heavy on the team: the brutish she-devil named Grinelda. The high point for me was a shower-room wrestling match with Jaclyn Smith, which she, of course, won.

All my friends were in the business, and we definitely ran in a fast crowd of celebrities, actors, and L.A. Rams football players. I went to all the hot discos, but I wasn't very interested in mindless partying. I preferred to talk with Melanie or other friends, and even when I went out, I usually ended the night in quiet conversation rather than dancing till dawn.

I wasn't exactly a cloistered nun, however, and I did my share of experimenting. I was up for just about anything and never lacked for boldness. When I was planning yet another party with my friend Linda Meyers, she jokingly mentioned that Jack Nicholson was on the same telephone exchange, so we could easily be patched through to him. Nicholson had just won an Oscar for *One Flew Over the Cuckoo's Nest* and was extremely hot. "Let's invite him to lunch," I said.

"Yeah, sure," Linda said.

"No, really," I told her. "Why not? The worst he could say is no."

Linda was game for anything, so she dialed the number. At the last second she tossed me the receiver. "It's your idea," she laughed.

A male voice answered. "Hello?"

"Hi, Jack. This is Heidi. I'm calling to invite you to a little lunch we're having."

"Heidi? Heidi who? Do I know you?"

"No, actually you don't," I said, adding quickly, since I already was in over my head, "But you do want to know me."

He didn't make the lunch, but he called soon after and asked for me. "I love your voice," he told me. I have a deep, throaty voice, so deep that when I answered the phone as a kid, people would say, "Is your mother home, son?" I always hated that, but now my voice was coming in handy. We talked on the phone for a few weeks, each call lasting a little longer and becoming more personal.

"I've just got to meet you in person," Jack declared finally.

"Well, then, you can come over."

A little later I was wearing jeans and a T-shirt and was washing the car out front when he appeared. I saw him walking up wearing sunglasses and the official Jack Nicholson smirk. He didn't know if I was the person he was looking for until I said, "Hi, Jack."

"Heidi," he said, and we spent the rest of the day together. We talked and laughed and drank some wine, and one thing led to another. There was heavy chemistry going on, a serious physical attraction, and neither one of us wanted to pass up the chance.

I didn't have a lot of time for romance, though; I was constantly on the go. I was on my own, living in a beautiful apartment above Universal Studios with a view of Hollywood that stretched forever. In fact, the giant Hollywood sign on the mountain was right in the middle of my living room window. I had more work than I could handle, although I've only had one nine-to-five job during my life, a brief fling at a computerized dating service. I did just about everything else, even selling steaks out of the trunk of my car for a while. I acted, modeled, and tried my hand at movie and television production. There wasn't a day when I wasn't running to castings or shoots or interviews. I was hired as a supervising producer on a CBS Sports special featuring stuntmen, which I loved, but it was working on *Roar* with Noel Marshall that finally convinced me that my future was not limited to being in front of the camera.

Producing and directing, traditionally, were seen as male jobs, but that's what really captured my imagination. I loved taking an idea and making it become real on the screen. I enjoyed all the details on the set: working with actors, learning the technology, struggling to keep all those high-octane personalities happy, well fed, and productive. Acting was fun, but it was limited. Modeling is more hard work than glamour, and the career of a model is extremely short. Helping to produce *Roar* allowed me to climb a little higher and to see a little farther: Now there were so many possibilities before me. My horizon suddenly was as vast as the view from my perch on the hill, the potential paths before me were many, and I believed it wasn't possible to see all the way to the future.

Chapter 3

ROUGH NIGHT
IN VEGAS

On the day that I crashed, before my mother received the news, she complained of feeling strange and vaguely uneasy. I was three hundred miles away, unconscious and being rushed to a hospital in Las Vegas, while my mom and Aunt Joanna were shopping for a wedding present for a friend. They wandered aimlessly around Century City but couldn't find a thing. Both women said they felt cloudy or preoccupied about something undefined, that their heads were on crooked, but they shrugged it off to their return that morning from a peaceful two weeks camping in the mountains. It must be the shock of civilization, my mother said. She didn't learn what had happened to me until later that night when the phone rang at home. Christy answered. A man from the *Cannonball* production office was on the line from Las Vegas, and my sister knew from his voice that something was wrong.

She called to my dad and handed him the phone.

"What is it?" Brad asked into the phone.

"Well, we've got some bad news."

"Heidi?"

"Yeah. Gosh. I don't know how to tell you this—"

"An accident?"

"Yeah, a car accident."

"Is it bad?"

"Really bad."

"How bad?"

"Umm . . . it's her neck."

"We'll be right there," Brad said.

"Good. That's good. I'll have tickets to Las Vegas for you and Patty at the airport. Come straight to the hospital."

My dad organized everything; he and Mom tossed a few clothes into a bag and went to the airport. My mother thought she was fairly calm upon hearing the news, but she had packed a bag full of shoes and not a single piece of underwear. Because they were preoccupied rushing for the flight, my mom didn't have a chance to think until they were at the Los Angeles airport waiting to board the plane.

"My God, it's her neck," she said, crying.

"It'll be all right," Brad said, suppressing his own fears. "Heidi's tough."

I was drifting in and out of consciousness. I don't remember getting to the hospital, only waking up in a darkened room. Then I drifted off again. Doctors. Nurses. Buzzing voices. Hospital smell. Tubes in my nose. The metallic taste of stale blood in my mouth. Flashes of light through the venetian blinds covering the darkened windows. If I just rest for a minute, I'll feel better. Sleep. I'm so thirsty. Doctors asked me questions but offered no answers. I slept. I knew there had been an accident but not much else. I just wanted to rest. I wondered about Cliff and Jimmy. Let me sleep.

A doctor stood over me and placed a stethoscope on my stomach. Then he moved to the foot of the bed and said, "Move your toes." I moved my toes. "Okay, that's good. How does that feel?"

"Fine," I said, not noticing anything unusual.

I had no idea that he had just buried a straight pin into my big toe.

When I was awake long enough to figure out where I was, I realized I was strapped onto a bed. It wasn't a bed, really, but a frame of some kind, made of metal tubes. I was flat on my back, and there were straps tight across my chest and arms so I couldn't move anything. I felt as if I were suspended, floating above the ground. Nurses fluttered by in sensible shoes, white uniforms rustling near my head, which was somehow locked in one position. Let me sleep. My head was misty, drugged, and fuzzy. Two nurses stood over me and without warning threaded a clear plastic tube into my nose. I retched and tried to turn my head away, but they held me steady and inserted the tube. I looked at them, eyes wide, but they were focused on jamming the tube into my nose. I couldn't find the words to speak. The tube fell out, and they shoved it back. It fell out again, and they put it back in and held it firm with tape. The room rolled as gently as if it were at sea. The fog rolled in and covered me warmly. Sleep.

A nurse held open my mouth and inserted a stiff plastic probe. I heard a sucking sound that reminded me of the dentist's office, and I felt her vacuuming the inside of my throat. Yellow phlegm shot up the clear tubing and dripped into a container shaped like a food processor. She closed my mouth. The fog rolled in again, and I slept.

A whirring sound and a click. Whirrrr, click. X rays.

I felt an annoying pressure on the back of my head. A dull, indistinct ache, the sort that comes from wearing sunglasses so long that they press into the backs of your ears. I needed water. My teeth felt like they were wearing little wool overcoats. Machinery hummed and beeped. Sirens from the street. The light behind the blinds was so beautiful. Cool flashes of color. Sleep.

My parents arrived at the hospital, and a nurse brought them immediately to my room in intensive care. Holding her breath in fear, my mother looked in and saw me covered with a sheet and suspended above the ground. The nurses explained that I was on a Stryker frame, which is like a surfboard on legs, and is used to immobilize people with spinal injuries. My hair had been shaved off the sides of my head in stubby circles around my ears. Stainless steel tongs were bolted into my skull there and connected to a halo that kept my head from moving. Plastic tubes ran into my arms from IV packs hanging beside me. Another tube ran into my nose, down my throat, and into my stomach. I was breathing through a hole in my throat. I was deep inside a drugged sleep.

As scary as the sight must have been for my mother, her first reaction was relief, and she describes the scene as more surreal than frightening. I looked like I was starring in a bad science fiction movie, otherwise I appeared to be fine, considering what she had expected. She had imagined that the crash had left me bloody and mangled, so when she saw me sleeping calmly, she felt a little less anxious and a lot more hopeful, as if already I were showing signs of improvement. She walked to my side and hugged me and kissed me, grateful that I was alive. I slept, unaware of her presence.

I woke up again sometime during the night staring straight up at the white ceiling, my tongue dry and bitter as burnt toast. I had no idea how badly I was hurt. I knew it was serious, though, and I figured I was going to be laid up for a couple of days at least. I wasn't in pain or afraid, just numb and tired. The miracle of morphine.

I saw my dad standing over me, and I smiled. "What happened?" I asked. My lips moved, but I didn't hear any sound. I spoke again. Nothing came out. I had no voice. I mouthed the words again. "What happened?"

Brad turned to my mom and said, "What's she saying? She's saying something. I can't understand her."

The hole in my throat allowed me to breathe but prevented me from speaking. My mother looked at my lips, and I repeated. "What happened? Did they get the shot? Did they finish the scene?"

My mother read my lips and translated for Brad. She never had any trouble understanding me. "She wants to know if they got the shot."

"Don't even worry about that now," my dad said, standing next to me and gently touching my head.

"What happened to me?" I asked. My mother translated again for Brad.

"You fucked yourself up really good," Brad said, "and you are going to have to get better. We're going to have to fix it."

I looked up into their tired, troubled faces. My mother's eyes were red and puffy from crying. I felt bad for worrying them so; I knew they must be horribly upset. I didn't want them to suffer. The sight of them was soothing. How many times when I was little had they come into my room at night to cover me gently and kiss me once more on the hair? How many times had they told me stories, eased my fears, and explained the world to me? Whenever I crashed my bike or fell off my horse, my mother was there to place her cool hands on my skinned knee or bumped forehead. Just like that, the pain was gone. I knew this injury was too big for that, but knowing she was there, I felt myself relax a little. My dad's eyes were clear, although he couldn't hide his concern. He touched my hair and held my hand. He promised me that I was going to get better, and knowing that, I never doubted it. Not for one minute.

"You don't have any scars on your face," my mom said. "Not even a cut."

I smiled at her. "How did you guys get here?" I asked. "Did Bobby call? Who called?"

We visited for a few minutes before the nurses shooed them out of the room. I plunged back into a muffled, black sleep.

Bobby and other members of the crew were standing around outside my room, drinking coffee and waiting for news from the doctors. Brad knew just about everyone from *Cannonball*, having worked with most of them on movies and television shows. Hal Needham had doubled for Brad years before in *Have Gun Will Travel*, and they had studied together in Richard Boone's acting workshop. In a series called *Riverboat*, Brad had replaced Burt Reynolds after he left the show.

The actors and technicians from *Cannonball* filed into the hospital to say hello to Brad and my mom and to learn about my condition. Jimmy Nickerson, the driver of the car I was in, also was hospitalized, but the doctors said he was going to be fine. Cliff Wenger, who was operating the smoke machine in back, escaped without a scratch. The driver of the van that hit us had been wearing a safety harness and suffered only a broken rib.

As soon as Brad had a chance, he took Bobby's arm and led him to a quiet corner of the waiting room. Bobby and I had worked on several projects together before *Cannonball*, including a stunt competition that I helped him produce for CBS Sports. Bobby was older than I was, but I was attracted to the combination of rough-and-tumble (he's a Vietnam vet like my brother) and well-organized businessman. He taught me about doing the right thing in business and the importance of little details such as being on time and finishing jobs when you promise them. He was hysterically funny and loved to tell stories, but unlike some of the other stuntmen, he was conservative in his off-camera behavior. My parents never understood why I was dating a man so much older, but I always had fun with Bobby and he was sweet to me.

Brad asked him point-blank, "What the hell happened?"

Bobby told him about the crash. Everyone assumed the stunt was going to be a piece of cake, that it wasn't dangerous, Bobby said, losing it now, choking back tears. He stopped to catch his breath.

If the stunt was so easy, Brad thought, then why did they use the mock-up instead of the real car? Did they care more about protecting the machine than the people operating it? Brad stood listening, a paper cup of cold coffee in his hand, shaking his head at the stupidity, the callousness of what they had done.

Bobby told him, meaning it with every bone in his body, "I can't tell you how sorry—"

"It's okay, Bobby," Brad interrupted. "Everything is going to be okay."

Brad turned and walked away from the crowd of people. He walked alone down a darkened, deserted hospital corridor, thinking about what Bobby had told him, about the crash, about me, about our future. His hands clenched into fists, and his shoulders stretched taut against his shirt. A deep rage began to surface. How could people be so stupid? he thought. How could this happen? Brad looked up and noticed his reflection in a darkened window. He stopped short and looked again. He didn't recognize the face staring back at him. He was horrified: It was the face of evil, the worst, most grotesque looking man-beast. Oh my God, Brad thought. What's happening to me?

He was overcome and had to sit down. I've got to stop this, he thought, fighting to clear his mind of the woozy, dizzy sensation and to erase the image of the beast. He felt nauseated, and his hands trembled. I've got to regain control, he thought. I've got to shake this thing and put it back in its cage. He knew what to do. Sitting with his feet on the floor and his back erect, he wiped his sweaty palms on the knees of his jeans and folded his hands in his lap. He closed his eyes and focused on taking several deep breaths, concentrating only on the passage of air, in and out, in and out. He quickly fell into meditation, repeating, "All is well. God is with me. If God is with me, who can be against me?" But the bitter anger inside him was shouting louder than the calming words: How could they have done this to my girl? How could they be so stupid?

Trying not to focus on the anger, Brad for some reason recalled a line he had used once in a script he had written about a gunfighter-turned-preacher. The passage was from Ecclesiastes 7:9. "Be not hasty in thy heart to anger, for anger resteth in the bosom of fools." It was strange to remember a script, but that line rang true to him, always had. Brad was no fool, and he knew that anger kills. The face he saw reflected was a face that would kill not only others but Brad himself; the monster would eat itself alive. "All is well," Brad repeated to himself, gently but firmly pushing the monster aside. "All is well. God is with me."

After a few minutes, a warm feeling took root at the bottom of his feet and worked its way up his legs. "All is well. God is with me." The warmth pushed up through his chest, cleansing everything in its path. "All is well. God is with me." It surged like a lump through his constricted throat, flushed his face, and burst through the top of his head. Brad jumped with a gasp, startled, and blinked open his eyes. For a moment he couldn't remember where he was.

He rose from the chair, slowly at first, but feeling stronger, more alert. He began to walk again, and he no longer felt tired. The tension was gone, and so was the anger. Maybe Heidi's awake, he thought, walking back toward my room. He noticed his reflection in the window. This time a familiar face stared back. Brad smiled, gave a brief nod of recognition, and returned to my side.

Gallons of coffee and cartons of cigarettes were consumed in the waiting room that night, and no one slept. The next morning everyone gathered, rumpled and weary, for breakfast in the hospital cafeteria, the light of dawn mercifully warming the pale waiting room after the long night. An older woman approached Brad. "Excuse me," she said, "I'm Mrs. Nickerson, Jimmy's mother."

"Pleased to meet you," Brad said, taking her small hand in his. "How's he doing?"

"I have a big favor to ask you," she said.

"What's that?"

"Would you mind coming up and seeing Jimmy?"

"No, not at all."

"Oh, thank you," she said, leading him to Jimmy's room.

"Wow," Brad said, seeing Jimmy's bandaged head. "That's some piece of work." The surgeons had needed dozens of stitches to re-attach Jimmy's scalp where it had been lifted off his head. Brad offered his hand and asked, "How're you doin'?"

"I'm okay," Jimmy said. "I can't tell you how sorry I am. I tried to turn, but the car didn't respond." Jimmy looked down at his legs stretched out before him in the bed. "I'm just so sorry it turned out this way."

"Hey, you didn't do it on purpose," Brad said. "I'm glad it was you driving instead of some novice they just pulled off the street."

"Thanks, man," Jimmy said, taking Brad's hand again. "That means a lot to me."

Walking Brad back to the waiting room, Mrs. Nickerson thanked him.

"That's okay," Brad said. "He's gonna be all right. And Heidi is, too."

Brad came back into my room with my mother. I only was allowed to see them for five minutes every hour, so they constantly hovered near the door to be there when I was awake. While they were standing by my bed, a doctor came into the room and said hello to me. Then he asked my parents to step into the hall for a minute. "See you in an hour," my mom said, kissing my forehead. "Sleep now." I closed my eyes and fell into a black canyon, deeper and darker than any sleep I had ever known.

My parents followed the doctor out of the room. They stopped in the bright hallway in front of a busy nurses' station. Doctors walked their rounds, stethoscopes hanging like necklaces; nurses rushed by with clipboards; families asked about relatives; and stooped orderlies wheeled clacking carts of plastic dinner trays. The doctor didn't offer my parents a chair or even a cup of coffee. He didn't prepare them at all for what he was about to say.

"Here's the situation," he said. "She has smashed several vertebrae in her neck. This is a very high injury, which means she will never again move below the earlobes. I believe she will be able to speak once we fix her throat. She won't be able to go to the bathroom or have her period or enjoy any normal bodily functions. She won't have any feeling, nothing, and she won't have anything even approaching a normal life. She won't ever have a sex life, and she won't be able to marry. We won't know about brain damage until she is stronger, but in that respect at least, she seems remarkably unharmed. Because of her looks and what people have told me about her life, how active she was and her potential, I have no doubt that psychologically she will be destroyed. When she understands her future, she'll want to kill herself.

"I'm afraid that in any case," the doctor said, "her life expectancy is very short. The slightest infection or even a bad cold could kill her, and it is very possible that she will last only a few months in her weakened condition."

My mother was beyond tears, shocked by the doctor's harsh manner and prognosis. "But she looks fine," she insisted. "She looks perfectly fine."

The doctor turned abruptly and grabbed a pad of paper from the nurses' station. "Look at this." He hastily drew a thick cable on the pad and said, "This is a telephone cable. Inside, it has thousands and thousands of lines. Someone comes along and whacks it in two with a knife," he said, slashing at the tablet with his pen. "Try to put it together again. You can't. That's it. It's over. She will live maybe five years, if she's lucky, and she will be permanently paralyzed."

Brad hadn't said a word, digesting what the doctor had said. "What you are describing," Brad said, "is a talking head."

"Essentially, yes," the doctor said.

Brad was silent for a minute and then looked the doctor square in the eye. "As long as she has a brain cell working, I won't have her described this way."

The doctor held his ground, convinced that the sooner my parents accepted the gravity of the situation, the better. "Be that as it may, I can't help the reality. I'm giving it to you straight. If she were in Russia, they would just put her out in the hall and let her die."

My mother couldn't believe what she was hearing. I looked so normal, so healthy. I was tired but alert, and she couldn't imagine that I would never get up again. It just didn't make sense. Her baby. Her Heidi. I was too strong, too athletic, too healthy. Just look at her, my mother wanted to say. She looks fabulous! Yet the doctor was so hard. He seemed to want to darken even the faintest hope my mother might have. Brad put his arm around her and hugged her. She sunk into his chest, and they stood there, together, for a long minute.

The doctor had other patients to see. He said that as soon as I was fully conscious he wanted to take my parents in to explain the situation to me. It would be best if they broke the news, he said, but he would be there to provide the technical details and explain the situation medically. The doctor said they would need to help me begin to put my affairs in order and to prepare myself for the future, which was not in fact going to be a very long time.

My mother's face was tormented as fear, shock, and anger crashed into one another with no escape.

Brad faced the doctor, silent as a stone, his face not revealing anything. I was his little girl. I was hurt, but I had banged myself up before and had always bounced back. Heidi will be fine, Brad told himself. This doctor was the one with the problem; he was so filled with negativity. Did he truly believe that predicting horror is more honest than offering hope? This poor guy couldn't heal her if he wanted to, and it didn't seem like he was even willing to try. Why did he want to give up on a young woman just beginning her life?

Brad would never give up on me. The idea was as inconceivable as giving up on a piece of himself. Love bound us as securely as the cord that once fed me and tied me to my mother. I was his flesh and spirit, a unique and separate person but never without him. He knew my time in this life had not ended; I still had many things to discover and accomplish. If the doctor wasn't going to take care of me, Brad decided, then he would do it himself. He would pick me up and take me home if he had to, but he was going to make me better.

"I've got to run now," the doctor said, "but maybe later today we can go in and talk to her. We need to explain the situation to her as soon as possible."

Brad's concern for me, and his anger at what had happened, rose hotly and without warning. The snarling, spitting beast that he had tried to lock away burst out of its flimsy cage as if the bars were made of paper. When he spoke to the doctor, he forced himself to be steady, and the words came slowly and deliberately.

"You son of a bitch. You tell her what you told us, and I'll kill you. I'll fucking kill you."

The doctor flinched as if struck.

"What kind of a jerk are you?" Brad asked him, staring into his eyes. "This girl is already in a devastating position, and you're going to go in and unload this pile of rocks on top of her? That in itself is probably enough to kill her. So I'm telling you right now, don't you or any of your nurses—and you better pass this around to them— don't you say anything to my daughter about anything."

The doctor was knocked back on his heels for a second, but only for a second. "She'll have to find out sooner or later," he said.

"She'll get it through the process of osmosis," Brad said. "It'll dribble in a little at a time. She's intelligent, and at some point she's gonna know that something really serious happened, but at that point she'll be stronger than she is now and she'll be able to handle it. Let her get used to it at her own pace. In the meantime, I'm telling you now, mum is the word."

It would have been extremely unwise to argue with Brad right then, and the doctor didn't seem to care that much one way or the other. He held his tongue, and thus my confrontation with reality was postponed.

Friends from the film crew were coming and going from the hospital, saying hello to my parents and asking about me. Half the set must have been milling around the waiting room, drinking coffee and talking. Hal Needham appeared out of the crowd of people and approached Brad. The members of the crew nudged one another and fell silent, following Hal with their eyes. By now, all of them knew that Hal had insisted on doing the stunt a second time and that there had been questions about the safety of the car. There was no doubt that their sympathies were with me and my family; the only unknown was how Brad would react.

The two men, who had known each other for years, stood face to face. The entire room was silent. Brad waited for Hal to speak.

"You know, Brad," Hal said finally, "I don't know why you don't just beat the shit out of me."

"Hal," Brad responded, "I'm not going to let you off that easy. If you want somebody to spank you to ease your guilt, you're gonna have to go get it from somebody else. You're not going to get it from me."

Brad turned his back on Hal and walked away. Those were the last words they would ever exchange.

Later that day my parents moved into the waiting room of Intensive Care. The production company found them a room at a nearby hotel, but they never left the hospital, not for one minute. The waiting room already was occupied by two dozen red-eyed strangers: the parents and friends of other patients. A twenty-year-old girl had nearly drowned and was hovering between life and death. Another young woman had suffered a brain hemorrhage during delivery of her child. An elderly woman was dying, and she was being cared for by her daughter, who worked as a surgical scrub nurse on the East Coast. When the scrub nurse found out what had happened to me, she recommended a certain surgeon who specialized in neck injuries. My parents thanked her for the advice. Everyone in the waiting room was as desperate as my own family, and the scene resembled something out of a bad version of *Ship of Fools*. My parents, the newcomers on board, were warmly welcomed into the hold.

My mother had begun to piece together what had happened to me by talking to various members of the crew and the hospital staff, picking up details that I still didn't know. For one thing, along the way to the hospital someone had stolen the diamond earrings out of my ears. Even more sadly, the thief also took my new tennis shoes, figuring, no doubt, that I wouldn't be playing much tennis. There was some good news with the bad. A member of the rescue squad on the helicopter that brought me to the hospital sought out my parents because he had something he wanted them to know. He said that during the flight I had reached up and yanked the tube out of my throat. That was a good sign, he said, because it meant I still had movement after the crash.

My mother soon regained her composure. She was quick to tears but just as quick to shake them off and get down to business. She was devastated by what the doctor had said, but the truth was, it didn't square with what she was seeing with her own eyes. Obviously I was hurt badly, but if I was still alive, then there was hope. She knew from experience that doctors paint the worst possible picture, and that the reality could only be better than their description of it. She firmly believed that the mind controls everything, and if my brain was not injured, which she was sure was the case, then recovery was possible, even certain. My mother never accepted that I would live only a few months or even five years. She never accepted that I would be permanently paralyzed. And she never accepted that I wouldn't have a perfectly normal life. She seemed steeled by the odds and declared to herself, "This is going to be a challenge. This is going to be tough and a lot of work, but this family is going to do it together."

My parents have always seen life as a series of steps to be taken one at a time. When something bad happens, they don't look for excuses or people to blame; they look for the next step, and then they take it. Already my mother was thinking about what it would be like to have me at home, and that among the challenges, it was going to be physically demanding to care for me. I would need to be lifted and bathed and carried everywhere, which wouldn't be easy with someone my size. She and my dad were physically fit but not fit enough for my mother, who immediately started them on an intensive fitness regimen right there in the hospital. They bought little dumbbells and bounced around in the bathroom, which fortunately was big enough to train an entire football team. They refused to leave my floor even for a shower, so after exercising, they splashed off in the sink and dried themselves with paper towels.

Christy arrived with her baby daughter, Allison, and was equally sanguine about the future. "If Heidi doesn't walk again, she'll be sitting on the beach in a yellow bathing suit and tan and healthy and great with all her friends around her. Forget the doctors," Christy said. "We don't listen to what they say." Jeff, who was editing a newspaper in Big Bear, California, was on the phone every minute for updates and promised to get there as soon as he put the current edition to bed. "I'm not worried about Heidi," he told my parents, "but you guys get some sleep."

The rest of the family agreed with Brad's gut instinct. For the time being it was best not to tell me about the doctor's prognosis. I would find out soon enough, but they wanted me to be stronger before that burden was placed upon my shoulders. I was heavily sedated, always the blink of an eye away from the deepest sleep. Night and day ran together, visitors came, nurses hovered. Eyes heavy. Mouth thick. Dark sleep beyond dreams.

A few days after the first doctor gave his prognosis, another doctor strolled into my room, cheerfully greeting everyone like old friends. I only assumed he was a doctor because of the white coat; he looked more like a high-stakes gambler in Vegas on a roll. He wore a gold watch, gold chains, and flashy clothes underneath the white doctor's smock. He was dark-haired and dashing, and in sharp contrast to the first doctor, he offered my parents a warm hand and a friendly smile. "Elias Ghanem," he announced.

If you were making a movie about Las Vegas and you wanted a doctor, you would cast Elias Ghanem. He not only looks the part, he's the real thing. He was the attending physician at the biggest prize fights, and his patients included Liberace and Elvis Presley. On a chain around his neck, Ghanem wore a gift from Elvis: a gold lightning bolt with the letters "TCB," which stands for Taking Care of Business.

After a few minutes of small talk, Ghanem excused himself to me and led my parents into the hall outside my room. "Did you talk with my colleague?" he asked.

"He paints a very dismal picture," Brad said.

"I don't think it has to be that way," Ghanem said. "Probably she'll never walk again, but she could have a lot of recovery. I've seen a lot of things in my day, and she could do well. It was a horrendous accident, but she's young, she's strong, and no one can say for sure what the prognosis is at this point. A lot depends on her—and on you."

Those were the words my parents wanted to hear. They were the first words of hope and the first sign of positive thinking from someone dressed in white. The hope Ghanem offered was modest, but his were words of kindness and love, and they helped my parents begin to pick themselves up after the beating they had taken.

More visitors looked in on me with cautious smiles, an endless parade of people flowing into my room during the five minutes allowed every hour. Just as quickly, the nurses herded the visitors back outside. I fought to stay awake for more than a few minutes, and I was so disappointed every time I slept through the brief visiting period. I couldn't talk, and I was barely aware of the world around me, but I loved knowing so many people were there.

I had trouble actually seeing who was in the room because my head wouldn't budge and I was staring at the ceiling. By now I had figured out that my head was bolted in place, a realization that frightened me at first. Maybe, I thought for an instant, this thing is worse than I know. I had seen people in traction and wired up like this on television, and I knew doctors didn't do it for just a little whiplash. I was so fit and active, though, that the thought of serious permanent injury was not really a concern to me. I figured I couldn't move because I was so tired, that my battered body had literally shut down to heal. I just needed to rest.

The doctors told me not to move, and I was too weak to even try. My body didn't feel any different. I wiggled my toes and clenched my fists. Everything felt the same. The problem was that with my head bolted in place, I couldn't see any part of my body. I had no idea that when I wiggled my toes, they weren't really moving. When I made a fist, my fingers didn't budge; it felt the same as it always had. My mind had no concept of what had happened to the body in which it lived.

My irrepressible sister, who makes a hummingbird seem calm, charged into my room with fashion magazines and snacks and makeup, everything she could think of to keep me busy. She kissed me, arranged the blinds, adjusted my bed, said hello to the nurses, dumped the magazines on my chest, flipped the perfumed pages with one hand while popping open a soft drink with the other, told me about her adventure getting to the hospital, examined the machines whirring next to my bed, kissed me again, and plopped into a chair. She jumped back up like she had sat on a tack to see if I needed any eye makeup. She stood over me to look at my face, wondering what miracles she could perform with eyeliner.

I looked up at my big sister. I remembered the long rides on horseback we had taken in the country. I remembered sitting in her room watching her get ready for a date, stealing her clothes before I shot past her in size. I couldn't speak, but I wanted to tell her I loved her, I wanted to tell her that I was scared, and mostly I wanted to tell her to get me the hell out of this hospital. I just wanted to go home.

I didn't know what was happening. Nobody was telling me anything. I didn't want to be bolted onto the stupid bed.

Christy says that my eyes flooded with tears, turning them into a pair of deep blue pools, so that I appeared to be looking at her from underwater. She snapped at the nurse for a tissue, but the nurse was busy with something, so my sister grabbed a towel from the sink and dried my eyes, her own tears streaming into the river of mine and wetting my frightened face.

Christy ignored the nurse's announcement that the five-minute visiting period had ended. The nurse wasn't too concerned, though, and was more interested in a conversation she was having with another nurse about their dates the night before, interrupting their boy talk just long enough to flip me over in the Stryker frame. They had explained that this was necessary to prevent bedsores from forming on my back, but the facedown position was annoying and extremely unpleasant. The frame was designed with straps across the chin and forehead, so when I faced downward, my body was held in place by thick straps across my chest and legs and my head was supported by straps across my face. The straps kept my face from clunking onto the floor, which was a good thing, but they sliced into my chin and forehead.

The nurse fastened the straps snugly across my face, and with cool efficiency she flipped me facedown, at the same time resuming her conversation with the other nurse. I was staring at the floor, half listening to the story about the nurse's boyfriend and half listening to Christy going on about something, when the strap holding my chin snapped down across my neck. Another strap strained against my forehead, but the weight of my head had collapsed almost entirely onto the strap across my windpipe. I didn't have the strength to lift my head to ease the pressure, which seemed to be increasing with every second. My eyes bulged and my tongue flopped out of my mouth. I tried to yell, but no sound, and no air, came from my throat.

The nurse continued to discuss her boyfriend, who apparently was a real doll but a bit of a problem maturity-wise. The nurse had wanted to go home after a movie, but the boyfriend wouldn't give her the keys or it was his car or something. Christy was talking away at my backside, until she noticed a puddle of drool spreading beneath my face. She bent her knees to look at my face.

"I'm choking," I mouthed.

"What?" Christy said. "What's wrong, Heidi? What is it?"

I tried again, slower. "I'm choking."

"Nurse!" Christy shouted. "Something's wrong! Get over here."

". . . so I go, 'No, you give me the keys,' and he goes, 'No, you give me the keys,' and I go . . ." The nurse reluctantly interrupted her story and ambled over to the bed. She bent down to look at me. When our eyes met I saw a flash of alarm on her face. She snapped to attention and flipped me onto my back, quickly loosening the strap across my neck.

I took a few deep breaths and smiled at Christy. "Thanks."

My memories of the first days are blurry, as though like Christy had said, everything was shot from underwater. Certain images are crystal-clear, neatly arranged in my brain, but they are surrounded by cottony morphine, exhaustion, and the trauma of the shock to my body. I remember people coming and saying hello. They cried and looked down at me with red eyes and serious faces. I tried to smile, but everyone was so sad. I loved them so much, and I felt sorry that I had upset them so. I smiled to say I would get better very soon. Sometimes I imagined I was in a coffin and this was an open-casket funeral. The more I saw the reaction of other people, the more I realized I was seriously injured. But their love and concern also helped me know that I would be better very soon. If only I could rest.

Chapter 4

MY HERO
FROM HAWAII

My parents set up a command post in the waiting room and commandeered the bank of pay phones. They took nourishment in the cafeteria, slept on plastic couches, bathed in the public rest room, and began a crash course in spinal injury, medical administration, and hospital politics. They drew strength from the other families, a group my mother dubbed the "victims of the victims." The families compared notes about what was happening in the hospital, about who the good doctors were and who to avoid. The young scrub nurse taking care of her dying mother went on and on about a surgeon she knew who could help me, but she was so small and mousy, with such a tiny little voice, that no one paid her much attention. The girl who had nearly drowned did not survive, but everyone cheered when the woman with the hemorrhage was able to leave for home with her healthy baby.

Despite the relentlessly positive attitude of my parents, I wasn't going anywhere for the moment. I realized my neck was injured, although I don't remember anyone actually telling me, "You broke your neck." If they did, it didn't register. For the doctors a broken neck had all kinds of serious implications for my health and future; for me it was just a broken bone that would heal in time. My spinal cord was what really mattered, and obviously that wasn't severed completely or I would have died on the spot. I knew about paralysis and people in wheelchairs, but that wasn't me. Maybe I'm thick or something, but I just didn't get it. I thought, this is bad, but I'll recover.

The doctors informed my parents that the immediate, most pressing problem was my neck. They said I had suffered a compression fracture of an area of the spinal column known as C-5–6, which is close to the head, with compression and maceration of the spinal cord. They didn't want to move me at all because bone splinters floating around in my neck could slice up the spinal cord and do even more damage, if that was possible. I also had a broken femur (which is the bone in my right thigh that had popped through my jeans), a severely dislocated shoulder, and a smashed hip.

My parents waited for the surgeons and specialists to get to work on fixing me. And they waited. And waited. But no one took a step in my direction. The doctors seemed to think they were doing enough by letting me stay in their hospital. No one ever said, "This is what we are going to do, this is our recovery plan for Heidi." My parents asked everyone in the hospital—doctors, nurses, and administrators—"What's going on? What is the plan?" No one had any answers. My parents are not very good at waiting, unless they know what they are waiting for. They like to make a game plan, map out the moves necessary to complete the plan, and begin to execute it. The hospital, however, had no plan.

On the day I was admitted, my parents marched down to the office of the acting administrator. The man occupying the position didn't even invite them in; he spoke to them from his desk while they stood in the doorway. "What is the plan?" they asked. He looked up briefly from piles of paperwork and said, "That's something you need to establish with your doctor." The doctors had no more answers than the administrator, except that we should be patient and wait and see how my condition developed.

When it comes to waiting, I'm even worse than my parents, and as consciousness started to return, so did my desire to get on with my life. After only two days of being strapped, pinned, irrigated,

...ort, with me strapped to the Stryker frame a... ...broiling tarmac alongside the plane, the ambulan... ...d that Dorothy had been right: The frame was too... ...They made a few adjustments, cleared the doorw... ...n. No way. There were a few more adjustments an... ...ssion, but it was physically impossible to get me ins... ...hout taking me off the frame, which was not an opti... ...se of planes landing and taking off around us g... ...asts blew thick, hot gusts of gritty dust. Dorothy beca... ...The ambulance drivers were getting cranky. The... ...wanted everyone to decide one way or the other. I wo... ...ld stay, but I didn't want to talk about it anymore. T... ...o hot. There was no air. I started to feel woozy and t... ...suddenly had been wheeled into an air-conditioned ro... ...and felt goose bumps raising on my arms. Dorothy loo... ...es and touched my cheeks. I smiled weakly.

...s getting heat pröstration," Dorothy said. "We've go... ...ut of here." The drivers scrambled to get me aboard... ...ce, and we sped back to the hospital.

...le the drivers futilely tried to wedge a six-foot wo... ...the three-foot door of an airplane, my parents took a c... ...flight to California to be at the hospital when I arr... ...nded in Los Angeles and sped to the hospital, only to... ...oper tell them, "She's not here. She couldn't make it o... ...gas. You've got to go back."

...ey returned to Las Vegas to find me in my old room, pal... ...nd feeling miserable, physically drained and disappo... ...was still there, back at square one. I hadn't been able t... ...he crash because of the hole in my throat, and now... ...ing was a great effort. A few days later we tried again to... ...urney to California, but on the second try my blood pr... ...p to the ceiling and I feared my heart would explode... ...do this," Dr. Ghanem said. "She's not strong enough."

...ut I wasn't getting any better waiting around in Las Ve... ...sisted on scheduling a third flight. I remember lying...

evacuated, and catheterized, I was getting antsy when I wasn't too tired to care. After more than a week, I was stir-crazy. Every two hours the nurses rotated my Stryker frame so I wouldn't spend too much time in one position, and I felt like a chicken roasting on a spit. Now at least they were more careful about the straps across my chin and forehead, because I would have strangled if Christy hadn't been there that time. How embarrassing for everyone.

When I was alone, I was stuck because I couldn't reach over and use the call button. I could see the controls dangling on a cord alongside the bed, but I couldn't move anything to operate it or even to touch it. I couldn't call out for help because my throat did not allow me to talk. Soon I devised a set of signals I learned from *My Friend Flicka*. Instead of stamping my hoof once for "yes" and twice for "no," I clicked my tongue. When I needed something, I made a series of clicks to get the attention of the nurses. I got so I could click loud enough to rattle the windows and make the nurses come running. Once they arrived, breathless at first and more slowly as the days dragged on, I mouthed my requests with careful enunciation so they could understand me. I called often because I was helpless: I couldn't even scratch my nose or rub my eyes. CLICK! CLICK! "Could you change the channel?" CLICK! "Would you get me a tissue?" CLICK! CLICK! "What time is it?" I had lots of questions that the nurses couldn't answer, most of them having to do with what was going to happen next and when I could go home.

Dr. Ghanem tried to get me some answers. He suggested the best course would be to find a neurosurgeon who could stabilize my neck—not heal it, but fuse the bones so there wouldn't be any more damage. My head was attached only with muscle, and during the ride from the crash site to the hospital it had flopped on my back because there was no support. The slightest movement could have killed me, so for the time being the doctors wanted to keep my head bolted in place with the halo made of canvas straps and steel.

Besides the major injuries the doctors had identified the first day, there were other problems we learned about by ourselves. One day Brad and I were talking about nothing in particular while he performed one of his regular checkups. He always liked to see me for himself, to touch my skin and feel my forehead, to make sure was well. When I was a baby he would get up in the night, pad into my room to look in my crib, just to make sure I was breathing. Now he lifted the sheet across my legs to touch my feet, and he jumped back. "This is unbelievable," he said. "What are they doing?" I couldn't see what he was talking about. He gently turned my fee and told me that he was looking at two open wounds on my heels He said they looked like exit holes from gunshots: bloody red cen ters rimmed with a black dried crust.

Brad was furious. He snapped at a nurse, "What are you goin to do about this?"

"Those are decubitous ulcers," the nurse said smartly, as if call ing them by their official name made them less ugly or dangerous "You don't really do anything about them except monitor them t prevent infection."

"I don't want you to explain to me what they are; I know what bedsore is. I want you to tell me why you let them happen. She ha to be moved. Even I know that. If you don't do it, I'm going to do myself."

Every day brought new grisly discoveries and new frustration frustrations that were hardest on my dad. Brad is a natural leade and has never been comfortable as a follower. He does not let thing happen to him; he makes things happen. But even he had troubl making things happen in the hospital. The whole system is designe the other way: Doctors act, patients are acted upon; doctors operat patients are treated. Families are advised, not consulted. Patient and their loved ones, are supposed to be patient.

We began to realize that if I was going to get better, we wer going to have to do it ourselves. I would have to stop being a passiv patient and start being an active participant in the healing proces No one cared about me as much as my parents did, and none of th "professionals," except Dr. Ghanem, seemed to think that gettin better was even a possibility. Dr. Ghanem's suggestion that a goc first step would be to find a neurosurgeon for my neck made sen

to us, but there was no one on the If there had been time, I'm sure Bra read up on the topic, and perform next best thing was a family friend, D son of our friend Frank Cooper and o surgeons.

My parents called Martin and e agreed that my neck needed to be wanted to come to Las Vegas to do it h was that he was at Cedar's Hospital in seriously hurt patients, and there was no v He tried to organize everything by teleph isfied and insisted on performing the sur because I trusted him and I wanted the be Martin told my mother, "and I'll stabilize her thing ready at this end."

That was a plan, and my parents jumped Ghanem agreed that I should go to Dr. Cooper, that I would have to be moved very carefully bec was so delicate. I had been in the hospital for abot although I was feeling much stronger, I was still we helped in arranging the special air ambulance by "Nurse Ratched" from *Cannonball*, who had a ton When she examined me before going to the airpo everyone that the Stryker frame was too big to fit into no one listened to her.

When the big moment arrived, Dorothy and Ghar he ambulance with me and we sped to the airport, into the blistering desert heat. The days were relentles loudless, and I had almost forgotten how hot it was o he way, Dorothy suctioned my throat every few Ghanem monitored my vital signs. I was tired but hought of getting out of Las Vegas and back to Califor irted shamelessly with me, promising me a night on the came back to visit.

At the air parked on the drivers realize for the door. and tried aga lot more disc the plane wi The noi louder. Jet b impatient. baked me. go or I wo sun was to cold, as if I shivered into my e "She get her ambular Wh throug mercia They Dr. C Las V weak that I since breat the shot can't

we i

frame a few hours before the scheduled departure, hoping that three was a charm. Then without warning the sky darkened and huge black thunderheads rolled over the hospital. The nurses all remarked on how strange it was to have a storm at that time of year. The sky split open and poured water down upon us, washing out the third and final attempt at moving me.

Shot down again, my parents worked on a new plan. If Dr. Cooper couldn't come to me, and I couldn't go to him, someone else had to do the surgery in Las Vegas. Unwilling to wait for the hospital to help us find a doctor, my mother grabbed a telephone book and started searching the Yellow Pages for a surgeon. I'm not sure exactly what she looked for—ads that promised "You fracture 'em, we fuse 'em"?—but she managed to find three likely candidates, whom she called from a pay phone in the waiting room.

One of the doctors listened to the story and decided nothing more could be done for me. The second doctor was on vacation. The third doctor wouldn't take her call. The next day the third doctor's nurse called back and said she had a message from the doctor: "The doctor asked me to tell you that he hasn't done a neck in ten years, but if your daughter ever gets a brain tumor to call him."

The frustration, uncertainty, and anger were building up inside my parents. They too were trapped in the hospital, afraid to leave my side for even a few minutes and unable to escape the pressure and biting worry. Before something snapped, or my mom punched out one of the nurses, they decided to call Mrs. S. I won't use her full name because she would consider it the height of vanity to single her out, even though she has done so much for us. Mrs. S. was our Christian Science practitioner back home, our toughest teacher and guide.

My mom dialed the number and stood in the waiting room with the phone to her ear. Mrs. S. was a stern old woman, with a spirit—and a voice—strong enough to travel across the desert and into my mother's body. My mom listened for a while to Mrs. S.'s long-distance wisdom, nodding her head silently (it was hard to get a word in with Mrs. S.). Then she passed the phone to Brad, who listened for a while and passed it to Joanna, who in turn gave the phone to Bobby, even though he's Jewish and didn't know the first thing about Christian Science.

My mother told Mrs. S. what was happening—basically nothing—and that we were going crazy with the lack of direction and the apparent lack of concern among the doctors.

"Turn away!" Mrs. S. yelled at my mom, repeating it like a mantra, or more like a bullwhip. The voice was so loud my mother held the phone away from her ear. "Turn away! Go to a movie. Read a book. Get out of there!"

My mother tried to interrupt, "But the doctor says—"

"Turn away!" Mrs. S. shouted back across two states. "Turn away!"

Bobby, who soon came to appreciate Mrs. S.'s brand of hard love as much as we did, took the phone and tried to explain our situation further.

"Bobby, turn away!" Mrs. S. commanded. "Don't listen to the doctors. Whatever they say, that's not something that the Lord made. The Lord only makes good, and if the Lord didn't make it, then it's man's idea of something, so turn away."

Mrs. S. meant that we should turn away from the material belief in the injury. Focus on a perfect neck, she explained, and that energy will create the matrix for the neck to conform to that perfect image. When Jesus saw the leper or the blind man, He saw the perfect man and therefore the man became perfect. Hold in your mind the perfection of being, and the spirit will work within you to heal. She told us that the healing process would take care of itself, but we had to turn away from all the negative thoughts and energy and allow God's work to be done.

"Whatever destructive things they tell Heidi, don't worry about it," Mrs. S. said. "She will not hear them."

We called her several times every day, and she sent us care packages of meditations for us to work with hourly. The words of Mrs. S. helped us find our way. Here I was in one of the world's most modern hospitals, surrounded by highly trained doctors, but my best help was coming from a little old lady hundreds of miles away, repeating the teachings of our ancestors. Her words were like a cool hand on my forehead, and I let them work their magic. I prayed and meditated, and I felt Mrs. S., and God, at my side.

My parents had learned about Christian Science as adults and were firm believers in the healing power of the spirit. My mother's religious upbringing had been very conservative. Her father was a Presbyterian minister, strict, stern, and intelligent, who read Greek and Latin and thought deeply about religion and expected my mother to do the same. The only time he ever lost his temper with her was when my mother innocently mentioned the name Darwin. Her father banged the dinner table until the plates jumped, forbidding her to ever mention that blasphemous name.

My father, too, had been raised in a traditional home, but he also had a longtime interest in Eastern religions, metaphysics, and what now are called New Age ideas. Largely because of my father's broad interests, my brother and sister and I attended Sunday school at the tiny Church of Religious Science. In what surely was a good omen, my first teacher there was the Good Witch of the North, the wonderful Billie Burke from *The Wizard of Oz*, who was married to Florenz Ziegfeld of the Ziegfeld Follies.

My mother had been skeptical at first about nontraditional religious ideas, but her view of the world changed drastically when I was only three or four years old and her dear friend Bette was diagnosed with cancer. The doctors told Bette they had no choice but to operate, and to most people at the time, surgery was a powerful, if slightly mysterious, cure for everything. Bette didn't want surgery, and she sensed the doctors were treating her symptoms but not the underlying problem. She had been reading a book given to her by Cary Grant about LSD and the mind, and she feared the doctors were concentrating too much on her illness and not enough on her as a whole, spiritual person.

Days before she was to have surgery, Bette asked my mother to go with her to a hypnotist named Dr. Hugh Case, who worked with the Religious Science minister Bob Scott. The treatment consisted of hypnosis and a series of readings designed to allow the body to heal itself. The theory was that hypnosis would open the mind and body to the power of the spirit. As soon as Hugh and Bob began and Bette entered the altered state similar to deep meditation, she felt the treatment was working, but she thought they had stopped before her body had time to really start healing. Back at home, my mother opened the text by Ernest Holmes and began to read. For five straight days she read Bette those healing passages and affirmations.

Bette felt much better when my mother drove her to the doctor for one last checkup before surgery. Somewhat embarrassed, Bette told the doctor what they had been doing. Instead of laughing at them, the doctor said, "I'm a Jew who believes Moses literally parted the Red Sea, so I wouldn't rule out what you're telling me. For that reason I'm going to send your samples to the lab one more time, but this time we'll send them in blind, without your name on it. At the lab they know you're supposed to have cancer and the test is supposed to come up positive, but we don't want their thoughts influencing the results."

A few days passed and there were no results, which was unusual because the previous cancer tests had come back quickly—and positive. When the doctor finally called the lab to check, he was told the unnamed patient's samples showed no signs of cancer. Bette was cured, and my mother began to undergo a spiritual change. A few years later she herself took a treatment from Hugh Case, who successfully relieved a horrible toothache and saved her tooth through meditation. I went to Hugh the first time when I was just a girl, and he cured my badly swollen tonsils.

Thus I was raised to think that hypnosis and the power of suggestion are perfectly normal medical procedures. I grew up hearing stories such as the one about a man in Africa who had his throat torn open by a lion. Far from any doctor, the man prayed and his throat was closed. These stories were not parables to me, but historical facts. The car crash, however, left me with injuries far worse than any we had ever seen. The long-distance guidance of Mrs. S. helped, but

I was strapped to a hospital bed, surrounded by doctors, and the only option seemed to be to place our faith in medical science.

My parents, like most of us, grew up with the image of the great god doctor who knows all and heals all. My dad's only major experience with doctors came when he was fifteen years old and was badly burned when a pan of hot linseed oil blew up in his face. He was rushed to the small-town clinic, and like the good boy that he was, he quietly took his place in line behind the half dozen people with cuts and bruises and various ailments who had arrived before him. When the doctor glanced out and saw a beet-red boy covered with rising blisters and frizzled hair, he told the nurse, "Get him in here, now!"

This was an Arizona mining town, and the clinic kept a precious supply of special, very expensive salve for serious burns. My dad remembers vividly how the doctor ordered the nurse to apply the cream immediately, and she delicately spread a thin layer on his skin, frugally wiping up the excess in order not to waste a drop. The doctor angrily grabbed the jar from her. "Are you trying to scar this boy?" He shoved her aside and slapped huge globs of the salve onto the burns. My dad healed quickly and without a scar, and from that moment his respect for doctors ran deep.

But now he was having his doubts. I think the medical staff was afraid of touching me, fearing that they would kill me and be accused of malpractice. They seemed to regard keeping me alive as accomplishment enough. There was no more discussion about when I might leave the hospital. No one had even bothered to comb out my hair, which was still matted and caked with Jimmy's blood ten days after the crash.

Brad approached one of the nurses, again, and asked, "When is someone going to do something?"

"That's hard to say," she said.

"Hard to say?"

"You haven't made yourself very agreeable."

"What do you mean, agreeable?" Brad said, almost over the edge with frustration. "Is this some kind of situation where you are supposed to be agreeable?"

"Let's just say you haven't been very nice."

"Well, nobody's doing anything, and nobody's been nice to us," Brad said, incredulous.

Joanna, my very capable and sophisticated aunt, gently but firmly pushed Brad aside. "Can't you understand," she said to the nurse, "we don't know what to do. I mean, we can't get her out of here until she has her neck stabilized, and we can't get anybody to do it."

The nurse said, "First of all, before you say anything to me, I want you to get down on your knees and apologize."

Brad thought the nurse was kidding, but she wasn't. He turned away. My aunt swallowed her pride and fell to her knees on the polished hospital floor. "I'm on my knees," she said, looking up at the towering figure in a starched white uniform. "Now tell us what to do."

"You will have to discuss that with your doctor."

All this effort, combined with the tension and uncertainty, was exhausting. The constant vigilance of my parents only annoyed the nurses, who regarded the hospital as their private domain and regarded me as something less than a guest, almost as an intruder. They couldn't exactly throw us out, and my parents weren't going anywhere, so tempers flared when the nurses didn't respond immediately to my calls or when my parents disagreed with the treatment, such as it was.

Then Bobby received a call from an old friend, a famous race-car driver named Stan Barrett, who had banged himself up regularly on the way to all kinds of records, including being the first person to break the speed of sound on land. Stan knew about my accident, and he wanted to tell Bobby about a special doctor who could help me. When Stan broke his back, he had been fixed by Ralph Cloward, whom Stan described as a legendary pioneer in spinal surgery and the man who had invented much of the equipment and surgical tools used by everyone in the field. The only problem, Stan said, was that Cloward was close to eighty years old and had retired in Hawaii. Stan gave us Cloward's home telephone number, and Brad called from the hospital pay phone. The old doctor picked up the phone himself on the first ring.

"We're grasping at straws," Brad told Cloward after explaining the situation. "Nobody will touch her, and we don't know what to do. I feel like a horse swimming a stream and trying to get up on a matchbook cover."

"When did it happen?" Cloward said.

"Fifteen days ago."

"Oh, God," Cloward said. He was silent for a moment. "I don't know if I can help you. I don't have clearance to practice in Nevada. If she were in California, there'd be no problem."

"What if I can get you clearance?" Brad asked.

"You do, and I'll come."

Brad hung up and called one of the hospital administrators. "We can get Ralph Cloward, but he doesn't have clearance for Nevada," Brad said. The mere mention of that name magically opened a huge door that had been closed until now.

"Tell Dr. Cloward that he'll have clearance by the time he gets here," the administrator promised, and she was true to her word.

Days later, Brad went to the airport to pick up the surgeon, and although we had no idea what he looked like, Brad said there was no doubt when Cloward stepped off the plane. A small, brisk man marched briskly through the crowd carrying a single metal case. He looked like Alec Guinness in *Bridge on the River Kwai*, and Brad half expected someone to start whistling the movie's theme song. The doctor introduced himself to Brad, who then had to hurry to keep up as Cloward smartly led the way out of the gate area, brushing past people who were moving too slowly with a crisp "Step to the side, please. Step to the side."

Cloward immediately charged into the hospital, parting the admiring sea of white-uniformed doctors and nurses. The word of his pending arrival had spread quickly, and the doctors bowed and scraped before his imposing presence. Cloward burst into Intensive Care and snapped my X rays up to the light. "This is no good," he said, tossing an X ray aside. He snapped another image up to the light. "Poor picture. Poor picture. Who took that? Better. Oohh. Good, really good. This is no good. Ahh. This is better. Hmmm. Okay."

The first time I saw Dr. Cloward, he walked directly to my bedside, said hello, bent over, and plugged the hole in my throat with tape and gauze. Just like that I could talk again. At the sound of my first words, the room, which had filled with doctors and staff wanting to see the legendary Cloward in action, erupted in applause. No one had thought to plug the hole before, and it was so simple that I was furious it hadn't been done earlier. (Now that I think about it, the doctors probably kept the hole open deliberately, thinking that with a voice I'd be even more of a pain in the neck, so to speak.)

"Heidi," he said, "as I'm sure you know, your injury is very serious. I've looked at your X rays, and you've got a couple of exploded vertebrae. This is a very serious injury, but we're going to do this thing, and we're going to do it under local anesthesia because that tracheotomy means we can't put you under with a general."

I remained motionless in bed listening to his words, staring straight up because of the bolts holding my head in place.

"I've brought a whalebone all the way from Hawaii," he continued, "and we're going to put it in there to replace the piece that's broken. It's gonna be tough. We're gonna have to work together on this. It's going to be a long operation, and I've got tired old legs, but you've waited long enough and we're going to start right in. We're gonna fix you up, little lady."

I couldn't move my head, but I shifted my eyes to look into his. From the moment he walked into the room, I had not a single doubt that he could fix me. I smiled and told him, "Go for it."

Cloward checked me out from head to toe and stopped abruptly when he saw my exploded heels. "What about these bedsores?" he asked the nurse, an exasperated look on his tired face. "Haven't you done anything at all for this girl?"

Cloward wanted to talk to one of my many doctors. Immediately. But the doctor was nowhere to be found. When a nurse explained that the doctor was busy with a previous appointment, Cloward said, "It must be awful important for him to keep me waiting." Then he went to lie down for a few minutes before the operation.

The little scrub nurse who was taking care of her mother came running up and said gleefully, "He's the one! Dr. Cloward's the one I was telling you about." We just laughed and told her that we should have listened to her in the first place.

When the orderlies wheeled me in for the operation, my mother's final words were, "Pay attention, Heidi. The good thing about a local anesthetic is that you'll be awake. Try to remember because someday you're going to write a book about this."

The surgery lasted nine hours. My parents sat in the waiting room, talking with the other families, calling Mrs. S., and meditating. They not only sought answers, and the peace that such guidance brings, but they hoped to lay down a field of positive energy to light the path for Dr. Cloward.

When it was over, I couldn't remember very much, despite my mother's urging, and I fell into an exhausted sleep. Cloward washed up, changed clothes, and went to see my parents. My neck was a mess, he said. He told them that he had vacuumed out some of the bone chips, but that scar tissue had formed already. He showed them how he had inserted the piece of whalebone and carved it down to fit my skeleton.

"She is paralyzed," Cloward said. "She is going to be paralyzed for the rest of her life, and it probably would be well to get used to the idea. She should be able to recover some of her breathing, but it is severely impacted because the injury is so close to the phrenic nerves that control the diaphragm.

"I took out all the bone chips I could get, and I put in stainless steel posts throughout. It works like bridgework to support her spine and make the neck rigid again."

Up until this point, all the doctors had told us that the spinal cord was badly damaged. Cloward was the first to actually have a look at it, and he said it was not severed at all. The only damage was a slight nick in the dura mater, which is the protective layer around the nerves. There was a minor leaking of spinal fluid, but not much more than would occur during a routine spinal tap.

"You've still got to be prepared for permanent paralysis," Cloward told them. "For the moment I gave her a big dose of steroids to help the healing process."

Brad was the first to see me after I awoke. I was in a regular bed, staring up at the ceiling, not sure what was happening. There were no more bolts in my head, and no more halo, but I was wearing a foam brace around my neck like the kind used for whiplash. Brad watched me quietly for a moment until he saw a fat tear well up in my eye, spill over, and roll down my face.

"What is it, honey?"

"I don't know what I can do," I said. "Can I move? What can I do? Is my neck okay?"

Brad walked out of the room and interrupted Cloward talking to another doctor and pulled him into my room. "Heidi wants to know what she can do," Brad told him.

"What can she do?" Cloward repeated. "Why, she can do anything!"

He bent over and pulled off the brace around my neck. "Move your head," he commanded, but before I could gather the courage to do anything, he grabbed my chin and yanked it side to side. It felt fine. I moved it myself. I looked up, I looked down. I looked around the room. I smiled a huge smile.

"It's all fixed," Cloward said. "You're gonna be great. I saved a couple of nerves, and we'll see what happens. Straighten up, sister. You're fine."

Then Cloward opened the silver case that he carried everywhere. Inside were his surgical tools and a single clean shirt. The case also contained a delicate lei made from real orchids, which he removed and gently placed around my newly repaired neck.

The next morning, Brad took Cloward to breakfast before his flight to Hawaii. "There is a lot of scar tissue," Cloward said. "The thing is, the sooner we can get to a spinal-cord injury, the better we like it. Scar tissue starts forming, and there is no way of telling what kind of damage it will do.

"There was one nerve I was able to clear that might give her partial movement of one of the arms, but that's it," Cloward went on. "She's going to be like that the rest of her life. The life expectancy is not good in these cases because there are so many complications. I'd have to agree with what the other doctors told you: She may last five years, or it may be even sooner. We've done all we can do."

"I respect your opinion, Doctor," Brad said. He took a sip of his coffee. "But my daughter's gonna get up and walk again."

Cloward gave Brad a little smile and said, "I have to admire your spirit."

"Is there anything else?" Brad asked.

"No, I think that about wraps it up—"

"No," Brad said. "Anything other than spirit?"

Cloward smiled again, broader this time. "Let's go back and let me say good-bye to the girls."

We said our good-byes, and Brad took Cloward to the airport for his flight home. As soon as Brad returned, we started making plans for us to go home, too. I wouldn't be able to return to my apartment yet, but with my neck fixed, we at least could transfer to a hospital in California. I felt like I had cleared a major hurdle, and we all were relieved to be thinking about leaving. I'm sure the nurses were equally relieved. The only thing that worried me was that every once in a while I saw little flashes of pink slipping through the tube that ran from my stomach and out my nose. Normally the liquid was clear, and it was only recently that I noticed this occasional pink. I mentioned it to my mom, and she told one of the nurses. "Oh, I'm sure it's nothing," the nurse said.

"I'm not so sure it's nothing," Joanna said. "It's the color of digested blood. I think it's coming from her stomach."

None of the doctors seemed concerned, though, and we let it go. Maybe it was just some aftereffect of the surgery that would pass. The big news was that a woman had arrived from the company that insured the producers of *Cannonball*. No one up to this point had talked to us about money or insurance, but we all knew that my care and surgery were costing a fortune. When the insurance representative arrived, my parents wanted to meet her right away. I was doing so well after my neck surgery that they were confident enough to leave me alone for the first time in two weeks and drive to the airport to meet her.

While they were gone, I watched television and dozed, thinking about going home, about my friends, skiing, playing tennis. I wondered how *Cannonball* was coming. I drifted off to sleep, the most peaceful that I had been since the crash.

I woke with a start to find several doctors and nurses standing over me. "Heidi," one of them said, "we're going to take you down for surgery."

"Surgery? What are you talking about?"

"There's a problem with your stomach. There is internal bleeding, and it appears to be getting worse. We need to do some work on it, and we're going to take you down right now."

"No, you're not," I said. "I'm going home. Where are my parents?"

"They're not here right now. We left them a message, but there isn't time to wait. We need to do this right now."

"I think we should wait until my parents get here."

"If we wait any longer," the doctor said, "you're going to bleed to death."

When my parents returned to the hospital and walked into my room, I was gone.

My mother ran out of the room. "Where's Heidi?" she demanded of the first nurse who appeared.

"She's in surgery," the nurse said.

"Surgery? What do you mean, surgery?"

"Yes, Mrs. von Beltz. She needed emergency surgery on her stomach. She just went down a few minutes ago."

"Oh my God," my mother said. "Where's the recovery room?"

"After the surgery she won't be awake for hours," the nurse said.

"Where is the recovery room?"

The nurse pointed my parents to the recovery room, where they waited for me to finish surgery. I was doped up and groggy, but I remember seeing my mother when they wheeled me out of the operating room. I couldn't speak, but I rolled my eyes at her as if to say, teasingly, "You leave me fifteen minutes and see what happens?" She smiled back at me, and I toppled into black, empty sleep.

The doctors explained that the steroids given to me after surgery had so irritated my stomach that they had blown a hole in the lining. The irritation could have been prevented by heavy doses of antacid, but no one had given me any. With my stomach spilling blood from the acid wounds, the doctors cut me open from the bottom of my rib cage to below my belly button in order to pull out a chunk of blistered stomach and cut the nerve that helps control digestion. All of my blood had to be replaced after the surgery, and I was left weak and feverish.

The insurance-company representative, Mary Alys Gilshrist, quickly sized up the situation and started barking orders. She swept through the hospital like a blast of pure energy. She was our kind of woman: someone with a plan and the means to execute it. She told us that we had two choices of hospitals that specialized in spinal-cord injuries, and she recommended either an excellent hospital in Colorado or another in Long Beach, California. We liked the sound of Long Beach, mostly because it was closer to home. She agreed with our decision and made the arrangements.

Even though I was the one who had been in the accident and suffered the injuries, I mostly was an innocent bystander to much of the discussion about my condition, my care, and my future. The doctors always talked with my parents instead of with me directly, and then to Mary Alys when she arrived to handle the insurance. Even when we all were gathered in my room, the nurses breezed in and said—to my parents—"How's she feeling today?"

I still didn't know how badly I was hurt. I was feeling better, more alert, although I wasn't going to be jumping out of bed anytime soon. I knew that I had been hurt the worst of those involved in the crash and that it would take a couple of months, at least, to get back on my feet. Cliff and Jimmy already had been released from the hospital and were going to be fine. I still couldn't move anything below my neck, but I had heard enough gory details about the crash to know that the trauma to my body had been tremendous. I couldn't blame my body for refusing to move for the time being.

I was confident that shortly I would be following Cliff and Jimmy home, and I still regarded my injury as more of a nuisance than a tragedy. One thing that truly upset me was that I had let down everyone on *Cannonball*. I hoped to fly out to the set for one more visit before they finished, just to see everyone again before the screening. If not, the screening party would be a blast, a chance for a great reunion. I just needed plenty of rest, some good healthy food, and I'd be on my feet.

That was exactly what my parents wanted me to believe.

Brad had convinced the doctors to say absolutely nothing to me about not being able to walk again, and the expression "permanent paralysis" was banned from the vocabulary authorized in my presence. Reluctantly the doctors had agreed. There was one nurse, however, who refused to play along. Although she was only about twenty years old, she was small and wizened, a little thing in a crinkly white dress. Her shoulders came up to the top of the bed as she bustled about me.

I had lost track of time and was floating in and out of sleep. The little nurse put her head close to my ear and whispered out of the darkness, "Heidi, there's something you need to know."

"What is it?" I said. The room was dark except for the blinking lights of the shiny machines humming beside me. My eyelids were heavy, and there was an incessant pressure on my head. I felt like my brains had been replaced by a wet blanket, bundled up and shoved in through my ears. Day ran into night ran into day. Dawn was dusk; brighten, darken, the light behind the blinds. Waking was like rising from the floor of the ocean: The world gradually came into focus, and the pressure lessened, the darkness turning lighter until I reached fresh air. I forced my eyes open and tried to look at the nurse's shrewish little face, her small eyes squeezed close to a perky nose.

"The doctors haven't told you because your parents don't want them to, but your injury is very serious," she said.

I was silent. For this she's waking me up in the middle of the night? I knew my injury was serious; that's why I was in the hospital. How much more serious could it be?

"I know it's serious," I said, trying to be patient.

Her tiny pointed face was almost touching mine. "Really serious," she hissed, her voice low to keep from being discovered. "The doctors don't think you are going to walk again. Ever. You are permanently paralyzed."

I jerked my face toward her. "What are you talking about? That's bullshit."

"I'm not supposed to be telling you this," she said, looking around the room to be sure we were still alone. "They're not being straight with you, but I think it's something you should know."

"I'm not going to walk again? That's crazy. I'm just a little banged up."

"I'm afraid it's worse than that, Heidi."

"Where are my parents? I need to see my parents."

"They're outside sleeping. You'll see them first thing in the morning."

"I want to see them now," I demanded.

"No," she said. "Now you need to rest."

"No, I'm getting up. I want to see my parents." I struggled to move, but nothing would budge. I shook my head from side to side. "No! No! No! You don't know what you're talking about!" Inside, I felt myself thrashing around on the bed, but the only part that actually moved was my head. The nurse grabbed my face with bony hands as strong as pliers and held it firmly.

"Don't move your head like that! You'll just make it worse. Your neck is not healed, and there are bone fragments floating inside there. You shake your head like that, and you're going to hurt yourself worse."

I shook my head again, and she held it firmly. Her tight hands were stronger than my weakened neck. My face was scrunched between her fingers. I breathed hard through my nose, my heart pounding and my face hot and flushed. I grunted and tried to move, but she had me pinned. I looked at her. I hated her and feared her. I mouthed the words, slowly so she would understand: "I want my parents."

"You need to calm down," she said, exchanging her conspiratorial whispers for the official nurse's voice. "You'll see them first thing in the morning. Now get some rest." She slid out of the room, satisfied that she had done her duty.

I was more angry than anything, and the anger protected me from the true impact of her words. The words hurt, but they bounced off me quickly because I didn't want to hear them. Never walk again? That possibility had never crossed my mind. Of course I was hurt, but I'd been hurt before. Probably not this badly, but I was very strong and resilient. I didn't even get colds, and I was in excellent physical condition. In addition to my professional skiing, I had been teaching aerobics for months before the crash, and I had felt the positive effects in everything from my digestion to my breathing, not to mention how the vigorous exercise had reshaped and sculpted my outer body.

After Dr. Cloward fixed my neck, I knew I was going to get better, 100 percent better. I had no illusions: It would be an uphill climb, and it would take weeks, maybe even months. I would start slowly and build myself back, and pretty soon I'd be doing aerobics again, then running and skiing. I just needed to rest. I was so tired. I felt like I had been awake for days. I slept without dreaming, my mind switched off and shut down.

The next morning Brad, my mom, and Joanna came into the room, greeting me cheerily and opening the blinds. I was waiting for them. "This little dipshit of a nurse, you know the one I mean, the little one, she told me that I wouldn't walk again."

Brad and my mom looked at each other. Brad bent down to my face. "Well, like you said, she's a dipshit," he said. "I'll admit, that does seem to be the popular opinion around here, but we don't pay any attention to that. We told them not to bother you with that now. You need to get well and healthy, and that's the plan."

My mother and Joanna jabbered at me explaining that the doctors didn't really know what I was capable of and that everyone agreed the level of recovery depended on me. "Of course you're going to walk and do everything," my mother reassured me. "Your mind is fine; it's just your body that needs fixing. There's nothing that can't be fixed. You're gonna be fine. Don't worry."

While my mom and Joanna were trying to get my thoughts off what the nurse had said—reminding me to turn away—Brad slipped out the door and headed directly for the nurses' station. I couldn't see him, but I can imagine the scene. I know he didn't storm out because he doesn't storm anywhere; he strides, and mountains move. He knew right away who the offending nurse was, and he practically grabbed her by the earlobe. "Get over here!"

"Yes, Mr. von Beltz?" she asked innocently.

"You were specifically told by the doctors and by me to never, never open your mouth," Brad said. "You are not permitted to do that. The rest of the staff has better sense than you. You for some reason thought that you could preempt my wishes."

"She's a grown woman, and I think she has a right to know what is happening to—"

"You butt out," Brad said. "And don't you ever go near her again."

If my life were a movie, this is the part where the camera would cut back to me, alone with the knowledge that I would never walk again. Cue up violins. Heidi cries tears of dark depression. Woe is me. A cripple. *Permanent paralysis*. Fade to black.

Forget about it! Never happened! It is entirely possible that I have some mental defect or personality flaw or something, but I never plunged into suicidal depression or thought that life wasn't worth living. Nor did I ever accept the diagnosis of permanent paralysis, the damning and damaging label that is attached to everyone in my condition. Permanent? I can't sit in one place for a few minutes without doing something. There's never been anything fixed or permanent about me.

What the nurse told me was a kick in the teeth, mostly because it was such a shock and because it came from her. When someone in authority, someone in a white uniform, tells you about your condition, you expect them to tell the truth. I'm sure this woman thought she was telling me the truth, and I'm sure she thought the truth was the best medicine. Normally, I would agree, and I know she thought she was doing the right thing. She was trying to predict my future, but I wanted to be the one to write my future. How could she know something that I had not yet determined? I pushed her words from my mind. I rejected them as false. I turned away.

I would love to meet that little nurse again. I only have one thing to say to her: Thanks. For one thing, she helped me understand why everybody around me had such long faces. They thought I was never going to walk again! No wonder they were moping around all depressed. More important, she made me so determined to prove her wrong that she gave me just the kick in the butt that I needed. I knew I should focus on positive energy—and rubbing someone's nose in her mistake is definitely negative energy—but maybe this was a time to use negative energy as a positive tool. That little nurse might just as well have fired a starter's pistol next to my ear: I heard her words like a shot, and I was off. I was going to get up just to show her how wrong she was.

Even with this burst of energy, I wasn't ready to leap out of bed. The nurse was right about one thing: I was badly injured. Not only were my bones broken, but I was running a high fever, so even though I wasn't moving, my body was working overtime and the effort left me exhausted. I couldn't even be helped into a sitting position because every time I tried, the room swirled, my eyes rolled back into my head, and I blacked out. I fell back limply onto the bed, and my parents had to slap my face until I regained consciousness.

The doctors weren't sure why I was unable to sit up without passing out, but they believed my blood pressure was too low. They wanted to give me medication, but I refused. There were so many things wrong with me that I didn't want them fiddling with my blood pressure, too. If I could just rest for a little while longer, I'd be strong enough to start recovering. Besides, now that my neck was mobile, this life wasn't so bad. I had a steady stream of visitors, and my parents were always there.

My mother was not so patient. She was getting frazzled living on a couch and dressing in a public rest room. She was trying to manage my care, her own life, the family, and things back home by long-distance telephone calls. The latest crisis at home involved our three dogs. The person caring for them had let them escape from the yard. Our dear Fiorello was instantly run over and killed. Lucy was never found, and Mucket, the mother of the other two, was missing for days.

Meanwhile, the doctors were telling my mother that I was going to be in that hospital bed for a good while because I remained too weak to be moved. Finally my mother—my sweet mother, blessed with the patience of a saint—lost it.

"Listen, young lady," she said to me. "There's nothing wrong with you," she said. "It's over. It's fixed. There are certain things that still need to be done. You're going to need a lot of plastic surgery to repair the scars, but you're not getting any better just sitting there. We need to get out of here, get home, and get on with this."

I knew she was right.

"Fiorello's dead!" she burst out. "Mucket's gone and everybody got away and the whole world is going to pot at home. Sit up in that bed and convince these doctors that you are well enough to get out of here so we all can go home. Right now!"

"Fiorello's dead?"

"He was hit by a car. I'm sorry, Heidi, but everything is a mess. We've got to get out of here, we've got to get home, and we can't leave until the doctors think you're strong enough."

"Okay," I said, immediately warming to the idea. "Yeah, I could go home. I might as well start getting better there. Okay. Let's do it."

I turned to Christy and said, "You heard the lady: Go to work."

Christy grabbed an industrial-strength brush and went at my hair. When she finished my hair, she went to work on my face. She scrubbed me until I squeaked and then troweled on enough makeup to hide the bags under my eyes, adding a burst of blush-on. She painted my lips and used eyeliner to lift away some of the weariness. We're talking Oscar-level makeup here. Pretty soon I looked like a million bucks. Or at least a few hundred thousand.

A doctor came in on his rounds.

"Hi, Heidi," he said, then he did a double take. I think he wondered if he was in the right room. Sitting on my bed, Christy and my mom bit their tongues to keep from laughing at his startled expression.

"Wow," he said, "you look great!"

"I feel great," I said.

"Do you really?"

"Yeah. In fact, I was wondering if I could go home."

"Home? Do you think you're ready? You know it hasn't been that long since your surgery."

"I'm telling you, I feel great."

"Well, you do look good. Do you think you are strong enough?"

"Strong as a horse."

"We'll see," he said, walking out of the room, shaking his head in disbelief. He stopped in the doorway and looked back at me one more time. "Boy, you do look terrific, though."

I collapsed, exhausted from the effort of looking good. I wasn't strong at all and I had no stamina, but my mom was right. I wasn't getting better sitting in bed. I knew that getting home would give me a lift. The sooner I got back, the sooner all of our lives could begin returning to normal.

HOSPITAL
HOSTESS

Getting back home to California nearly killed me. The doctors in Las Vegas finally decided that I was strong enough to leave, but just to be on the safe side, Dr. Ghanem wanted to fly on the plane with me. I honestly did feel much stronger, although I wonder if my efforts to convince everyone how healthy I was didn't end up deluding me into thinking that I was better than I really was.

I was quiet during most of the flight, which in itself was unusual. Dr. Ghanem and the others were looking out the windows of the air ambulance and reporting on our progress. I remember when we passed over Big Bear, and I smiled at the thought of my big brother as the town's crusading newspaper editor. As usual, the dapper Ghanem was carefully coiffed and dressed for business: gold chains, gold watch, diamond ring, and the little TCB lightning bolt around his neck. He promised to give me the pendant on the day I walked again.

"You look gorgeous," Ghanem said. "A goddess lying there on her throne, surrounded by her waiting attendants."

"You're not looking so bad yourself," I told him, forcing a laugh. I wasn't up for our usual flirtations, and mostly I stared up at the ceiling of the plane, anxious to land.

When we finally landed and the door opened, a furnace blast of hot air rolled into the plane. As I was being wheeled to the waiting ambulance, I began to feel light-headed, spacey. The California air was thicker or more humid or something, and I couldn't get enough into my lungs. The harder I tried to breathe, the less oxygen made it into my bloodstream. Waves of sticky warmth washed through me, as if hot syrup were being pumped into my veins. "I don't feel so good," I told Dr. Ghanem.

"Don't worry, Heidi, just hang on for a minute and we'll get you to the hospital." He barked at the ambulance attendants: "Let's move it, you guys. We've got to get this girl to the hospital."

Unlike my other doctors, Ghanem never questioned or doubted what I said. If I told him I didn't feel well, he knew I wasn't well. I felt safe with him, and I was so glad he had come with me—taking care of business. The doors slammed, and the driver stepped on the gas. The ambulance squealed out of the airport and shot down the road at full speed, lights on and sirens wailing. Ghanem leaned over the partition that separated us from the drivers. "This is Code four. Step on it," he barked. I don't think they could have gone much faster.

I arrived at Long Beach Memorial Hospital with a fever of 105 degrees. I was unable to move anything below my neck, unable to control any of my bodily functions, and in immediate need of various operations just to stay alive. The hospital staff, to say the least, was not very excited to see me. Lying on a gurney, I could hear doctors and administrators down the hall debating about what to do with me, questioning Dr. Ghanem about why in the world he had brought me there in the first place. I rolled my eyes, imagining I had found myself in an overpriced hotel with a surly staff. Ghanem started yelling back, wondering what kind of two-bit operation they were running and who was in charge anyway.

I went first to a private room, but the doctors became alarmed at my condition and tried to switch me to Intensive Care. There was no space available, and while they tried to make room, they deposited me on a gurney parked in the hallway. Busy doctors bustled by; orderlies pushed patients in wheelchairs. I was hot and tired.

The hall was so stuffy that I couldn't breathe. There was no air, and I had no energy to suck in what I needed. I felt like someone had shoved me into a cardboard box and left me to bake in the sun. I stared up at the tiles in the ceiling, trying not to breathe too hard because that only seemed to make things worse. Finally, they found me a space and connected me to another battery of machines and tubes. My mother and I called our new home Memorial Island because it felt like the prison Terminal Island: I wondered if I would ever escape alive.

After a few days in Intensive Care, my condition stabilized enough to allow my transfer back to a private room. Immediately following my arrival in the new room, orderlies began to wheel in flower-filled gurneys that had been circling in a holding pattern. Flowers weren't allowed in Intensive Care, but everyone I had ever known had sent them. There were bouquets of wildflowers, fancy arrangements, plants, and boxes of roses, which soon were bursting forth gloriously from every corner of the room. From our flowered perch on an upper floor of the hospital, we could see all the way to the ocean, and although the windows were designed to remain closed, Brad managed to pry open mine. We figured that even the polluted air of Long Beach was better than recirculated hospital air. From the parking lot, the hospital was a pristine tower of glass—with a single window pushed open.

Photos of friends and family went up on the walls; my parents brought in a hot plate for cooking. I wasn't going to wear an ugly hospital gown that showed my butt to the whole world, so my mom bought me cute shorts and T-shirts. She soon realized how difficult it is to dress an immobile person (So that's why hospital gowns are open in back!), and she ended up slitting the brand-new clothes up the backs to drape them on the front of me. The first friends began to arrive soon after the flowers, bearing cakes and goodies and bottles of champagne. For the next few months, I felt like a busy hostess and never a helpless invalid. I was rarely alone, there were no dull moments, and I was so busy I had no time to think about what the future held.

Since the accident, my parents had not left my side long enough to visit their house in Hollywood, which was several hours away. Christy had put all their things in storage, and they moved into an old doctors' quarters at the Long Beach hospital. I was furious when I heard they had moved out of their own place because I was planning on resuming my life as soon as possible, and I didn't want them stopping theirs. They insisted that it was easier for them and that they wanted to be near me. There were decisions to be made every day, papers to fill out, and doctors to watch over. Joanna drove her mobile home into the hospital parking lot, where it became the family office equipped with a typewriter, files, and a telephone.

All this effort seemed excessive to me, since I expected to be walking out of there in a month or so, but my parents usually knew what they needed to do, and I trusted their judgment. What I didn't know was what the doctors were telling them: I would need constant, round-the-clock care for the rest of my life, a period of years that probably could be measured on one hand.

The doctors put so little faith in my recovery—*recovery* was a word that was never used in my case—that no one bothered to fix any of the broken bones other than my neck. My femur had popped out of my thigh, and my left arm had been yanked out of the socket. Both injuries would have caused enormous pain in a healthier person, but I didn't feel a thing. I only knew about the injuries because people told me. The doctors figured that I would never use my arms or legs again, so it was a waste of time to set the bones or encourage healing. To them, fixing my shoulder and leg would have been as extravagant as painting a house that had been condemned.

Dr. Eric Widell didn't feel that way. I don't know if he really believed I would get better or if he was just playing along, but from the very first time he walked into my room, he treated me as if I were a world-class marathoner who needed to be strong enough to run right out of the hospital. His main concern was that three weeks had passed without my leg being fixed; if the bone had started to heal by itself, he might just have to let it go. He wanted to do surgery, and I agreed. When he opened the leg, he was surprised to find the fracture as fresh as the day it had occurred. He also took great professional pleasure in discovering what he called the "densest bones" he'd ever seen. My bones were so solid that he worked up a sweat jamming in the metal pins necessary to support the leg, and he apologized for leaving me with a black-and-blue bruise on my thigh. "I just want you to know that I fixed your leg perfectly in case you ever want to use it again," Widell said.

Widell ordered that I be taken downstairs to the rehabilitation center, placed on a special table, and tilted forward ever so slowly to begin applying weight to the leg. It was not normal for a leg to be weightless, and he feared that it wouldn't heal properly unless I was able to push down on it for at least a few minutes every day. I could only be tilted a few degrees off horizontal, because for some reason I still blacked out whenever I started to go vertical. But I knew it was important to have some weight on my leg, and I fought to remain conscious for as long as possible.

More worrisome than my leg was my spine. I was as limp as a bag of sand, so the only way I could lie in bed was flat on my back. This was a good way to develop bedsores, and it also was boring to stare at the same part of the ceiling all day. Being the engineer that he is, Brad figured out how to pack a dozen pillows around me so I could at least lie on my side for an hour or so every day. The first time was wonderful; just to see things from a different perspective was refreshing. My enthusiasm for something as minor as a change of scenery from the ceiling to a wall shows how low the threshold had fallen for what I considered to be progress: Simply changing position felt like a breakthrough.

When Brad turned me over for the first time, he closely studied my back. I had been lying face up for so long that flipping me over was like digging a big stone out of the ground and finding all kinds of surprises underneath. One of the surprises was a knot the size of a golf ball on my right arm. Brad prodded the lump and said it felt tougher than fat and softer than bone. I couldn't see it, but it sounded extremely unattractive. When he rolled me a little farther onto my side, Brad exclaimed, "Holy shit, Heidi. Your spine is shaped like an *S*."

That was news to me. I had always had very good posture and never suffered any back problems or pains before the crash. I think I would have noticed if my spine, as Brad kindly informed me, was as curved as a snake crossing the road. My mother gently traced the side-to-side curve with her finger, but I couldn't feel her touch. Brad called in the doctor, who looked at my back but didn't seem terribly concerned. The spine wasn't supporting anything except my head, he explained, so it didn't really matter if it was a tad crooked.

"Why don't we turn her over onto her stomach to see it better," Brad suggested. "Maybe it's just the position she's in."

"Oh, no!" the doctor said, alarmed at the thought. "She'll never be able to lie on her stomach."

"What are you talking about?" Brad asked, incredulous.

"In fact, no one should lie on their stomach," he said.

We all looked at one another. The doctor pulled the sheet over me and excused himself to continue his rounds.

"Never be able to lie on your stomach? What a bunch of bullshit," Brad said, and my mom and I burst out laughing. He said to me, "Do you want to lie on your stomach?"

"I would love to lie on my stomach." After weeks on my back, the possibility of lying facedown sounded as delightful and exotic as a Caribbean getaway.

I already was on my side, so Brad simply removed the pillows supporting me in front and pushed me over. A healthy person falls into place naturally, but I had to be arranged like furniture: the arms here, a leg here, head this way. Brad didn't want to leave me in a position that would cut off the circulation to any part of my body. A healthy person knows when an arm "falls asleep" because the blood is cut off, but I wouldn't know until the arm turned blue. What a relief to be on my stomach! I felt perfectly fine, despite the doctor's warning, and I had no trouble breathing. The only problem was that I couldn't move my head very easily, so all my visitors had to stand on one side of the room. As for the lump on my shoulder, the doctors said it was just some kind of growth (obviously), but they couldn't know for sure without surgery, which I didn't want.

Every morning at what seemed like the crack of dawn (I'm sure it was more like 7:30 A.M.) the door to my room burst open without even a knock of warning or of courtesy, and a professionally cheery doctor would announce that another day had begun. Oh, joy. I moaned and groaned, not from pain but from being awakened so early. I never knew why we had to start so early. After all, I was going to be there all day for them to poke and prod. The nurses followed the doctor in to help me urinate by inserting a catheter and filling a little plastic tray with pee.

Then I had breakfast, which was surprisingly good and included bushels of fresh fruit, thanks to an excellent hospital nutritionist who helped me plan my meals. Another doctor making his rounds would stop in on me later, glance at my chart, and ask how I was feeling. Fine. Okay, good. Sometimes he would test my level of feeling by sticking my foot with a pin. I was aware this was happening because I could see the pin entering my flesh, and the first few times I winced in anticipation. But I felt nothing. I would see the pin and brace myself. Then the doctor would say, "Okay, good," and he was finished before I realized he had started.

One of my parents was at my side whenever I woke up, and one of them slept in the room with me. An orderly who saw them sleeping stiffly on an uncomfortable chair kindly brought in another small bed. If my mom spent the night with me, she would leave in the morning to shower and change, and Brad would take her place. They both would come for lunch, along with Joanna or Christy or Jeff or some of my friends.

Although I was eating well, my digestion was not good. The visible parts of my body—my arms and legs—were no longer working at all, and the inside parts weren't working much better. My stomach churned up buckets full of bitter acid that sloshed around inside me, causing the most unpleasant indigestion. Some days I didn't feel like eating because I knew what awaited me after the meal. Even the blandest food inflated my stomach with gas, and I could not make myself burp. My mother tried to rub my back and pound me gently, but that didn't work. I finally figured out that by taking a big drink of 7UP I could trick my body into burping to allow some of the gas to escape. The only food I really enjoyed was french fries slathered in ketchup. The hospital cafeteria had great fries: not the stringy fast-food variety but big hunks of potato cooked to perfection. Unfortunately, they were not easy to digest.

Part of the problem was the damage done to my stomach in Las Vegas, and everyone tried to make me eat Rolaids. I had never taken medicine for anything, not even aspirin for headaches, and I couldn't bear the taste of digestive tablets. When the manufacturer finally came out with a much tastier, spearmint-flavored tab, I thought someone had answered my pleas and invented them just for me. They did seem to help keep down the acid, but I didn't want to become addicted to antacid and preferred to fix my stomach rather than cover for its weaknesses. The lower part of my digestion seemed to be working, although without my knowledge or control. The doctors were excited to hear "bowel sounds," which is the fancy name for gurgling, but I still couldn't control my bowels. I no longer knew when I needed to go to the bathroom, so the nurses would insert a suppository and return a little later with a bedpan.

I was incontinent, too. I couldn't tell when my bladder was full, and I couldn't hold my urine. There are a lot of muscles down there that you don't even realize you have until you can't use them. The nurses "cathed" me every few hours, but I still had to guard against leakage. The normal solution is to wear a bulky adult diaper, which I didn't want to do, so with my mother's help I figured out how to make an infant diaper into a pad for the front of my cut-off jeans.

Another bodily function I had lost was the ability to cough. I simply didn't have the strength in my diaphragm to force out enough air to clear my throat. I could feel the phlegm building up, but I couldn't make it budge. I had no relief for the most annoying sensation of needing to cough, until we figured out a Heimlich-style technique that helped. "Give me a push," I'd say to my mom. She would make a fist, set it just below my rib cage, and push firmly. That forced out the air, which I channeled through my throat into something like a cough. Once we figured out the timing, it was an effective expectorative.

I know that none of this is very appetizing, but these were the kinds of things that occupied my energy. For the moment, I no longer worried about casting calls, ski races, or tennis matches, or where to go dancing, or about my career or my larger goals in life. I worried about not wetting my pants. Everything I had learned the first time as a baby: how to feed myself, how to blow my nose, and even potty training, had to be learned all over again, this time with my hands tied behind my back.

After a few days trapped in a sterile room high above Long Beach, I had almost forgotten what it was like to be outside. The first time Brad wheeled me out of the hospital, I felt like I was entering a new and magical kingdom. He stood at my feet pushing the gurney, the automatic glass doors popped open, and the bright sun hit me like a shower of light. A pleasant chill started at my feet and raced up my whole body, making me shake and shiver like a big dog climbing out of a cool stream. I didn't actually move, of course, but I felt as if I were tingling all over.

That first blast of sunshine, unfiltered by thick windows and hospital air, was as glorious as the clanging of church bells. A simple experience, really, but it opened my eyes to something that had momentarily drifted from my sight. The burst of sunlight made me thankful to be alive. I thanked God for saving me and for having sent me to such wonderful parents. I thanked God for Jeff and Christy and Joanna and all of my friends. I was only sorry that I made everyone worry so much.

Since the day of the accident, I never once had felt that my life was over or that I might as well be dead. I was sad sometimes but never suicidal. If there was a single dominant emotion at this stage, it was boredom. The doctors kept looking for depression and obsessively quizzed me on my state of mind, but I honestly didn't have the serious emotional problems they expected. The sunshine reminded me that, for the moment, it didn't matter if I couldn't run on the grass—or even sit up on it. I was alive, my mind was strong, I was protected by friends and family, and I was happy. The sun felt so powerful and good; it felt like life itself.

I tried to sit outside every day, and since I wore shorts and halter tops, I soon developed a fantastic tan. People said, meaning well, that I looked healthier than a "normal" person. We talked and napped and enjoyed the sunny afternoons, debating such momentous issues as what to do about dinner. The ladies from the coffee shop would see us and wave, and often they sent out snacks and pots of coffee on the house. My mom and Joanna rode bikes after lunch, went for walks, or waded through my paperwork, which was piling up in boxes in the trailer. Brad was working on various projects, writing scripts and doing some acting. Bobby was still my boyfriend, at least in name, and he was a regular visitor when he wasn't working. I knew we were growing apart and our relationship couldn't last, but I doubt it would have lasted even without the crash.

If we were expecting company, and we normally were, Christy came after work to do my hair and fix my face. For fun, she liked to add streaks or coloring or something fancy. The impact of the crash was so fierce that all my hair had turned gray. When it grew back, it was blond again, but in the meantime Christy had fun experimenting. I have photographs from those days of me sitting in bed made up like a runway model. Actually, I looked more like a Barbie doll or Baby Jane, and the whole ritual was kind of surreal. The photos make me wonder about the sanity level in the room—not mine, but everyone else's. Everything was a game, a project, and a laugh. I kept up on the news of my friends, the world, and the movie business, and I always knew what scripts were going around and who was doing what. I didn't talk about my condition any more than I would talk about a cold or the flu. It came up, but dwelling on it would have been terribly boring for everyone, me included. My memories of those days are filled with fun and hugs and loving family, endless parades of visitors, parties, and adventures.

One of my few vices was cherry candy, the more sour the better. I had drawers full of sweets, and people kept adding to the collection: cherry candies, cherry cubes, cherry gum, and cherry sticks.

My tastes broadened into watermelon sticks and cinnamon sticks and Sweetarts. After the drawers filled up, we stacked the candy in piles around the room. Someone brought me an entire tree made of candy. There was so much candy that the sugar began to attract other, unwanted visitors. I remember a nurse, wearing a cute yellow outfit, coming in to turn me one day. She had to get up close and personal to do this, and I watched her as she dug her arms under me, her face next to mine. I noticed something moving on her shoulder. And on her breast. And on the waist of her yellow uniform: They were ants, armies of them. The woman was alive with ants. I tried to look away without laughing, but I wasn't going anywhere.

"Uh, nurse?" I said, barely able to restrain myself. "Could you ask my mother to come in here, please?"

I told my mother and we laughed hysterically, until she searched the room and discovered that the candy tree housed an entire colony of ants and little winged bugs. We had to have the whole room fumigated. Soon after that, my parents were snooping around the top floors of the hospital (they are natural explorers) and found a beautiful empty room, far nicer than mine, with new carpet, fresh paint on the walls, and huge windows. Just out of curiosity, they called the administration to see how much the room cost. Amazingly, it was the same price as the comparatively dingy room I was in, and in a few days I was moving to a new, deluxe suite.

Parading all my belongings to the new room was a major production, as were most of the events in my busy part of the hospital. We were constantly goofing around and joking, entertaining the staff and inviting the other patients and nurses to join the festivities. We invented games and played tricks on the staff, such as the time Brad wheeled me down to X Ray and pulled up the sheet to cover my face. Then he placed a pair of Ben Franklin–style glasses on the sheet over my nose so that I appeared to be a cadaver wearing glasses. He left me, absolutely still, until the orderlies stumbled upon us. We thought it was terribly funny.

Friends arrived every afternoon, bearing more flowers, food, and with luck, champagne. The nurses never said anything about drinking in the room, and I never bothered to ask for permission. Some evenings we ordered pizza delivered or someone went for Chinese food. We played cards and talked or watched television. When I was little, I always managed to put myself at the center of every game. That wasn't going to change just because of a little spinal injury.

We celebrated special occasions, too, and I managed to throw a birthday party for Melanie without ever leaving my bed. I had a lot of help, of course. We had cake and balloons in my room, and her family and dozens of friends drove down to the hospital for the celebration.

If we planned on being really bad some night, we asked Jean to stand guard. Jean was one of the private nurses we hired to help care for me, because the staff nurses weren't able to be there all the time. Nobody messed with Jean. She was as big as a football player but with the pads in all the right places: Her waist was teeny, and her breasts were enormous, and she squeezed them into pointy bras that made her look like a Viking opera singer. Rounding out the package was a high, full bottom that pushed against tight jeans. Jean was shaped like a very large figure eight, and when she stood in front of the door with her arms crossed like Mr. Clean, nobody got into my room without an invitation to the party.

Jean became part of the family and loved to flirt with Jeff. He would lob her sweet nothings, which became increasingly suggestive and imaginative, and she would slam them back with, "Not even in your life dreams, sweetie," batting false eyelashes as big as butterflies. Inside the room, we cranked up the stereo, popped the champagne corks, and stuffed towels beneath the door to keep the cigarette smoke from triggering the alarms in the hall.

Things got so wild that one afternoon when Christy arrived, Jean shoved her into the room and quickly locked the door behind her. Christy picked her way around twelve empty champagne bottles before she reached me in my bed, and I was not alone. Lying on one side was Bobby Carradine, passed out, and on the other was Melanie, drifting in and out of sleep.

A strange coincidence had further tightened the link between Melanie and me. I vaguely remember being in Las Vegas shortly after the crash and asking about Melanie. My mother told me she too was in the hospital. She also had been in a car crash and injured her leg. My mother said the injuries were not that serious and Melanie would be home in a few days. We remarked on the weird coincidence, and I asked my parents to send her flowers and a card so she would know I was thinking about her. Melanie had recovered quickly, and of course she wanted me to do the same. She tried to will me up out of the hospital bed, and every once in a while she started to cry. Then I ended up being the one consoling her, which made us both laugh.

Melanie and I had celebrated and suffered through so much together, and the crash wasn't going to change that. We plotted our careers, voiced our secret dreams, and tried to figure out what to do with the crazy men in our lives. Melanie was only fourteen when she met Don Johnson, who was working on *The Harrad Experiment* with Melanie's mom. Don fell for Tippi's teenage daughter from the moment he laid eyes on her. Melanie reciprocated the crush, and when she was old enough, they embarked on a romance that was, even by Hollywood standards, volatile.

I love them both and have spent a good amount of time over the years holding hands and stretching myself between them, trying to bridge the gap between two whirling personalities. I've talked for hours with Melanie about why Don is worth fighting for, and I've told Don why Melanie really isn't such a pain in the butt, just a little frisky.

Years before, when Melanie and I were young roommates and she called me, giddy in the middle of the night from Las Vegas, I immediately feared the worst.

"You'll never guess what, Buddess," she said. She calls me Buddess, as in a female buddy.

I already knew. "What?" I said, playing along.

"We got married!"

I probably said, "That's great," or something like that, but sitting on our couch, I rolled my eyes and thought, "Oh God!" They married for all the wrong reasons, and I knew it couldn't last. In six months they were divorced. They couldn't remain apart for long, though, and for years they were together and not together, together and not together. Their relationship was sort of like the weather, and I simply accepted whatever the current conditions were, knowing they soon would change.

Melanie's career took off when she did *Night Moves* with Gene Hackman. She invariably was cast in the role of nymphette, but she had a strong presence on the screen and I knew she would make it as an actress. She got another good break with *The Drowning Pool*, starring Paul Newman and Joanne Woodward, in which Melanie played the home wrecker. Then she did a picture with a cast of unknowns called *Smile*, a behind-the-scenes look at a beauty pageant. Melanie played a ditsy type, but she was cute and was emerging as a talented actress.

The best thing about Melanie was that she never treated me differently after the crash. She was upset, of course, and she cried all the time at first, but it didn't change our relationship. She felt bad but not sorry for me. That's all I wanted from anyone.

Some of my other friends tried their hardest to treat me normally, but they just couldn't. I noticed that people began referring to me in the past tense, as in, "Heidi used to be six feet tall." I still am six feet, although I suppose that in the hospital I looked six feet long. When people saw me, I watched them trying to adjust to the new image, and the disconnect flashed across their faces. I was me, but I was different. My voice and my face were the same, but the body was frozen. Everyone expected the worst, but I looked fine, just frozen. My body appeared perfectly healthy, my color was good, and my eyes shone like always, but I was limp, as if everything but my head were asleep. "You look so good," they said, partly in relief and partly in disbelief. "You look fine."

I wasn't exactly Quasimodo. Some people have a stereotypical idea of what a quadriplegic should look like—a skinny fetal ball, all knees and elbows—but I never looked like that. I was different-looking, but not in the way people expected. My friends knew in their hearts that I had not changed, but in an instant my body had become something completely different from what it was before. It took a while for the thoughts and perceptions of those around me to catch up with the new reality.

After the crash, talking with good friends or "losing myself" watching a movie, I forgot about my physical body. This was a new experience for me because I am such a physical, active person. Other people always had reinforced the importance of my body because, even when I was growing up, they reacted to my appearance: I'm a tall and healthy, sun-burnished California girl. People noticed me, and I liked it. Such attention to my physical attributes seemed particularly absurd now. I thought that if my personality were generated solely by this body, I wouldn't be a very interesting human being. And if my personality—even lying in a hospital bed—wasn't strong enough to lift another person above and beyond my body, then I wasn't communicating very well.

My parents were upbeat with my friends and never showed the slightest sign of doubt that I soon would be walking. I was the same way, mostly because I believed in my heart that I would get better but also because nobody—myself included—likes to be around someone feeling sorry for herself or wallowing in sickness. The truth about my condition was no secret, however; news of the accident had been all over television and in the papers. The crash itself had been captured on film, and the scene was repeated with every story about what had happened. All the gory details were well known in Hollywood, and since most of my friends worked in the business, they often surprised me with the things they knew about me.

Watching television one day, I saw a commercial for one of the supermarket tabloids. STUNT GIRL PARALYZED FOR LIFE! the headline screamed. The camera cut to a darkened roadside. A car crash. A body on the ground, under the car. Hey, that's me! I thought. The screen flashed DRAMATIZATION. Then the accident was reenacted, with plenty of screeching and crashing. Even if I had wanted to avoid thinking about what had happened, it would have been impossible with that commercial reminding me three or four times a day.

The publicity caused a wave of support from people I had never met, a wave almost strong enough to lift me out of bed. I received bags of mail from all over the United States and from as far away as Europe. Everyone wished me the best and hoped for a speedy recovery. People offered prayers and lighted candles. Among my friends the assumption was that I would be up and around; it was just a matter of time. The shock of seeing me frozen in suspended animation must have given them doubts about my chances, but most of them went along with the idea that I would recover soon. I'm not sure everyone believed it, but I wasn't about to let them down.

The doorway to my room filled one day with black leather and hair, dirty jeans, and heavy boots. Two guys who looked like woolly mammoths pushed their way inside. "Mule!" I shouted. "Cisco! How's it going?"

"Okay, okay," the first one said, ambling over to the bedside and looking around the room. "How long they gonna keep you locked up in this place?"

I knew from his question that Mule was on my wavelength, at least about my incarceration. His real name, of course, is not Mule. His real name is Animal, but his friends call him Ani-Mule, or just plain Mule for short. He has long hair and a beard, and he's as big as a Dumpster, only not so tidy. (Just kidding, Mule.) I've never seen him dressed in anything other than oily jeans and a leather jacket emblazoned with HELL'S ANGELS.

I had met Mule and Cisco on a movie set and had gone to visit Cisco at his home near San Francisco. Cisco looks like Grizzly Adams on a bad-hair day, so I was shocked to see his home: It was so normal. He had a sweet wife who kept everything neat and tidy. The garage was cleaner than some hospital rooms, and I've been operated on with tools that were less well cared for than his.

"So, they treatin' you okay?" Cisco asked.

"Yeah, it's okay, but I'm ready to go home."

He looked at me with the tenderness of a mother bear caring for an injured cub. "If you wanna get outta here, you just say the word and we'll bust you out."

"No, that's okay, Cisco, really."

"I mean it. They mess with you, and we'll come busting in here with our bikes and we'll get you out."

"No, no, no, no. Really. It's fine. I'm fine. I'll be fine."

I was flattered but afraid they really would do it. I was having a hard enough time with the hospital staff without a pair of Harleys bouncing up the stairs to my room.

I was glad to have so many guests, and the nurses knew that it boosted my spirits. I couldn't sleep until midnight, anyway, and I preferred to have people around me. I did get tired because my body was still digesting the injury. My diaphragm was so weak that my breathing was slowed and talking sapped my energy: I simply didn't have the wind. I could only make sounds when I exhaled, so I had to pause often to inhale for the next burst of words. The words came more slowly than before, pause, because I had to think about, pause, breathing. But I was fine.

When it was time for bed (for sleep, actually, since I rarely left the bed), I liked to put on a tape made for me by my friend Michael Gregory, who did such a good job playing a doctor on *General Hospital* that he still gets mail seeking medical advice. "Peace and tranquillity," his voice soothed. Buddha bells chimed, ding, ding, ding. "Peace and tranquillity." Despite the chants, there wasn't much peace or tranquillity during the night because the nurses constantly came in to turn me or cath me or check my vital signs. They used little flashlights to avoid turning on the bright overhead lights, but I always woke up.

The most worrisome thing about my condition was that every night at around one o'clock my body temperature spiked up to 104 degrees or 105 degrees. The nurses would pack me with cold towels, and eventually the temperature would return to normal. In Intensive Care there was a great toy that I loved: a plastic cooling pad that slipped underneath me. When the fever was burning its hottest, I could lie on the pad and imagine I was on an iceberg floating in the Arctic Circle, penguins hopping happily around me. The doctors had no explanation for the temperature spikes, and their only suggestion—literally—was to take two aspirin and wait until morning.

The fevers were more proof to me that my body was working overtime. I appeared to be motionless, but inside the healing process was fully mobilized. The system was overwhelmed at first and couldn't begin to deal with all the injuries at once, but the healing forces were scurrying around to assess the damage and begin the repairs. All this effort, even though it didn't appear on the surface and was invisible to the doctors, was exhausting. I understood that occasional tiredness was a normal side effect of the healing process, a symptom of something else, but the doctors became alarmed when they tested my blood and found that I was anemic. Even though I felt fine, they immediately prescribed Inferon, an iron supplement. My mother vehemently opposed this, insisting that they treat me like a healthy person with an iron deficiency. Why not give me iron-rich foods instead of drugs? But this was a hospital, not a restaurant, so they wanted to shoot me up with something.

I didn't see any harm in it, and they were bugging us so much about the danger of anemia that I finally told my mom not to worry. Getting the Inferon inside me was the next problem. By this point, the doctors had injected me so full of stuff that I didn't have a single vein left that wasn't collapsed. The doctor poked around like a desperate old heroin addict until he found the last round vein—between my toes. The needle went in and the fluid began to drip into my foot through a tube. In seconds, I felt a pressure in my chest, like a cat was sitting on me. Then the cat was the size of a dog, and then as heavy as a full-grown man. I took deeper breaths, but I felt my chest was being turned inside out. Now the man on my chest was standing with thick boots, crushing me into the bed like a cigarette butt. "Mom," I said, exhaling weakly.

"You're all gray," my mother said. "What's wrong?"

"I can't breathe."

The doctor yanked out the tube dripping Inferon between my toes. He replaced the drip with a clear fluid to flush my blood.

My mother shouted to Joanna to call Mrs. S.

"Who's that?" the doctor asked. "Your lawyer?"

Soon the pressure lightened. The doctors later said the pressure was the onset of a full cardiac arrest and a rare side effect of their treatment. The experience drained me completely, and I slept straight through for several days. Sleep was what I had wanted after all, but I think I would have preferred less drastic means. I wanted to start getting better by myself, but the doctors insisted on medicating me for everything. They focused on stabilization; I wanted improvement. They counseled patience; I knew we were burning daylight.

Most of my stay in Long Beach was not so dramatic, and my life consisted of languorous days punctuated by meals and medical procedures, and being entertained by friends and family. I was the queen and my room was my kingdom. All my needs were cared for and everything was done for me. If I was hungry, someone fed me. If I was tired, I dozed. When my nose itched, someone scratched it. There was plenty to drink, games to play, and gossip to share, with little thought of the future. The future, I figured, would take care of itself. I occasionally thought about the past, but not with sadness. My life had been fantastic so far, and I didn't see any reason for that to change. I reminded myself that no one can return to the past, so it's best left behind. My time was the present, and there I reigned.

Melanie announced one day with great fanfare that she knew my future. Melanie does everything with great fanfare. She doesn't just enter a room, she fills it. She comes in like a tall ship with billowing sails entering a harbor; the other boats get out of the way, and their crews stare in reverent admiration. She learned this from her mother, whose tiny frame can barely contain her effervescence.

Melanie's approach to life inspired us deeply, and whenever my parents felt they were getting the runaround from the hospital, they asked, "What would Melanie do?" What Melanie does is whatever she damn well pleases, and if you don't like it, then get out of the way. She doesn't act impetuously or without thinking, but once she decides what needs to be done, she does it. Melanie has always been our fearless leader.

Long Beach was ninety minutes from Melanie's house on the beach, but she made the trip every single day. That's the kind of friend she is. On this particular day Melanie announced that she and our friend Buddy Joe Hooker, another legendary stuntman, had gone to a psychic, an astrological forecaster who made predictions based on birth signs and that kind of thing. Buddy Joe was going to have a romance in his future, the psychic predicted. That was not such an amazing prediction because Buddy Joe always had romances. The psychic insisted that this romance was going to be different, however. A short time later, Buddy Joe abruptly gave up a lifetime as a ladies' man, got married, and became the father of beautiful twins. As for Melanie, the psychic predicted she would become a world-famous actress, heaped with recognition and awards. That, too, came to pass.

"We did your future, Buddess," she said to me. "We told her your birthday and everything, but we didn't say anything else about you."

"What'd she say?" I asked, curious and without a clue as to what the prediction could be.

"She said you are going to be a teacher," Melanie said.

"A teacher. Right," I said. "You know I wasn't crazy about school when I was a kid. I'm sure not going back when I don't have to."

"Not that kind of teacher, Buddess. She said you are going to be a teacher to many people, that what you say is going to reform entire areas of philosophy. Things that are thought of as absolute will be changed because of you. She said you will have a great impact on masses of people."

I laughed. "A teacher, huh?"

"Don't laugh. This woman is really good, Buddess." Melanie, at least, was convinced that the prediction would come true.

Chapter 6

GIVE ME FALSE
HOPE, PLEASE

The doctors also had a prediction for my future, and it was grim. They did not expect me to live very long, and the few years I had remaining would be under the constant threat of lethal infection, disease, and minor illnesses that could prove fatal because of my weakened condition. Even a common cold was dangerous because fluid collected in puddles in my horizontal lungs and could drown me.

The spine and the nerve impulses it carries are so essential that the slightest damage can disrupt not just the ability to move arms and legs, but every biological and chemical system that maintains the body. The medical solution to my problem was not to fix what was wrong—this was not considered possible—but to replace the systems I had lost with drugs and machines and twenty-four-hour care. For example, instead of letting me try to move in bed to improve circulation, they gave me a bed that rocked and tilted automatically. The tilting bed didn't really make my blood circulate; mostly it just sloshed the blood around and washed me with waves of nausea.

The medical approach was not only annoying and uncomfortable, I was beginning to realize it was dangerous. When I first arrived in Long Beach and was in Intensive Care, a tube dripped constantly into my arm. I didn't think much of it; at the time it was the least of my concerns. I figured the drip was to keep me hydrated or provide nourishment or some other essential life support. I was only the patient; how was I supposed to know what I needed? When out of curiosity I finally asked a nurse about the drip, she replied matter-of-factly, "Oh, that's morphine."

"Morphine?" I shouted, furious. "Why do you want to put morphine in me?"

"It's to keep you calm," she replied.

"Well, it's not working," I snarled. I knew that morphine was only a chemical process or two away from heroin, something I had been exposed to in Hollywood but never, ever would have put inside my body. I thought morphine was a painkiller, anyway, and I didn't have any pain. "I don't want it anymore."

"I'll see what the doctor says," the nurse replied.

She came back a little later. "The doctor says it's okay to take you off the morphine."

"Great," I told her. "I don't really think I need it."

"But he's going to start you on Valium."

I rolled my eyes, but I didn't argue right then. I still held to the lingering belief that the members of my vast and growing medical team knew what they were doing. In any case, Valium sounded a lot milder than morphine. Shortly, I would stop taking that, too.

The one medicine the doctors would not let me stop taking while under their roof was antibiotics. They constantly worried that my weakened immune system would open me up to infection, and the drugs were supposed to create an artificial barrier. The problem with drugs, however, is that they don't form a living, flexible barrier like the body's own natural defenses, which adapt and respond to new threats. After being exposed to a particular antibiotic for a time, infections learn how to get around the barrier. For that reason, doctors must repeatedly change the type of antibiotic before the infections can figure out a way through the defense.

A major source of infection for all people, but especially for people who cannot control their bladders, is the urinary tract. To prevent infections there, every time I needed to urinate, the nurse tore open a new package containing a narrow rubber tube to insert into my urethra, a tray to catch the urine, and a piece of cotton with a container of Betadyne to disinfect the area. I had this done as many as eight times a day, and each time the charge to the insurance company was twenty dollars.

I complained that this was stupid and wasteful, but the doctors' proposed solution was worse. They wanted to install an "indwelling" catheter, which meant permanently sticking a tube inside me that would be connected to a little bag worn alongside the leg. The doctors said this would be easier for everyone and would make me more "independent," another of their favorite words when discussing my future of "permanent paralysis." I wouldn't be able to insert the tube or empty the bag myself, so I didn't know how a built-in catheter made me any more independent, and I could think of three reasons right off the bat why it was a horrible idea.

First, it was not very attractive. Imagine me relaxing in the sun, sipping champagne with friends while a little plastic bag, sitting inertly on my leg, slowly expands with pee like a bright yellow jellyfish. What a great conversation piece: "My goodness, Heidi, you're looking a little cloudy today!" The doctors' answer to the unsightly bag was to have me wear baggy jogging pants instead of shorts. No thank you.

The second reason the in-dwelling catheter was a bad idea was that it would create a breeding ground for bacteria. I never disagreed that the urinary tract was a problem, but having a piece of rubber in there seemed like it would only attract more infection. The doctors explained that it wasn't in fact a permanent catheter; it had to be changed often and the area "irrigated." Thank you, but no.

Third, I wanted to control my own bladder. I did want to be independent, but really independent, which meant me deciding when I would go to the bathroom. I wasn't sure I ever would be able to control the necessary muscles, but there was no way to know unless I tried. I hated the idea of my urethra being open like a spigot. I knew enough about physiology to understand that even with a perfectly healthy urethra, if it were kept open all the time, the muscles would atrophy. The very fact of having the permanent catheter in place meant that I would become dependent on it. Just as the longer I took antibiotics, the more I would rely on them, the longer I used a catheter, the more I would come to depend on it.

I realize that for some people a permanent catheter is the only alternative, and I don't mean to make light of it, but I knew that I was a strong, healthy twenty-four-year-old woman, and I was stubborn enough to think that I could regain my own bladder control. I was convinced that whenever possible it was better to encourage my body to do what it was supposed to do, instead of replacing a natural, built-in system with a drug or a machine. Otherwise the body says, "Oh, something else is taking care of it, so we don't have to bother." The doctors insisted on installing the new catheter, and I was equally insistent in saying no, thank you.

This was the wrong answer.

As usual, the medical campaign to make me "independent" and self-sufficient began with my parents, instead of with me. People talked about me as if I weren't even in the room, or they talked about my "injury" instead of about me. The rich and complicated being that I am—that we all are—was reduced to a broken neck in a wheelchair. The urologist warned my mother in hushed dark tones about what would happen if they didn't install a catheter: "When her skin breaks down, which it will, when her bladder breaks down, which it will, then it will be too late."

The predictions made my mother nervous, but I told her to hold the docs at bay for just a bit longer. I had a plan. I was going to fix this thing by myself and end the debate once and for all. The next time the nurse came in to cath me, I closely followed every step. I couldn't lift my head enough to see her, but the procedure had been done so many times that by listening I could follow what she was doing. Right before the part when I would hear the first tinkling into the plastic tray, I said, "Wait a minute. Hold it."

"What's wrong?" she said.

"Just hang on a sec. I want to see if I can stop the flow."

She laughed. "You can't do that. The muscle is either too flaccid or spastic. It's out of your control."

"Let me just try, please."

"You really don't want to play around with this," she said. "You don't want to get a distended bladder. That's why we have you on a strict four-four."

I think that's what she said, a "four-four." Whatever that means. What she intended to say was that I was cathed every four hours, a concept I understood, but everyone in a white uniform insisted on talking in an obscure medical code. I have learned the language now (through the immersion method), but when I was first injured the alien tongue only made the doctors seem more remote and my condition harder to understand. Along with their strange language, they had an obsession with recording data, with quantifying and measuring everything, even my pee. They always measured my pee and would praise me or scold me depending on the quantity. I never understood what the "right" amount of urine was and how that was something that could be measured, but I filled up cups and vials with urine, and they filled up page after page with notes and charts.

"Just this once," I said. "Let me try to see if I can stop it."

"Suit yourself."

I heard the tinkling sound and squeezed. More tinkling. I squeezed again. Still tinkling. I gritted my teeth and strained like an Olympic weightlifter. It felt like the muscles were working, but I still heard the darn pee rushing into the tray without interruption. I was powerless to control the flow. The tinkling eventually stopped by itself. I heard the ripping sound of the cotton being opened, and I knew the nurse was cleaning me. "There we go," she said. "All set."

I sat back defeated; the nurse hadn't even noticed my strenuous efforts to stop the flow. Still, I could feel the muscles. I knew what to do and the muscles knew what to do, but somewhere between my brain and my bladder a link was missing, a connection was broken. The doctors said I really wasn't feeling anything; only remembering the feeling I once had. They called this "phantom feeling" and said the sensation was the same for people who lose a leg and swear they can still feel it. But I knew it was more than that. My muscles weren't amputated; they were still there. I just couldn't get them to work.

Whenever the nurse took urine, I discreetly practiced flexing the muscles. Watching television, I flexed, relaxed, flexed, relaxed. Even talking to my friends, I clandestinely exercised the muscles around the urethra. I couldn't tell for sure if the muscles were responding, but even if the tubelike urethra was in fact closing a little, it apparently wasn't enough. Every time the nurse cathed me, no matter how hard I squeezed, the tinkling sound remained steady.

The inability to control my bladder was one of the limits on me that the medical experts accepted as unavoidable. The fact that I was not so prepared to accept this or any limitation was a source of tension. When I said, "I feel this," they said, "You cannot possibly feel that." So after a while, I stopped telling them anything and stopped listening to what they said. They were the highly trained experts, but nothing they said matched up with what I was feeling, so I came to realize that maybe *I* was the expert. I didn't care about their statistics or the fact that in "ninety-nine percent of these cases" something was true. I wasn't a statistic, and averages don't say anything about individuals. I learned to lie in bed with an interested look on my face, totally ignoring their pessimistic prattering.

There were realities I couldn't deny, though, and being cathed every four hours was one of them. This was a major pain and a short leash because no matter what, I had to return to the hospital every four hours to expel my urine. I knew it wasn't good to allow waste to remain inside my body, and at first I watched the clock and reminded the nurses to cath me when they forgot. Later, I learned how to read the new signals my body was sending me. Instead of having the feeling of pressure and the discomfort that used to tell me to go to the bathroom, now I noticed goose bumps and sweat in my hair when my bladder was full. It was as if my body were overflowing and squeezing out the waste wherever it could. Soon I knew when I needed to urinate, even if I couldn't actually do it myself.

I didn't get discouraged, and this was just one of many examples of goals that took longer to achieve than originally expected. Before the accident, I was not an exceptionally patient person, and it seemed I always was rushing places and doing three things at once. Now everything was slower, and the progressive steps were much, much smaller. As long as the steps were in the right direction and built upon one another, I was satisfied. The one thing I had in abundance was time. So I worked on the urethra muscles every day, squeezing that little sucker to make it close. And one day it did close. I was stunned. I was being cathed, I heard the tinkling sound while the nurse stood next to me, and I squeezed. The sound stopped. I couldn't believe my ears. I had stopped the flow. I had regained control of errant muscles. If I could control my bladder muscles through practice and exercise, then why couldn't I control all of my muscles?

Before I could congratulate myself too much, I realized I had an immediate problem. I had stopped the flow, but I didn't know how to start it again. I tried to focus on relaxing the same muscles I had spent so many weeks trying to close, but they wouldn't budge. I was afraid to say anything to the nurse who was cathing me because she'd know I was playing with my urethra again (Bad, Heidi!). I just stared up at the ceiling, Little Miss Innocence. The nurse noticed that the pee had stopped, although she never dreamed I had done it myself. I didn't say a word, and she jiggled the catheter, starting the flow again. But I, Heidi von Beltz, had stopped it. By myself. It took a little longer to learn to open the muscles as well as to close them, but I did learn, and in time I was 100 percent able to decide when to urinate. That was two years after the crash.

Until then, I was cathed every four hours. No matter how many times the procedure was performed, I never felt comfortable, and I certainly never allowed it to be done when someone else was in the room. I've always been modest and dreaded visits to the gynecologist.

Melanie was visiting one day, sitting on the edge of my bed, when the nurse came in, pointed to her watch, and announced, "You're ready."

"Melanie," I said, "I gotta do this thing where I pee." I was hoping she would get the hint and leave the room for a minute, but she sat there on the edge of the bed.

"What do you do?"

I didn't feel like going into all the disgusting details, even with my best friend, but to my horror the nurse chimed in, "Maybe you would like to watch and learn how to do this because there might come a time when you will be alone with her and you'll have to do it."

I winced and thought to myself, Very helpful. Keep your suggestions to yourself, Nurse.

Melanie, of course, thought this was a great idea, and pretty soon they had the sheet down and my legs spread wide. The nurse was on the left side and Melanie was on the right, both of them crawling on the bed, looking up at my crotch like it was a science exhibit.

I stared at the ceiling, thinking that if I didn't look at them, then maybe they couldn't see me, and all the while praying this horrible indignity would end quickly. Maybe there'd be a fire alarm, or I'd have a heart attack.

"Now, you see this here," the nurse said to Melanie. "Okay, now this one here . . ."

"Yeah, yeah," Melanie said.

"Now that, as you know, is the vagina, but right up here—no, here. Look up here."

I can't believe this, I thought. I rolled my eyes, mortified.

"That's your . . ."

"Oh wow!" Melanie said. "Is that where you go? I thought it all came out of the same thing."

"Oh no," the nurse said. "You have one for the pee and one here and the other for this."

"Buddess," Melanie said, looking up like a mechanic coming out from under the hood. "Did you know this? This is really cool."

"Sure, Melanie." I tried to count the little holes in the ceiling tiles.

The nurse continued. "What you do is you take this tube, and you apply a little lubricant to insert it like . . . this . . . Now you take this end and put it in there . . . and push . . . There we go."

"Wow, Wooowwww! Oh my God!" Melanie could barely contain herself.

"Make sure this part goes in here so the tube goes in the pan. Get it in the pan. There you go. Little more. There it is. Very good."

"Wow! Oh, Buddess. That is so cool."

"Yeah, it's great, isn't it?"

Actually, it was great, because Melanie did learn how to cath me, and it gave me new freedom. Now I didn't have to worry about drinking too much champagne and filling up my bladder. I wasn't going to train all my friends to perform this procedure, but Melanie was different, and somehow I didn't mind as much as I thought I would.

Other friends helped me over less intimate medical hurdles. An old family friend who was a dermatologist was kind enough to look at my heels, which remained exploded and open. They weren't infected, but they were exposed: bloody flesh with the skin removed. The doctors considered them a fact of life, however unpleasant, and didn't seem too worried about them. Our friend the dermatologist was horrified. He brought some special creams and applied them to my heels. In a few days the sores disappeared. I don't remember the doctors even noticing.

Unfortunately, not every problem was so easy to fix.

An eager physical therapist walked into the room with a flourish at first light one day, clutching a plastic contraption with a Ping-Pong ball bouncing around in a hollow tube. I groaned inside: another toy. I closed my eyes and tried to wish her away. I opened them, and the therapist was still there, stretching a toothy grin from ear to ear. "You're gonna have some fun with this," she said.

"I doubt it."

"Come on, Heidi, this is a great game. It's really fun. The object of this game is to blow into the tube and see how high you can make the ball go." She spoke to me in the upbeat voice they all adopted in my presence. It must have been part of their training. "Let's give it a try. I'll do it first so you see how, and then you try. Okay?"

She put the plastic elephant trunk into her mouth and blew. Her breath pushed the ball up into a narrow cylinder, which had little marks on the side to record the distance traveled by the ball. She blew again, and the little ball hovered near the top, reaching what I supposed was a perfect score in this "game."

"Can you do that, Heidi? Can you make the ball go to the top? Let's try."

I made a face, but she stuck the tube between my lips. I didn't have much choice, and I figured that if I just did it, she would leave me alone. I blew. I blew again. Nothing happened. The ball didn't budge. "Lemme try that again," I said, placing my mouth more firmly around the tube. I blew again. Nothing.

I laughed about it to the therapist, but inside I was scared. This was the first graded test of my condition, and I failed miserably. I knew I was short of breath; people always thought I was whispering because I could only speak when I exhaled. But this test meant I was worse off than I had imagined. Boy, I thought, I've got some work ahead of me. I'm going to have to fight this one, and it won't be easy.

After the failed test, I was ready for breathing exercises or whatever rehab program the therapist had planned. But there was no plan. She gave me a test, and I failed, and that was the end of the story. There was no breathing therapy, no exercise program, no drills to make my lungs and diaphragm stronger. They assumed that I always would be short of breath, and people would just have to lean closer if they wanted to hear my words. Do not pass Go. Get used to it. You are *permanently disabled*. I grumbled and complained, but they just smiled and patted me on the head, each pat like a sharp kick to the sides of a racehorse who wasn't going to stay behind for long.

The one place I could breathe easily, and get some peace and quiet, was inside the hyperbaric chamber, a machine that was the therapeutic rage in 1980. The chamber is a completely enclosed capsule into which high concentrations of oxygen are pumped, the theory being that oxygen aids the healing process, whatever the problem or illness. The theory of oxygenating the tissue made sense to me, and at least it felt like we were doing something positive to get better. My parents faithfully wheeled me down every morning at ten, and the technicians slid me into the capsule and sealed the hatch like they were sending me off to the moon. I stretched out there like a ship in a bottle watching David Letterman, who in those days had a daytime show, listening to the sound through little speakers inside the capsule.

The therapy on my leg went well. Dr. Widell, the surgeon who had repaired my broken leg, was closely involved in trying to make sure it healed properly, and he directed the therapists to apply more and more pressure and to continually work on improving the range of motion. Every day my parents wheeled me down to the first floor of the hospital to the therapy area for this treatment. Other people with injuries were there to exercise or, as in my case, to be exercised. They stretched me flat on a table, and the therapist bent the ankle and straightened it, bent the knee and straightened it, pushed the knee into my chest and straightened it. Each time, he used a triangle and a measuring stick to record how far I had moved.

He also tried to "impact" my leg, which meant pushing it up into the hip, but here I wasn't able to help very much. The best way to apply weight to the leg would have been for me to stand, and the next best way was to tilt the entire table upright until my feet touched the ground, but both options proved impossible because when they raised me vertically I felt woozy and thick, and a curtain of blackness fell across my brain. My eyes rolled back into my head and my teeth clenched. I had no choice but to surrender to the rather pleasant, floating sensation of going completely limp and unconscious. The therapist slammed the table back into a flat position and shook me gently. "Heidi, Heidi." I heard my name off in the distance. Slap; someone hit me in the face. "Hey, what are you doing?" And I blinked awake.

Every time I came close to being vertical, I passed out. The doctors diagnosed that sufficient blood wasn't reaching my brain, and they prescribed amphetamines to push the blood higher. When I refused, arguing that I didn't want to speed up my entire system with potentially dangerous drugs, the therapists accused me of impeding their progress. Not even *my* progress, *their* progress. "We can't help you if you don't help us," they said, in a vaguely threatening manner. The doctors didn't like me passing out every ten minutes, so they decreed that if I wasn't going to take speed, then I shouldn't be allowed to sit up anymore.

To keep me horizontal when I wasn't in bed, the therapists found me a wheelchair that reclined like a rolling La-Z-Boy—very snazzy and reasonably comfortable, but a wheelchair nonetheless. They couldn't understand why I wasn't more grateful, and they muttered about a problem with my attitude. To the therapists, giving me a wheelchair was the equivalent of giving wings to an angel: The chair was to be a defining part of me, an essential element of my being. The wheels were meant to become an extension of my torso, just like legs extend down from a healthy person.

"You've got to learn to love your chair," the therapists said. The really sick thing about that suggestion was that they meant it.

The therapist who worked with me most was Susan, a big, raw-boned young woman with thick glasses and an earnest manner. She would put her hands on my muscles while a doctor directed me to move various limbs. When she put her fingertips on my right biceps, the doctor said, "Heidi, move your right hand to your mouth." I made the effort, and it felt like something was happening, but the hand didn't budge. The doctor would then ask Susan if she felt anything. Usually she didn't, but sometimes she said, "I think I felt a flicker." I felt flickers, too, and I knew that some of my nerves were firing. Even if I couldn't move, I was sure the muscles were being fed because I was still round and curvy after so many weeks in bed. If the nerves were dead and the muscles had been completely cut off, I would have started to shrink down to the bone and go fetal like someone with polio.

After testing the right biceps, Susan would put her hand on my triceps. "Now move your arm back," the doctor would say. I pushed the arm backward, but nothing moved. "Good, that's good."

Susan would move her hand to my stomach. "Now sit up." I grunted with the effort. Nothing moved. "Good, Heidi. That's good." Susan's fingers on my chest. "Flex those pectorals." I felt everything move on the inside, but I couldn't see anything move on the outside. "Good, Heidi. Excellent." The doctor would tap my knee with a rubber hammer to test for a reflex. Nothing. He'd tap again. Not even a jiggle.

At the beginning, this was fun because it seemed like we were doing something constructive. After four months, the fun had gone out of it. I liked the tests because they were as close as I came to real movement; at least I was moving inside. I wanted to go a step further and try to work the muscles, but the therapists just wanted to keep testing them, no matter how many times they failed. Maybe they were expecting some sort of spontaneous regeneration. If that's true, then they were even more idealistic than they accused me of being. Even a healthy person doesn't build muscles just by flexing them once a day. You have to work them, push them, make them hurt and break them down and engorge them with blood. You build muscles by pushing them until they burn, until sweat pours out of your forehead and stings the eyes. I craved long workouts and burning muscles, and the relaxed, calming hum that followed. How I missed that feeling.

My mind wandered out of my bed, and I thought about how to make something move, anything. I already was regaining control of my bladder, so I knew improvement was possible. With all those muscles, I thought, there must be a couple that were strong enough to do the job. I did a silent inventory, muscle by muscle, looking for a response. I wasn't discouraged yet; this was still new, and it was kind of an adventure. My mother says that I must have been reincarnated from a pioneer woman who didn't stay in Boston because she knew nothing would happen there, who didn't think the world was flat and who wanted to open up the West. Most of all, who didn't take anyone's word for anything. This first exploration of my own body didn't turn out to be as bountiful as the opening of the West, however. I couldn't even wiggle a toe. My facial muscles were fine, and my neck was getting stronger. I could lift my head and turn it, but there was almost nothing else I could do.

Dr. Cloward had managed to save a single nerve in my left shoulder and arm. That was the arm that was bracing against the dashboard at the time of impact and it had jammed up into my spinal cord. Even though that shoulder was separated and severely damaged, I was able to move it slightly. I wasn't going to be pitching in a major league baseball game, but I could shrug my shoulder a little and pull my left arm up slightly. Once I got the hand to move toward my face, however, I didn't have the muscle control to push it back down. To me that meant I had at least part of the biceps muscle, which is used to curl the hand and arm upward, but not the triceps that's needed to extend the arm. I joked about doing Dr. Strangelove with my hand choking my neck, but at least it was progress. The other arm, the one that was not injured, was completely lifeless and immobile.

I was excited to have the tiniest movement below my earlobes because my first doctors had insisted that I would never move again. There wasn't much I could do with an arm that moved only slightly, and only in one direction, but to me it meant that there was hope for further recovery. If I had that one arm muscle and the tiny ones that controlled my urethra, why not more muscles? If I eventually could bring back a whole arm, then why not two arms and a leg? To me, this was a sign that there was life in my body. I never lacked confidence that I would get up, but this clearly was proof that recovery was possible, a reason for hope.

My doctors, however, were not impressed with my plan to build on those first-recovered muscles. In fact, one of the doctors went out of his way to discourage my hope.

"I'm sorry, Heidi," he said. "If you want to call this hope, then it's false hope. There is some residual movement, and that's a good thing, but there is no guarantee that it will last and definitely no sign that it will increase. False hope is worse than no hope because it will only lead to disappointment. The sooner you accept the reality, the sooner you can learn to adjust to it."

I thought a lot about what he said. It seemed contrary to everything I had ever believed. When I was growing up, we were taught to make the best of our situation, not blindly accept it. On the other hand, I didn't want to waste my time on something that was impossible. I knew there would be adjustments necessary in my life, and maybe the doctor was right. The sooner I recognized my limits, the quicker I could deal with them. Later, sitting in the afternoon shadows with my mother, I said, "Mom? Can there be such a thing as false hope?"

"No," she said. "How can hope be false? That's like saying the sun isn't shining just because it's cloudy or that the sea is calm, when in fact it's always moving and changing. Hope is the fuel that keeps us going. We decide where it will take us, but it's hope that powers the engine.

"Even if the only hope is false hope," my mom said, "then give me false hope, please."

I complained about my pessimistic doctors to Dean Ferrandini, a stuntman I knew from *Cannonball* and other projects. My litany was becoming a familiar, and probably tiresome, topic for my friends. "I know I'm in there," I said, searching for the words to explain the sensation I had. "I can feel I'm in there. I don't care what they're saying; I can feel my toes wiggling. I can feel squeezing my knees together. You just can't see it yet. So what are they talking about? They're not in here. They don't know what I'm feeling. They've never been in this position, and how are they the experts?"

"Can you move anything?" Dean asked, trying to get me to be more specific.

"Yeah," I said. "I can move my left arm. I can pull it up almost to my face, but I can't push it back down. That's it. It started as a tiny movement, but now I can at least pull my arm up. Believe me, I've been working on it."

"Well, that's a start," Dean said, rubbing his chin and staring at my arm.

"What?" I said.

"I'm just thinking. Maybe we can fix up something to help you. So it goes up but not down, right?"

"Right."

"Okay. Lemme work on it."

A few days later I got a call from Keefe Millard, an actress who now is married to Dean. She said they were on the way to the hospital. "Dean's got a surprise for you."

They walked in, and Dean was carrying a fishing pole, some string, a plastic water bottle, and a few pieces of Velcro. He went right to work measuring me, cutting the fishing pole into pieces, and lashing them along my forearm with the Velcro. He ran the string through the eyelets of the pole and tied the dangling end to a water bottle on the floor.

"What're you doing?" I said, cracking up. The contraption reminded me of those machines in the Rube Goldberg cartoons with twenty levers and slides all to make a piece of toast that pops up and rings a bell.

"Just wait."

He fiddled some more and stood back to admire his handiwork. "See, the way this works is you pull your arm up, and with this water bottle it's like a pulley, and it'll pull it down again. As you get stronger, we can add water to the bottle to make it heavier and increase the resistance. It'll be like you're in traction."

"What a great idea," I said, enthusiastic about the prospects of the Dean machine.

The machine worked, but my arm didn't. At first the bottle was too heavy for me to lift. Then the poles wouldn't sit right, and they needed a hinge or something to allow them to bend more.

"Thanks for trying, Dean," I said.

He fiddled a little longer before finally giving up and taking his stuff home with him. What I loved most about Dean's contraption was that it was physical proof of his faith in me and his love. He knew I would get better, and he wanted to give me a hand; that's all I could ever ask of a friend. Interestingly enough, ten years later I was fitted with a special orthopedic brace that did exactly what Dean's contraption was supposed to do, only it cost more.

Working on my new muscles inspired this song, which I sang for every visitor:

> I've got my deltoid and my biceps
> but no triceps . . .
> . . . my brachialis . . .
> My wrist is moving kind of slow,
> my hand is just about to go,
> and soon I'll have the use of this
> aaaarrrrrmmmm.

Okay, it's not ready for Broadway, but it shows that I was feeling confident about my recovery.

The therapists were excited about the biceps muscle I found, but for a different reason. I saw it as the first step on a long march, one thread in a large fabric I was going to weave. They saw it as the best I could do, an end in itself. Instead of helping me work on other muscles, they wanted to leverage the one I had. "You can run an entire household off a single muscle," one of them told me. Their idea was to design machines that I could operate with that single muscle, and they immediately set to work building elaborate, expensive contraptions that were just about as effective as Dean's fishing pole. They had warehouses of machines in mind, and they flipped through entire catalogues of devices that might be useful. Excited by the prospect of a new customer to outfit, the therapists circled eagerly around me, clipboards in hand, debating which apparatus to attach.

"I'm thinking a PT-409C," said one.

"What about an F-02?"

Another said, "You know what they say about the PT series, 'the right to keep bare arms.' "

They laughed and circled some more.

I think this was some kind of primitive physical-therapist humor. Like the nurses, they talked in code. They didn't use the code to keep me from understanding; they didn't care if I understood or not. I wasn't even there. All they saw, as they circled me like architects walking around a construction site, was the one muscle that could be used to power their exoskeleton. I was not a whole person, just the motor for their machines. They were most proud of what they could build and attach to me: a giant erector set that would run off my single working biceps.

I tried to be enthusiastic about this kind of occupational therapy, or as it was called in the hospital, OT. This was the future everyone in rehab looked forward to, and I figured that there must be some value to it. So far the value remained hidden to me, but I tried to keep my mind open to what they were doing. Still, I couldn't help but think we were avoiding the problem rather than helping me solve it.

They never sought the underlying cause of any problem, and they always were willing to settle for the least amount of advancement. Instead of helping me walk, they were thrilled if I could brush my teeth. If I wasn't positively bubbly about all this "independence," they blamed me for the lack of progress and marked on my chart that I was uncooperative.

My chart itself was another point of contention. Even though it recorded my condition, it was not *my* chart. How silly of me to think so. This was the doctors' chart, and I wasn't even allowed to look at it. This absurd secrecy didn't last very long, however.

Brad insisted on taking me everywhere, even when orderlies came to wheel me to X ray or Rehab. Brad always pushed me on the gurney or in my reclining wheelchair, and an orderly or a nurse usually accompanied us, just to carry my chart. We became such fixtures at the hospital that one day on the way to the therapy room the orderly didn't bother going with us and handed Brad the folder stuffed with charts and reports. Brad and I looked at each other and smiled, and he wheeled my chair into an empty room. He locked the door and started flipping through the file, reading me the juicy parts. The notation I remember best, perhaps because it appeared so often, was "Family continues in close attendance." This is medical code for "Family continues to be a major pain in the butt," but to me it was a badge of honor.

Afraid we would be missed if we tarried too long, Brad closed up the file and we continued on to the dreaded therapy dungeon located on the lower level of the hospital. The stark white room was furnished only with exercise tables, rings to pull up on, and games to test dexterity. I imagined forgotten patients, with ragged clothes and flowing beards, hanging from mossy stone walls, stretched on creaking racks and tied to rowing machines.

Arriving on the reclining chair with Brad at the helm, I heard one of the therapists announce to the others, "The quad is here."

"Heidi," I said.

"What?" the therapist asked.

"Heidi. My name is Heidi."

"Oh, yeah. Sure, Heidi. How ya doin'?"

"Great," I said. "How are you?"

"Okay. We've got something new for you to try."

He started to attach yet another new device to my chair. They never explained how the appliances worked; they just started attaching them to me. The latest was a shiny metal trough that held my arm alongside the chair. The therapists envisioned that my one working biceps muscle would power the trough and allow me to lift a toothbrush or a fork to my mouth. I had to get the arm up by myself, which I could do, and then a motor on the trough would lower my arm. "With this you will be able to feed yourself," the therapist said proudly.

"Great," I said, glad to at least be doing something besides lying in bed. "I'm ready."

First I had to be fitted for my new device. I lifted my arm by myself, and the therapist pulled it back down again to adjust it in the trough. I lifted it again, and he pulled it down. He pulled some straps and tightened some screws. After making this upward motion a few times, the muscle became so contracted that I was doing Dr. Strangelove again, and I no longer was able to move the arm.

"That's enough for today," the therapist said. "We'll start again fresh tomorrow. I think I've got it lined up okay now."

"Maybe if you just massaged my arm a little, I could get it to work and we could keep going," I suggested.

"No, don't worry," he said. "We'll do it tomorrow. Let me just try to fit this thing a little better, and you'll be all set."

I wanted to keep going. Getting better was at the center of my focus, and I didn't want to be doing anything else. I wasn't interested in resting. The therapist was kneeling down next to the chair, adjusting the trough. Brad was fidgeting, watching the whole thing with increasing frustration. His hands tightened on the grips of my wheelchair. I looked like Robocop.

"I really think I could make it work if you just flex my arm a little," I said. "It's like I've got a ball or this knot up there. I just need to loosen it up a little."

The therapist kept working on the trough without saying anything.

Brad couldn't keep still and blurted out, "I don't see what the point of this thing is if someone has to be standing there to put the spoon in her hand and then put food on the spoon. If they're going to be there anyway, why don't they just put the food in her mouth? This is an unbelievably idiotic concept."

"Mr. von Beltz—"

"This is not independent," Brad said. "This is a joke."

I felt myself getting smaller in the chair, my arm lashed to the trough. I wanted it to work, I wanted to be good, but it just didn't seem right. I agreed with Brad. I wanted to feed myself. I wanted to be really independent. I tried to be brave, but every time I started to get up, someone in a white uniform knocked me down. I felt like I kept getting the wind punched out of me. Why didn't anybody listen to what I was saying? Why can't somebody just exercise me? All they want to do is busywork. It makes them feel like they're doing something, but it's not helping me. Tears of rage and frustration splashed onto my legs, onto my arm, and plinked into the shiny metal trough. I felt sobs welling up and spilling out of me. I sat there and cried, defeated and alone, and I couldn't even wipe the tears off my own damn cheeks.

Chapter 7

GRINER
THE GREAT

Days became weeks, and weeks became months. I rarely doubted that I was going to get better, but I did come to realize that the healing process was going to be harder and slower than I had first expected.

When a person breaks her leg and the leg heals itself, no one says, "It's a miracle!" Indeed it is a miracle, but so is everything the body does. Why should healing a broken neck be any more miraculous than healing a broken leg? A neck might be more complicated than a leg, but it's still made of bone, muscle, and nerves. I already felt myself getting better, so slightly that I was the only one who noticed. I had been scared when I couldn't move the Ping-Pong ball in the lung tester, but after a few months my wind was coming back, probably from all the talking and laughing. I was feeling stronger every day and building stamina.

But now a new, subtle sensation was taking over. It was a faint but gnawing unease. I was uncomfortable, fidgety without being able to fidget. I felt a burning or a humming inside my body, like it was filled with static electricity. I imagined that I glowed in the dark. Instead of the impulses jumping across the nerve cells like they were supposed to, I saw them bouncing into one another and causing little electrochemical crashes. I felt haywire, like an electrical storm was trapped inside my body.

The impact of the crash smashed my internal thermostat, and my temperature continued to shoot up at night. Without warning, I would suddenly feel hot and then cold and then hot again. The other strange thing was that, no matter how hot my skin felt, I didn't sweat anymore, except for a little moisture under my hair when I needed to urinate. Before the crash I used to enjoy the feeling of being bathed in sweat after a hard workout; I felt cleansed. Now even my sweat was bottled up inside, adding to my discomfort.

Some of this feeling was psychological. I was used to being on the go all the time, burning the candle at both ends and only resting when I absolutely had to. Now all I could do was lie in bed. I craved activity and exercise, any movement. My internal motor was racing at the same high speed it had operated at for twenty-four years, but the gears had been thrown into neutral.

What kept me going was the knowledge that *something* was still working; if it wasn't, I'd be dead. Is my heart beating? Yes. Am I breathing? Yes. So what is the problem? How could I determine which systems were working and which ones were down, which ones were switched off temporarily and which ones were destroyed? Were there systems that could be circumvented with new powers, the way blind people report more acute hearing?

I took inventory. Are my bowels working? Yes. My metabolic system is processing food, and the waste is going to my lower intestine. My senses of taste, smell, and hearing are in order. Instead of focusing on what wasn't working, I was determined to focus on what was and to build from there.

I knew that all these bodily systems are related in a wonderful, complicated network inside a network inside a network. This seemed to me to be the most basic concept in all physiology. At that point I didn't know very much about science, but this much seemed obvious: In my body, and in everything else, all the parts are related, and the sum of the whole is greater than the parts. No part can be separated or changed or damaged without affecting other parts, sometimes in ways no one can imagine. While this theory, which I now understand to be a basic concept of holistic medicine, was obvious to me and my parents, no one else seemed to agree with us.

Until we met Tom Griner.

When Griner was a young structural engineer at Purdue University, a group of doctors asked him to map the human nervous system, believing it was the type of integrated system that could be understood through architectural renderings and blueprints. Griner began his research and fell in love with this most complicated and efficient of structures: the human body. He gave up designing buildings and bridges and dedicated himself to studying people. The only problem was that he didn't have a medical license, so by law his work was limited to theory. Instead of spending years at medical school, Griner earned a chiropractor's license and went to work on real people. Soon he was well known among professional athletes as someone who could fix even the worst injuries without surgery. Melanie had gone to him for back trouble, and so had Buddy Joe. Robert Blake of *Beretta* fame was a regular.

"Griner's great," Melanie told me. "After I see him, I feel like I'm floating. He puts everything back in place. Everything feels straight and leveled and where it's supposed to be." I was convinced he was worth a try, so Melanie picked up the phone at my bedside and called Griner. He agreed to come.

Griner could visit the hospital but not practice there because he lacked a medical license. I told him we were spending every afternoon sitting in the sun, so he could meet us on the grounds. At the appointed time, a smallish man with a strong face walked over to our worn place on the grass and said hello.

With little by way of introduction or small talk, he started to work. Griner never said much and communicated best with his hands, moving them across my body, squeezing here, rubbing there, almost without a word. I was used to being poked and kneaded by complete strangers, and I watched him in patient silence. I looked at my mom, and she smiled. Brad was fascinated.

Griner set his fingers on my bare, deeply tanned leg and wiggled them. Then he pushed harder and jerked his hand away as if he had burned his fingertips.

"What can you feel?" he asked finally.

"Mostly I feel this burning," I said. "I feel haywire. I feel these sparks and flashes, but they're not firing the way they're supposed to. Everything is simmering or sizzling or something."

"Good," he said. "That's a good sign." He placed his fingers on me again. Wiggle. Wiggle. Push the muscle, jerk the hand away. Wiggle. Rub. "Can you feel that?"

"I feel the pressure. Or at least I see you putting the pressure on and it seems like I feel it. I can't even feel a needle going in; it's like they're sticking it in the arm of a couch and not into me, but it still makes me flinch. Or if something is coming at me, like a dinner tray brushes my hair, I duck and raise my arm, even though the arm doesn't move. Do you know what I mean?"

"What else?" he asked, still touching me.

"There's something in there moving. When I make a fist, I feel the flexing of the muscle, even though the hand doesn't move. I feel myself inside my body. I feel myself move, only other people can't see it. The only time I don't feel anything is when I close my eyes. Sometimes when I lie in the dark I forget I have a physical body. It's like I have a body within a body, which I guess is my spiritual body. I think of it like this: When someone is standing there and they get shot, they drop to the floor and they aren't there anymore. Whatever was in there moving, animating the body, that's what I feel."

Griner took all this in, nodding and prodding. His touch was firm but gentle. What he was doing looked like massage, but it was deeper. I felt as if he were reaching in and touching my core. He wasn't just moving my body; he was grabbing that thing inside me and making the circuits fire. I felt that he was on the right track, and I felt comfortable with him personally, more comfortable than with anyone since Dr. Cloward, who had come from Hawaii to fix my neck. As I had with Cloward, I knew right away that Griner could help me.

When he had finished, Griner looked up at me. "If you want me to work with you, I think I can help," he said. "It might take a long time. Nothing is instantaneous. It's not going to be easy for you, but if you want me to try, I'd be happy to."

"Yes," I said. "Please. I'll do whatever you say."

"You'll have to come down to my office. I can't work on you here. Will they let you out?"

"Yeah. We go out all the time. It's not a problem. You just say when."

My doctors didn't approve of Griner, however, and for that reason the insurance company refused to pay for his services. That wasn't going to stop me. I liked him so much that we decided to go anyway.

A few days after Griner's first visit, Brad wheeled me out of my room as if we were going to take some sun. He smiled and waved cheerfully at everyone. Just another glorious day at the hospital. When we got outside, instead of walking me to our spot on the grass, Brad turned sharply and pushed me to a back corner of the parking lot. My mom, glancing around to make sure the coast was clear, was waiting for us there in Joanna's Jeep Cherokee, the engine running.

Quickly, Brad opened the rear door and slid me inside like a pizza into the oven. He slammed the door, threw the car into gear, and we were off, laughing and cheering at our successful escape from Memorial Island. We didn't bother asking permission to see Griner because we knew we would be denied. Then, if we saw him anyway, it would be wrong. This way we weren't really breaking the rules, just bending them a little.

Brad scooped me out of the car and carried me into Griner's dark and ratty little office. It was cluttered with gadgets, stacks of books and magazines, telescopes, and a large sound system, including one of the first compact disc players I had ever seen. Brad loved all these toys. I wasn't put off by the office; on the contrary, I've found that the quality of care often is in inverse proportion to the luxury of the surroundings.

I was too weak and limp to get up on the table, so Griner worked on me in the reclining wheelchair while my mom and Brad stood at his side, curious about his techniques. Griner's first test was to take a small rubber hammer and tap my knee. In all the tests of my reflexes at the hospital so far, nothing ever had happened. The doctors bopped me with the hammer, but nothing flinched. After a while they had stopped testing. Griner pulled back the hammer, took aim below the knee, and struck. My leg jumped like it had been shocked. He tapped the other knee. That leg also jumped up from the footrest. Then he tested the Achilles reflex and got my foot to move.

My mother's jaw fell open when my leg jumped.

"This is not spinal injury," Griner said. "This is not paralysis."

My mother started to say, "But the doctors have been telling us—"

"I know, I know," Griner interrupted. "I know what they say. Phantom feeling, residual movement, blah, blah, blah. They say it's over. It's not over. The spinal cord is operating. She has all these reflexes."

He continued to check me, touching the muscles and wiggling. I felt stronger in his presence, inspired. The fact that he had found a reflex that the doctors had given up on was proof to me that I really was getting better.

"The problem isn't just the nerves, it's the muscles. She probably has a thousand muscles in spasm, maybe more," Griner said. "Some of them are tiny, but they're bunched and knotted. Take a rubber band and twist it, and twist it some more. It gets shorter and balled up. That's what's happened to her muscles. When the muscle is in spasm, it's sickened by the overproduction of lactic acid, and that inhibits the firing.

"You see this lump here?" Griner asked, touching the knot on my shoulder, which Brad had been asking the doctors about since the accident.

"The doctors say that could be a calcified blood clot," my mother said, "but they don't really know. They say they'd have to do surgery to be sure."

"This is what I'm talking about," Griner said. "This is a muscle in spasm. See how she's got these Popeye arms? All skinny at the top and big on the bottom? That's because there is no activity in that area."

"The other thing the doctors can't figure out is her temperature," my mother said. "It jumps all over the place, and at night it spikes up to a hundred and four or higher."

"You've got a pretty good tan," Griner said to me. "Do you really sit out in the sun every day?"

"Every day," I said. "It feels so good to be outside in the fresh air."

"Your temperature feels normal now," he said. "Does it only go up at night?"

"Around one in the morning," I said, "and then it goes down to normal in a few hours."

"I think it's because your body is retaining the heat," he said. "Your skin feels hot and dry because the heat is trapped inside, and you can't sweat normally, which is the body's way of cooling itself."

I told him that when the fever started my nose ran; the phlegm seemed to come from nowhere and then disappear when the fever left. The fever was scary, not like the general burning sensation I'd had at other times. The usual burning felt like something positive, and I kind of liked it because it made me feel alive. This fever, however, was beyond my ability to control, and it threatened me.

"Sit in the shade for a few days and see what happens," Griner advised.

"Okay," I said. "I'll do it." I meant it, too, even though staying out of the sun would be a sacrifice.

I felt safe with Griner and knew that his was the voice of wisdom. He made everything pathetically simple and perfectly reasonable. This wasn't hocus-pocus or some bogus theory he had made up; Griner was a scientist. The more time I spent with him, the less sense the doctors made. The doctors believed what they were saying because they were repeating the accumulated information that fills their canon. They had statistics to back up their predictions about "permanent paralysis," but I knew the statistics were based on people who had been told the worst and expected the worst. Those people had been sold a bill of goods about never getting better, and they bought it. I have no doubt in my mind that for many people with this kind of injury, the diagnosis becomes a self-fulfilling prophecy. Patients live up to—or down to—the expectations of their doctors. Griner didn't predict I would get worse; he challenged me to get better.

I went to Griner's office whenever I could, and he continued to visit me at the hospital, discreetly working on me outside on the grass. We would make picnics of the sessions, and my parents and friends would sit on a blanket alongside us with sandwiches and champagne or pots of coffee. One afternoon before Griner arrived, I noticed a young man watching us from a few steps away, staring intently. "Can I help you?" I asked.

He was blond and tanned, very casual; he could have been a surfer between waves. He introduced himself as a friend of one of my good friends, and obviously he had heard all about me. We invited him to join us on the grass. He and my parents hit it off right away because the young man, whom I'll call Tim, was well versed in alternative healing, hypnosis, and metaphysics. He was very serious and earnest, although I did catch him sneaking a furtive glance at me every so often. I smiled back. I was paying more attention to the lovely day, but Tim seemed cute and nice enough, if a little intense.

He was encouraged by what he heard about my situation and thought he could help me with hypnosis. He was sure that my body was capable of doing more than my conscious mind allowed it to do. I was up for anything that might have the remotest possibility of helping, so I agreed, even though I felt a little funny about giving up control.

The first time Tim hypnotized me, I tried to keep one eye open, but he put me under easily and I remember very little of what happened next. My mother had been telling me from the beginning that hypnosis could help, that eliminating the conscious mind from the brain-to-muscle equation might facilitate movement. She was right. When I was in a state of hypnosis and Tim suggested that I move my legs, they actually vibrated and jiggled. He went around my body, ordering different parts to move, and I moved very slightly, without being aware of moving or remembering it later.

When I woke up after that first time, my mother told me what had happened and I was encouraged. I knew that all the bodily parts were there and able to function; I just needed to make the connection work again. Tim's efforts seemed to reinforce what I was doing with Griner because they both made the muscles perform in the hope that the motion itself would remind my body what it was supposed to be doing. Tim and Griner seemed to be a perfect combination, and I was prepared to go under anytime Tim was willing.

Tim began to come to the hospital more often, and the treatments became more concentrated. Whenever he arrived, he ushered everyone else out of the room because he needed total focus for these journeys, which he said were going progressively deeper into uncharted territory. I looked forward to his visits. We were making real progress, and I appreciated his help.

One day I came out of an unusually deep trance and was startled by Tim's face. His nose was only a few inches above mine, and he wore a strange, beatific look, a mask of pure bliss. I had never seen him that way, and I was a little frightened. I looked around the room, but we were alone. "Are you okay?" I asked.

He kept staring into my eyes. He turned a worn Egyptian coin in his hands, rubbing one side, then the other. His face remained close to mine. "Don't you recognize this?" he asked.

"Recognize what?"

"This coin. I was to bring this back to you. It is how you will know me."

"What are you talking about?"

"When we were together. Before. And we were lovers."

"Are you okay, Tim?"

"Yes, Heidi. We were lovers in that life, and we are lovers in this life. It was meant to be. You told me to bring this coin so that when we met again you would know me."

He was completely off the wall. I smiled. "Sure, Tim."

I suggested to my parents that Tim seemed kind of tired and maybe needed a little vacation. I didn't go into detail, but I said it might be better to take a break from hypnosis and just stick to Griner's massage treatment for a while, to let things gel. They were too excited about my progress, though, and Tim said that if anything, we should step up the pace and intensity of the treatment.

The next time I came out of hypnosis, Tim's face was crushed against mine and his tongue was in my mouth. I gagged and shook my head, but he held me and kissed me deeply, beyond mere passion into a consuming desire. He told me he loved me, that he had always loved me, in this life and in past lives, and that we were meant to be together. He would make me walk again; his mission was to lead me out of the darkness of injury into the light at his side. He kissed me again.

I wanted him to stop, but I was so shocked that I didn't know how to respond. He was such a good friend to my whole family. Everybody was crazy about him. He had been so patient and kind with me. I shook my head but couldn't escape. He had me under his control. Should I yell? Bite his tongue? Before I could decide what to do, he stopped and pulled back.

"I love you, Heidi," he said. "I have loved you forever."

"Mom," I called through the closed door, "could you come in here, please?" My mom came in the room. I smiled as best I could. "We're done for the day," I told her. Tim left.

I had to tell my parents exactly what had happened, otherwise they never would have understood why I didn't want to see Tim ever again. I felt bad for Tim and for having to disillusion my parents. They had been so encouraged by Tim's work, and they enjoyed their long, philosophical talks with him. They were saddened that his concern for me had crossed over into something else. I could no longer stomach the sight of him.

The experience with Tim slammed shut one of the doors of my consciousness. I had not appreciated how vulnerable I was, being unable to move. I knew I couldn't fend for myself, but I never imagined that I would have to defend myself. I had been treated with nothing but kindness until this point, and the people around me, starting with my parents, were loving to the point of being selfless. I've always been an open person, and the crash forced me to open myself more, emotionally and physically. Everything had to be done for me, and the most intimate elements of daily life were being performed with strangers. Now the first bricks of a protective wall were laid, and I would have to find the balance between opening myself to loving care and defending myself from wrong intentions.

I felt relief when I returned to see Griner, whom I had sometimes suspected of being from outer space, because after what had happened with Tim, Griner seemed positively normal. Griner was as intense as they come, but he was professional and he never saw me as anything but his patient. Actually, he saw me more as a client, because he never considered me to be ill.

Several months later Griner fitted me with flotation boots, which are inflatable plastic sleeves similar to those used to read blood pressure but much longer. He slipped them on over my feet, stretched them up to my thighs, and pumped them full of air. When inflated tight, the sleeves caused pressure along my entire legs, and Griner began to pump them rhythmically to imitate the effect of walking. The pumping got the blood circulating and stimulated the legs, but Griner wasn't satisfied. He said the boots were not pumping hard enough to truly imitate walking. Legs are made for walking, he said, and their enemy is immobility. "We've got to get some weight on those legs," he said.

"Every time I try to stand, I pass out," I told him. "As soon as I'm limp again, I snap out of it and feel fine. I don't want to take any more drugs. I figure I'll get stronger by myself."

"Let me see," he said, lifting my head and shoulders slightly forward as if I were going to sit up straight. "How does that feel?"

"Okay right there, but any higher and I'll pass out."

He squeezed my bad shoulder and rubbed around my neck. The shoulder was lumpy and out of whack. He moved me up and down, back and forth, with his hand on my shoulder.

"I think this is the problem," he said, pushing on my shoulder. "Every time you rise up, this shoulder shifts. It hasn't healed properly, and the shoulder blade is sort of floating around in there. When it shifts it puts pressure on the artery and cuts off the flow of blood to the brain. When the blood stops, you black out. That's why when you go limp, you wake up. When you relax, the shoulder drifts back out of the way of the blood flow and relieves the pressure. So you snap out of it."

Griner started working on the shoulder, relaxing and stimulating the muscles to get everything back into the proper place. His concentration was absolute, his effort ceaseless. The treatment was exhausting for him, even though on some days he focused entirely on a single, small area of my body. He rubbed using the tips of his index finger and middle finger, switching hands when he tired. I thought he was pushing hard, but he insisted that he was barely touching me. He said he could feel the knots under my skin, decipher how they were shaped, and most amazing of all, he could untie them. He didn't talk at all during this process, concentrating on my body. The only time he spoke was when Brad would ask him questions, which at first was every two seconds. Brad's curiosity is one of the things I love about him, and I expected nothing less.

Along with getting me moving again, Griner believed that he could also fix my internal thermostat with massage, and that I could control the fevers without medication. The key was my sinuses, he said, a concept I didn't understand at first. Just watch, he said. He bore into an area at the base of my skull, digging in his fingers. This hurt like salt on a wound, and I winced, but he assured me that it only hurt because the tissue was not healthy. Then he moved his fingers across my face, alongside my nose, and on my forehead. The pain was fierce on my head—I had plenty of working nerves there—and I yelped.

"You've got to let me in," he said. "You've got to let me in."

The pain was so intense and he was so persistent that when his hand pushed near my mouth, I wanted to bite him. I bit my tongue instead. I wasn't sure exactly what he was doing or what my sinuses had to do with fevers, but I trusted Griner. I knew immediately that he was making something happen because for about an hour after this treatment, my nose would spill out so much mucus I was tempted to have Brad tie a bucket under my chin. I had no idea so much stagnant fluid was backed up inside me, and the release made me feel better, more clear-headed. Griner explained that the blockage was impeding the flow of air and creating pockets of infection. Since the sinuses were involved in the body's heating and cooling mechanism, he said, damage there altered the regulation of temperature.

At the end of every session, Griner announced, "Now we'll give you a couple of shots to penetrate the whole system, and then we're finished for today." Those words always put me on guard because I knew what was coming next. I couldn't actually tense up to defend myself—I remained as limp as a bag of water—but I instinctively tried to protect myself. This closing treatment was meant to send a shock wave through the entire body, through the dense muscles and the organs. Griner said that no matter how hard he pushed, he couldn't reach some of those inner muscles by rubbing, so he'd aim the heel of his hand at my solar plexus and *whump*. The first time he did it I was so startled I couldn't speak. After the shock wore off, I felt ripples of energy ring out from the point of impact. *Whump*. The ripples spread throughout my entire body, like he had plunked a heavy stone into the pond of my inner being. The whumping itself was extremely unpleasant, but immediately afterward I felt energized and relaxed at the same time, strong enough that I didn't even mind returning to the hospital.

Griner began to teach me about the human body and about what had happened to mine. Healthy nerves fire at a certain rate, he said. Mine still were firing but at a reduced rate. Normally, an impulse starts in the brain and works its way through the nerves and muscle to cause a movement. In my case, the connection was broken. He rubbed the muscles to imitate movement, which would send a message to the brain to contract the muscle. Then he would rub a different way to send a message to release the muscle. The technique was designed to operate the system backward: Instead of me sending a message from the brain to the muscle, Griner was sending a message from the muscle to the brain. This was the best way to stimulate the muscles, he said, and it was essential for them to be able to function normally again. Later he would add electrical stimulation of the muscles and other treatments, all to trigger the memories buried in the tissue.

The treatments were so fierce that black bruises swam to the surface of my skin, but the deep massage worked. Griner helped me realign my body so that in time my shoulder blade moved clear of the artery carrying blood to my brain. Now, finally, I could sit up in bed or propped in a chair and not spend my entire life horizontal. What a relief!

Griner's explanations made sense to me, especially the part about how the mind controls movement. Finally someone was speaking my language. He gave all of us hope, and I allowed myself to think, "This guy is going to get me up. Once he starts stimulating the nerves and the muscles and everything, they're going to jump back and it's going to be a done deal." Griner never made any promises, though, and he gave me just the right mix of encouragement and sobering caution.

"I don't know how long this will take or what the results will be," he said on one of my first visits. "All I can do is start and see what happens, but I think you'll walk again."

Chapter 8

DENIAL
AND ESCAPE

My positive outlook and my conviction that I would be up and running very soon, a conviction shared by my parents, was well known among the doctors, nurses, and administrators throughout the hospital. We considered having a positive mental attitude an essential part of the healing process. Everyone else called it denial.

Susan, who was doing my physical therapy, and all the doctors who saw me were very concerned about my mental attitude: I wasn't depressed enough. If I had cried myself to sleep every night and announced that I felt like cutting my wrists, I think they would have been relieved. That would have been a "normal" response to my accident. It was not normal to have parties in my room and to expect to hop out of bed any second. They were so concerned about my "denial" that they insisted I see a staff psychiatrist.

"He can give you a better idea of what happened to you and what you will have to deal with in the future," Susan said. "The sooner you start confronting the reality, the easier it will be."

"Easier for who?"

"For you, Heidi. Denial is blocking your acceptance of the situation."

"I don't care what you call it; if denial means not accepting this as a done deal, well then, yeah, that's what I'm doing. What's wrong with a little denial?"

"That's why you should see the psychiatrist," she said, not hearing me. "He can help you work through those feelings."

"Don't you understand, I don't want to work through these feelings. I don't have mental problems; I have physical problems. I want to work on my physical problems, and no one is letting me. You guys are picking and choosing what I can and can't do, and mostly I just lie around waiting for something to happen."

"The range of therapeutical options open to you are limited, Heidi." She sat down on the bed. People always did this, even complete strangers. The same mentality that leads people to touch the stomach of any pregnant woman also led them to sit on my bed. Susan continued in her earnest way. "That's one of the things the psychiatrist does in cases like this. He'll walk you through an anatomy book and show you some of the things you can expect in the future. I can tell you one thing: It's not going to get any easier."

This discussion went on for weeks. The more they experimented with my body and realized that no one was home, that almost nothing was moving, the more they were determined to convince me to accept the worst. They thought they were doing me a favor and that telling me I would never take another step was simply stating the obvious.

To me, saying I'd never walk was as cruel as telling a little boy he'll never fly. Why tell him at all? If the boy is so convinced he can fly that he wants to jump out the window, then probably you have to tell him the truth, but if he simply wants to see how fast he can run and whether by running faster and faster he can lift himself off the ground, then why not let him try? He'll find out sooner or later that he can't fly, but allowing him to find out for himself means that his outer limits will have no artificial or imposed bounds. They are the real limits, his own natural limits, not the ones laid out by his parents or coaches or society. With luck, he'll run faster and faster, pushing himself toward the goal of flight. Along the way, he might not fly, but he will run as quickly as he possibly can and stretch his little legs as if they had no fetters. Or maybe, just maybe, he'll surprise everybody, spread his arms out wide, and fly.

I wasn't flying, I wasn't running, I wasn't even moving. Not only was I unable to move myself, no one in the hospital was willing to help me move, even just to flex my legs a little or to pump my arms. I had to sneak off with Griner if I wanted to get a little exercise, which was an absurd situation: I had to hide the one thing that was helping me. The only exercise I was able to do on my own was to lift my head off the pillow. Trying to make the best of the situation, I figured that if I could move my head, I'd darn well do it as often as I could. So I practiced lifting my head again and again, as if I were working out and my head were the weight. (I'm sure my nurses will appreciate the analogy of my head as dumbbell.) I practiced turning side to side and then lifting my head sideways. When friends were in the room, I'd ask them to push down on my forehead so I could lift up against the resistance. It wasn't much of a workout, but it was better than nothing, and I now have a *very* strong neck.

My whole argument was that unless I tried to move, I'd never move. If I accepted my condition, that was the condition I deserved and the condition I would achieve. You either set standards for yourself (or for others) that are comfortable and within easy reach, or you raise them a little higher and try to live up to them. If you ski the bunny slope every day, you will become a very competent bunny-slope skier, but you won't know how good you can be until you fall off the side of a mountain into a field of moguls as big and round as igloos.

My muscles were still in my body, waiting to be told what to do. They had memory, and they remembered how to flex and contract and power my body. They formed a perfect machine. The power had been cut off, and I knew the master switch was in my mind. Even in the earliest weeks when the doctors checked my muscles for "flickers," I felt responses in some areas and not in others. In some places there were flashes of energy, and in others nothing. That meant that something real, something physical, was happening in-

Qualifying for the aerials in freestyle competition. Skiing taught me to "find my center," imparting a sense of balance that was later helpful as I learned to stand again.

Me and Melanie, the early years. Here we are plotting world domination in my Hollywoood Hills apartment.

Modeling had its moments, but I was more interested in producing and directing films. (*Michael Childers*)

Celebrating in my Canadian Mountie costume after saving the shot on the set of *Smokey and the Bandit II*. All in a days work!

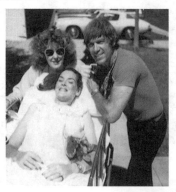

Worshipping the sun on a commandeered gurney with Mom and Brad when I couldn't even sit in a wheelchair without blacking out. I hadn't been outside the hospital in months.

My first time in a wheelchair. Looking at these two photos years later, I was shocked by how devastated my body had been and how far I'd come.

Talking with Tom Griner in 1981. His innovative chiropractic technique played a major role in my recovery. (If only he'd been able to do something about my hair.)

Pushing me one step further, Ray took me to New Jersey
to meet his terrific parents.

Ray and me cuddling in a limo.

Ray and me today.

With my niece Chelsea on my lap, surrounded as always by the love and support of my "true dream team": (clockwise from bottom left) Brad, my mother, my sister-in-law Saundra, my friend Kay, Kathleen Quinlan, my aunt Joanna, and my brother Jeff.

Megaproducer Steve Reuther (at far left), who always encouraged me, supervises as I am launched out to sea.

With author Jess Stearn, whose metaphysical writings inspired me.

Michael Gregory, me, and Buck Henry. Both of them have been vitally instrumental in many ways.

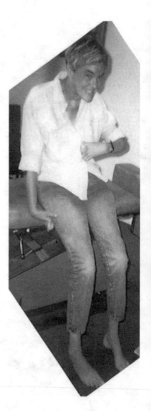

A landmark moment: half-sitting, half standing on my own on the edge of Dr. Eliot Griner's table in 1990. The look on my face says it all.

Visiting with Melanie and her daughter Dakota.

Taking a stand: unsupported in the standing frame for the first time, flanked by Mom and Brad.

Eliminating gravity in the Pepperdine pool: Paul and Marilyn Stader teach me hydrotherapy.

Doing fly presses. My formerly separated left shoulder is now strong, intact, and even with my right. (© *Scott Downie/Celebrity Photo*)

Working out on the hand bike under the watchful eye of Dr. Eliot Griner. (© *1996 Annie Leibovitz/Contact Press Images*)

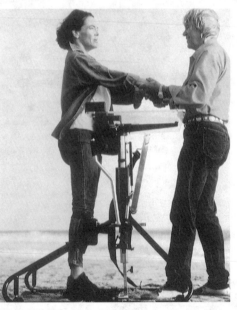

Today I am finding my center again: The standing frame's straps are undone, and with just a pad against my shins and a handclasp from Brad to hold my arms steady, I'm standing, legs locked, under my own power. (© *Annie Leibovitz/ Contact Press Images*)

side my body. If it were only "phantom feeling," why would I feel it strongly in one part of my arm and not at all in another part? If these flickers and sensations were merely ghosts of feelings past, as the doctors insisted, then I guess I've always believed in ghosts.

The same was true for the burning sensation I felt. Some days I felt myself heating up, sizzling and snapping inside. I imagined the scene in *Frankenstein* where the monster is strapped to the table and the doctor directs the flow of lightning into the lifeless body, shooting arcs of electricity and fiery sparks. Something was energizing me, but the system wasn't wired up properly. I complained to the doctors about the burning because some days it was so hot and searing that it was unbearable. I felt as if my blood had been replaced by dry ice; it was that kind of simultaneous hot and cold. I was tossing and turning inside, feverish, but I couldn't move on the outside. Some days the burning pain swelled and threatened to overwhelm me.

Doctors know about pain. When I said *pain*, they said, "Now, pain is something we can deal with. We'll give you painkillers." "No, no, no," I said, "I don't want to kill the pain, I want to make it work for me." Anyway, *painkiller* is a misnomer. I've taken enough of them to learn that they don't really kill the pain; they kill your capacity to care about it. The pain doesn't go away; it just doesn't matter anymore. The same is true of sleeping pills: They don't help the mind rest and heal itself; they shut it down completely. I was encouraged by this energy inside me, this pain, and I wanted to redirect it into the proper channels. The energy was spilling out of the circuits and burning me inside, but the goal was to focus the power, not turn it off.

The doctors weren't going to help me, so I had to help myself, the only way I knew how. My only hope was to use my mind to focus the energy and to get it on track. I began to imagine the energy traveling the proper pathways. I tried to redirect the energy and mentally reshape my nerves and muscles. For guidance I turned to anatomy books to understand the nervous system. I saw that the nervous system isn't really only electrical, it is also chemical. Millions of reactions involving chemicals called neurotransmitters are required for the slightest movement or nervous response. The brain is at the center, but many other parts of the body are involved, including glands I had never heard of that release chemical cocktails to control the body. Even the tiniest nerve cell, the last link in the chain, is an enormously complicated universe in itself. It was amazing, and I couldn't absorb the information fast enough. I asked my parents to go to the library, bring me more books, and turn the pages for me. I quizzed the doctors, and some of them enjoyed sharing their knowledge once they knew I was serious about learning.

I wasn't satisfied reading about the nervous system, however, nor was it enough to do mental exercises trying to restore the electrochemical pathways. I wanted to move, not just read about it. I assumed that concentrating on only the mental or only the physical wasn't going to be enough. I needed to combine the two, and through moving my muscles and working my mind, I was going to heal myself and get up.

My belief in the power of motion is not just a theory. This gets at the core of my personality. I move, therefore I am. My metabolism and energy level have always been extremely high, but now I imagined myself swathed tightly in bandages like a mummy. When my body decided to stop moving, my mind never got the message. Just because I wasn't able to move, that didn't diminish my desire, my need, to move. I remember a great line from an old movie where a man asks a woman, "Why do you dance?" She looks at the man, her expression a mixture of incomprehension and pity, and she says, "Why do you breathe?"

The doctors continued to fret about my attitude. I tried to ignore them, and my parents cheered me from the sidelines. What we regarded as a healthy, positive mental attitude was seen by the doctors as obstinate and obstructionist. I was interfering with their plans for me. I countered that they were the ones with a bad attitude, which of course didn't endear me.

If you think my denial of my denial and my consistent objection to seeing a psychiatrist were enough to keep a shrink out of my life, you obviously haven't been hospitalized. The psychiatric staff must have drawn straws to see who would get the onerous task, and the designated hitter strolled into my room the first time lugging a fat book the size of an encyclopedia. He walked right in, unannounced and uninvited, and introduced himself. Imagine walking into a stranger's home without knocking! (Some days I asked Brad to block the door with a gurney. The staff always pushed by the barrier, but it did give me a few moments' warning.)

I didn't offer the young psychiatrist a chair, fearing that he might get comfortable and stay. I immediately felt protective barriers going up around me, and if the administration really expected to get my attention, they should have sent a more accomplished psychiatrist or given him a bigger bat.

"They told me all about you down in rehab," the psychiatrist told me with a winning smile, starting his pitch with the friendly approach.

"I'm sure they did."

"I just thought I'd come up for a minute and see if I couldn't paint a little picture for you of what's happened, and show you exactly what's wrong with you." He reached for his thick book.

"I'm not interested in seeing your books," I said. "I'm not interested in seeing what's wrong with me, either. I've got my own books. I know what's wrong with me."

"Down in rehab they tell me that's not exactly the case, that you don't, in fact, know what to expect." His tone was stiffening; I wasn't the only one with protective barriers.

"Throwing yourself into denial is perfectly normal in these cases," he continued. "I see it all the time. It's one of the essential transitional stages that everyone must pass through on the way to acceptance. This is not the end of the world. They told me that you have enough strength in one arm to power an electric wheelchair, and you'd be surprised what people can do with just a couple of muscles and a quality chair. You'll come to love that wheelchair like a dear friend."

"I don't want to love my wheelchair," I said. "I want to throw it in the garbage. Frankly, I'd rather walk."

"Look," he said, ratcheting up to a very serious tone. "It's too bad this happened to you, but it did happen, and you've got to learn to live with it. You are not going to walk. You aren't even going to move without help, and no amount of wishing it away will make it go away. This is your future. But don't get me wrong: It's not hopeless. There are lots of people in your condition who, with the proper care, lead perfectly normal lives."

"I don't want to lead a normal life."

He sighed. "Come on, Heidi. This isn't helping."

"You can't tell me that my life is over. I know what's happened to me. There was an impact to the body, and it's been thrown for a loop. The connection is cut, and I've got to wait until it grows back. I mean, don't tell me that life stops there, the life of the body. It just doesn't make sense, what you people are telling me. I'm not interested in your information. You don't have any idea of what you're talking about."

I truly was hopeless; I was in complete denial, and there was no way to convince me that I was in bad shape. So the doctors and psychiatrists ignored me and tried to convince my parents. Mary Alys from the insurance company joined in the campaign, because part of her job was to help arrange for my life after the hospital. The normal procedure, she explained to my parents, was to choose a facility equipped to handle "people in my condition." For the rest of my life, I was going to be extremely delicate and vulnerable to disease and infection, so I would need constant and immediate access to quality medical care, she said. I also would need people who could feed me, bathe me, turn me over, brush my teeth, and help me go to the bathroom. With luck, I could learn some new skill and lead a happy, productive life again.

My parents, however, were in denial even before I was born. They've spent their entire lives in denial. Brad and my mom are President and First Lady of Denial. They always assumed that I would be going home; not to their home or to a home but to my own home. They never once considered putting me in an institution, although that apparently is what the professionals had assumed they would do since the very first week after the accident.

Mary Alys tried to reason with my dad. "Do me a favor," she said. "Just talk with these people I want you to meet, and then we'll all decide together."

Brad sat down with a young man and woman from the Craig Institute in Colorado, a very respected institution for "people in my condition." There was coffee all around and a little chitchat to break the ice, but Brad was impatient and told them, politely, to get down to business. The people from Craig apparently had the same training as the psychiatrist who visited me, because they immediately reached for a thick book filled with glossy photographs illustrating the medical horrors that awaited me. The man plopped open his copy of *The Book of the Living Dead* and flipped through the pages, turning it so Brad could see the best pictures.

"Their skin breaks down like this," the man said, pointing to a particularly vivid photograph of something that looked like a pizza run over by a truck. "They get infections and they have digestive problems. There is hair loss. It goes without saying that she'll have bedsores. Look at this. This happens all the time. It's not pretty, I know, but we have years of experience with these cases." The young man sat back, satisfied that he had Brad's attention. Then he moved in to close the deal. "She'll have to be rotated, and turned and cathed, and that's all day, every day. She will need registered nurses in attendance and quality medical care on the premises. Mr. von Beltz, we've got the trained and professional staff with the experience and competence that your Heidi needs."

Brad tried to avert his eyes from the museum of horrors before him, but the young man kept sliding the book closer.

Brad said, "I really don't think we'd be interested—"

"Excuse me, Mr. von Beltz, but you've got to start accepting that your daughter is going to be crippled for the rest of her life."

"Wait just a minute," Brad snapped, looking hard at the young man. My dad always taught us to have good manners and to be polite, but this guy had just stepped across the line. "What are you talking about, 'crippled'? What does *crippled* mean? As a student of metaphysics, I understand that the mind controls the body, and there is nothing whatsoever wrong with her brain. So what are you talking about, *crippled*?"

"Yes, sir. I understand. I'm talking about paralysis."

"A man ran this world in a wheelchair," Brad said. "Would you classify him as being crippled? Of course not. Nobody ever thought of Franklin Delano Roosevelt as being in a wheelchair."

"Well, that's true," the man agreed, although he was far too young to remember.

"I don't think, knowing Heidi, that she is going to go for this situation. I really don't think that we are going to be interested."

"I hope that you will at least talk to Heidi," he said.

"You can talk to her yourself," Brad said. "She's the one who has to decide. I'm just telling you what to expect."

They marched over to my room and showed me a beautiful brochure about the institute. It looked like a country club, but I wasn't interested in becoming a lifetime member. I smiled and said thank you very much, but it wasn't for me. I rolled my eyes at Brad, and he just shrugged.

If the ultimate form of denial is escape, then that was my goal: I had to get out of this hospital. And I wasn't going to a rest home or retirement village, either. My life was just beginning; I wasn't about to give up on it now. I knew I was strong enough to be on my own, with a lot of help, but I needed to convince the doctors that I could survive without them hovering over me all the time. I decided to make a trial run outside the hospital, just to see what I could do.

Jeff had invited us up to Big Bear for a rodeo. He was covering the show for his paper and was going to enter the bronco-riding contest to write about it firsthand. Seeing him go eight seconds on a wild horse was not something I wanted to miss, and it also seemed like a perfect chance for me to test my wings. The hospital agreed, but only after we signed a piece of paper relieving them of any responsibility once I left the grounds. To make the journey, Buddy Joe Hooker let us borrow one of the mobile homes he used on location, Brad rented a tank of oxygen in case I had trouble breathing, and we were off.

On the day of the rodeo, I had a place of honor sitting in the back of a pickup truck with a terrific view of the ring and the surrounding crowd. Jeff was something of a celebrity in Big Bear, and it seemed that just about everyone in town came by to say hello. "So this is Jeff's little sister," they said. "We've heard all about you." I knew that was true.

When it was time for Jeff's event, the announcer told the crowd that Jeff was dedicating his ride to his sister. I beamed from my throne. Jeff jumped on the horse like he did it every day, even though the only thing he had been riding for years was a desk. The horse burst from the chute and pounded into the ring with Jeff hanging on like a bushy weed growing out of the saddle. A few good kicks and bucks began to dislodge him, and he thudded to the ground just before the eight seconds had ended. He rode fearlessly, and I was proud of him.

The best thing about the trip was that someone else was the center of attention, even if only for a few hours. I always like being at center stage, but only when people are applauding, not fretting. The two-day trip also was proof that I could survive outside the hospital. My breathing was shallow and my respiratory capacity was only about 20 percent of normal, but I never needed the oxygen; Brad returned the tank full. For the second time in my life—the first time was during high school—I felt like I was ready to launch myself out into the world on my own.

I wasn't sure if the doctors would agree, but I knew my parents were ready to go home as soon as I said the word.

Early one morning, five months after the crash, my mom and Brad came into my hospital room for the last time.

"Brad," I said.

"Yes, honey?"

"I want to go home."

"What do you mean?" he asked, thinking that we already were home in California.

"I've had enough of this hospital. I just want to go home. To my home."

He considered this only for an instant. "When do you want to go?"

"Right now."

"Okay," he said. "Let's go."

With that, he started piling up my flowers and candy on the gurneys and stuffed a suitcase with my clothes. In a few hours we were strolling out the door of the hospital forever. We had done the impossible: We had escaped from Memorial Island.

I had kept my apartment on the mountain near the Hollywood sign, never doubting that I would return there. My mom had gone back to tidy up, and it was just the way I had left it five months before. Another thing that hadn't changed, unfortunately, was that the apartment was located on the second floor, and even though I had lived there for two years, I suddenly realized that there was no elevator. We laughed at this oversight, until Brad had to get me inside. He walked slowly backward up the stairs and pulled me in my wheelchair, bumping me along after him, step by jolting step, until we reached the door. I decided to give up the apartment and move into my parents' house.

I loved being home and sat for long afternoons looking out the window at Hollywood. A person doesn't always appreciate a change of scenery until she hasn't had one for a while, and I had been looking at the same ceiling for a long, long time.

The first few months of being at home were a training process. We all had to learn to manage the new me. I had help from a team of professional nurses, some of whom were more helpful than others. The agency called them "floaters" because they came in temporarily, drifting in and out of my life. One of them doubled as an Avon lady, and she was delighted to have a captive audience. She perched on the edge of the bed, spritzed perfume all over me, and offered me a rainbow of lipstick and eye makeup. The only thing more annoying than the thick, sticky, cosmetic cloud that followed her was the way she walked. She refused to lift her slippered feet off the ground. Shhh, Shhhh, Shhhh, across the floors, all night long. Another nurse left in a huff because my mother kept looking over her shoulder, especially while I was being cathed. My mother had never cathed me, but she knew how it was supposed to be done and she warned the nurse to be careful to avoid infections. The nurse took offense and stormed out the door into the darkness, with me half cathed. That night my mother learned how to cath me.

Even being cathed regularly, I still had accidents, and it seemed we always were changing the sheets on my bed. My mother had stocked up on new linens and sheets decorated with all sorts of different styles and patterns, in silk and cotton. Unfortunately, she spent a good deal of time keeping the new sheets clean and dry, and nearly every day she bundled up another load of dirty linens to lug down to the cleaners, paying the bills out of her pocket.

When Joanna saw my mom going to the cleaners and realized that we were paying for it, she was appalled. My aunt immediately picked up the phone in my room, called the insurance company, and demanded that they pay for a laundry service with home delivery. The company representative appeared to balk at this "extravagance." Joanna stiffened. "I know where your office is, and I know where your desk is," she warned the woman on the line, "and if you do not want me to deliver to you by two o'clock this afternoon a bag of wet, stinky laundry, I suggest you authorize this. My sister did not do diaper laundry when Heidi was a baby, and she's not going to start it up when she's twenty-five years old." Happily enough, the insurance company agreed.

During the first few months at home, I returned occasionally to the hospital as an outpatient and for treatments in the hyperbaric chamber. On one of those visits, I passed (or failed, depending on how you look at it) my final exam. The exam was required by the insurance company to certify that I was "permanent and stable," meaning that my condition would not get any better or worse, and that my level of disability was frozen in place forever.

Brad wheeled me in to see Dr. Mike Accord, who was one of the good guys. No matter how much I disagreed with some of the things that were done to me by doctors and nurses, I never held it against them personally. Well, almost never. Many of them meant well, and some were truly wonderful. Dorothy Vitale saved my life. Dr. Cloward saved my neck. Dr. Widell saved my leg. Dr. Accord was a decent man, and on this, our final visit, Brad had brought him a present. Brad knows everything about western films, and he knew that Dr. Accord's uncle was Art Accord, one of the great cowboy actors from the days of Hoot Gibson and Tom Mix. Brad had found a picture of the late actor and had it framed.

"You've been nice to us, and we appreciate it," Brad said, handing the gift to the doctor. Accord was pleased and seemed happy to see us, surprisingly enough after all the trouble we had been for the hospital.

"This is just a formality for the insurance, Heidi, but I've got to go through a few tests," he said. "You really do look good."

"Thank you," I said. "I feel good."

"Can you move this?" he asked, pointing to my right arm.

"No."

He pointed to my left arm. "How about this arm?"

"A little. I can pull it up but not down."

"Can you move these?" he asked, pointing to my legs.

"No."

"Can you move your fingers?"

"No."

"Toes?"

"No."

I told him that I spent most of my time lying in bed or in a wheelchair. My body was completely limp, and it took at least two people to carry me or bathe me. I could not control my bowels. I had difficulty digesting my food and had horrible gas pains. I suffered from high fevers and sinus trouble. I did not sweat normally because the glands did not operate properly. My damaged left shoulder appeared to have slipped out of the socket and fallen into the body cavity down to my waist. My shoulder looked upside down: instead of a rounded bone on top, there was a dent that appeared to be the armpit.

He pulled the point of a needle across the skin of my arm. "Can you feel this?"

"No."

He dragged the needle across my leg. "Here?"

"No."

He took out a little hammer and hunched down in front of me. "I'm going to check your reflexes now," he said.

He drew back the hammer and popped me firmly below the kneecap. My leg shot out like I had been hit by lightning, and my foot caught the doctor squarely in the chest. He rolled backward and clunked his head on the wooden desk. "Whoah," he said, looking up from the floor. "Isn't that something?"

Brad announced proudly, as if I had taken my first step, "Doctor, I give you the knee-jerk reaction."

We were excited by the response of my knee, which Tom Griner had discovered, but Dr. Accord was not moved. He completed his report classifying me as "permanent and stable," meaning I would be paralyzed for the rest of my life.

I continued to see Griner, the only one impressed by my recovered reflexes, for chiropractic treatments for three years after I left the hospital (until he retired), as often as three times a week. For the first few months he concentrated on my sinuses, rubbing the back of my head and my neck, digging in his fingers to smooth the muscles, release the built-up lactic acid, and restore my internal thermostat.

One warm sunny day, a few months after Griner's treatments began, I felt the strangest sensation: sweat on my face. The really strange thing was that the sweat appeared only on half of my face; one half was perfectly dry and the other was damp. I knew Griner was doing something right, and after a few more months I was sweating normally. Eventually I stopped getting fevers at night and was able to sit in the sun again without raising my body temperature, which was a big boost to my morale.

Then I made another discovery.

I called my parents into the bedroom in my apartment. I was on my back, limp as a rag doll. My arms were resting on my stomach where the nurse had arranged them. I ordered everybody—my mom, Brad, and Joanna—to gather around the bed. "Watch this," I said. I focused everything on my right arm, concentrating all the energy I had, which wasn't much. The firing of all the signals, which should have happened in a nanosecond, was occurring in slow motion, but it started to happen. My right hand, which appeared to be immobile and lifeless on my stomach and had not budged in nearly a year, fell off onto the bed.

My mother shrieked with joy and fell on me with kisses and hugs. "I can't believe you did that!" Joanna yelled. "I can't believe it." Brad let out a whoop, bent over, and scooped me out of bed. He whirled me around, laughing and shouting, dancing a jig with me in his arms, my hair flying out and twirling. I glowed, proud of myself and grateful for my family.

"That's amazing," Brad said, putting me back into bed and catching his breath. "How did you do that?"

"I don't know," I said. "I honestly don't know. But I'm going to keep doing it."

Now that I was free of the pessimists in the hospital and could choose my own therapy, I surrounded myself with people who shared my belief that the only limits on my efforts to recover were those I set myself. One of my new physical therapists, Bill Hunt, suggested that it wasn't too early to start thinking about standing. He wanted me to get some weight on my bones and joints, so he found me a metal frame that I could use to practice standing. Strapping me onto this thing was like hanging a jellyfish, and it took four people to get me in position. I was so limp that I couldn't be upright unless people were holding me on all sides. I had no infrastructure, no supporting muscles, to keep me in place. There is a bumper sticker that says, "Gravity: It's not just a good idea, it's the law." In my case, gravity was the only law. Each part of my body sought the lowest possible place and settled there.

I wanted to be ready, though, for the day when I would be stronger, which wouldn't be long. I worried that my bones would become brittle without any weight on them and without the cleansing and refreshing action of the blood that pumps around them during walking. So I recruited a couple of strong men, usually Brad and

Jeff, to help me into the standing frame and gradually increased the weight on my floppy legs. They held me up and strapped in my legs and hips. I could feel the blood and energy pumping into my legs, and it was encouraging. I couldn't "stand" for long, but even just for a second was a thrill.

I also needed to boost the circulation in my arms, which was easier now that I had slight movement in both of them. To capitalize on the movement, I bought a skate table to exercise with. Basically, a roller skate was fastened to my arm, and when the skate was placed on a flat board in front of me, I rolled my arm back and forth. At first I needed help to even budge the skate, but after a few months I had enough strength (it didn't take much) to move the wheels by myself.

Christy found a gym that specialized in rehabilitation, and the first time she took me, I fell in love with a special bike machine that I could operate sitting in a chair. The machine was motorized so the pedals helped move the legs, the idea being that any movement was better than none, even if the bike was doing most of the work. This seemed like a machine designed just for me, and I wanted to try it immediately. Four people were needed to get me aboard and to hold me there, but even then I couldn't make the pedals turn. I wasn't even able to allow the machine to turn my feet. My legs were too lifeless; they flopped heavily when they were bent and snapped straight when they were extended. The thought of being able to move my legs—or to have a machine move my legs—was wonderful, and I really wanted a machine of my own.

We immediately bought one of the bikes. Brad set it up for me on the beach, and he held me while I sat there, reclining backward and facing the waves, focusing all my thoughts on my feet and legs. Even before we turned on the machine, I tried to imagine my feet going around in steady circles: point, flex, point, flex. The first stage was to visualize movement. I wanted to mentally remind my muscles what they were supposed to do, hoping that by sheer force of will I could power them someday.

Brad strapped my feet to the pedals and turned the machine on to a low speed. It made a gentle grinding noise and carried my feet around in easy circles. At first Brad had to manually help my legs around, but after a few minutes at a time over the course of many months, I gradually built up to where I could be pedaled easily. I didn't have any force of my own, so the bike was doing all the work, but it felt like I was doing something. This was yet another sign that I was getting better: first my right arm had come back, now my legs were sturdy enough to be pedaled. The hardest part of using the bike was that I couldn't balance my body on the chair without people holding me because I didn't have any muscles in my torso, which meant I couldn't work out unless someone was willing to help me. Sometimes when no one had the energy to do the bike, I cajoled Brad or any reasonably strong visitor to lift my legs and "pedal" them by hand, anything to keep moving.

My left shoulder continued to hurt, which was the downside of Griner's good work. I suppose I should have been happy for any feeling, even pain, but it ached so badly that I couldn't sleep at night. The skin on top burned, and the muscles below throbbed with every beat of my pulse. I felt as if the shoulder blade itself were gouged into my heart. I slept so much on the good right shoulder that I was rubbing off the skin on that side. There was one point on my good shoulder that seemed to attract all my weight, and I was scraping it raw. The bad shoulder was so out of whack that I was lopsided: My left side dipped deeply and my hand practically touched the floor. When I was in bed, I constantly asked people to pull down hard on my good arm to get my shoulders more or less aligned.

In the morning when I woke up, I couldn't just jump into the day. First I had to lie in bed and concentrate on getting my shoulder aligned, straightening my back, and arranging all my muscles. If I moved too fast, my muscles jerked into contractions. Everyone knows the feeling of biting pain when you kink a muscle by moving abruptly with your body out of position. There is a sharp pain, a muscle contraction, and a tight, paralyzing stiffness. Multiply that by an entire body, and you realize why I took so long to get out of bed.

My deadened nerves didn't allow me to feel most things, but I did feel hot and cold, although not always at the right time. For example, I sometimes felt cold when the room was warm, or I felt hot when it was chilly outside. One thing I enjoyed very much was the feeling of warm air on my head when my mother dried my hair. I asked her to move the dryer down my arms and legs so I could bask in the warmth. The air felt like tropical wind, and I could key on that and block out the rest of my body. I closed my eyes and let myself be swept away by the warm steady breeze from the blow-dryer. At some point I realized this was as significant as feeling pain: If I could feel the subtle change of warmer air, it meant that at least some of my nerves were healing.

I asked my mother to put the blow-dryer under the covers, and I felt the warmth on my legs. The feeling was incredibly soothing and relaxing, and I begged her to just leave the dryer with me. She set it, whirring, by my side and went into the kitchen, leaving me to drift off into a trance of warmth and relaxation. A few minutes later I smelled popcorn cooking, and I figured my mom was going to propose we kick back and watch a video, which sounded perfect to me. I closed my eyes again and focused on the warm air against my leg and side. So soothing. My mom returned to my room with a strange look on her face, sniffing the air.

"What's that smell?" she asked.

"I don't know," I said. "I thought you were making popcorn."

Suddenly alarmed, she bent down and pulled back the sheets, yanking the blow-dryer out of the bed.

"Oh my God!" she said.

"What? What is it?"

"Your hand! Look at your hand!"

She held up my arm and turned my hand toward me. Red blisters were bursting on the backs of my fingers where the blow-dryer had burned them.

My mother and I thought this was hysterically funny, and we laughed about it for days. Other people found our reaction rather strange, and when we told the story, they got this pained look on their faces that was more grimace than grin. Most people found little humor in my condition. The only people who came close to understanding were the stuntmen, who regularly broke bones as a part of their work. They regarded injury, as I did, as something temporary that heals, not something that defines people. I was still Heidi, not a quadriplegic.

Surprisingly enough, another person with a good attitude was our friend Steve McQueen. He had remained close to our family, and when I had stopped being Brad's skinny little kid, he had given me a part in the movie *Hunter*, which, sadly, turned out to be the last picture he made before he died. Steve took illness seriously, but he had been banged up plenty of times making movies and driving fast cars and motorcycles. Then, as he had always feared when I was growing up, he got cancer. While he was undergoing chemotherapy, he sent me a big basket of roses with a cute card wishing me a "seedy recovery."

Now that I was home again, I was anxious to pick up my life where I had left it—with some accommodations to my new lifestyle. Not only did I have a mobility problem, but I also didn't travel lightly anymore. Parents with small children know how much gear you have to lug around anytime you go somewhere; I had the same problem, only in bigger sizes. I needed a wheelchair, medical supplies, cathing trays. I needed someone to drive me, and I needed someone to care for me.

The insurance company proposed to buy me a special van for "people in my condition." They showed me pictures of this thing that looked like the vehicle the pope uses, with a glass bubble on top and a five-hundred-pound lift for the wheelchair. Instead of getting out of the wheelchair and sitting in the seat like a normal person, I was supposed to stay in the wheelchair (which I hated) and be bound to the floorboards with hooks and chains and straps. The rig looked like a float in the Orange Bowl Parade, and I couldn't imagine rattling around town in that contraption.

"What about a limo like they sent to take you to the hospital? You know, that ambulance-limo kind of thing," Christy suggested.

"It would be big enough for you and all your stuff. You could even stretch out. You want to be in a regular car, you don't want to be in a bubble-top thing with everyone looking at you like a garbage truck."

The insurance company had once sent a sort of medical limo to pick me up at home for one of my regular hospital visits, and we were impressed. The car was long and gold, with flags and sirens and all sorts of fancy stuff. We didn't need a fully equipped ambulance, and usually a regular car was fine, but the idea of a limo made sense. The insurance company agreed, and occasionally we were given the use of a brown stretch limo with a sunroof, tape deck, and a bar, which we immediately stocked. By day we had a sophisticated, businesslike means of transportation. By night we had a disco on wheels.

Christy and I were getting ready to take the limo out for an evening on the town when Melanie dropped by for a visit. She decided to go with us, and the three of us piled into the car. First, of course, we had to stop at the dry cleaners for Melanie's laundry, then run a dozen other errands she just had to do precisely at that moment. We didn't mind, though, because we served ourselves drinks, put on a little music, and enjoyed the ride. Then Melanie wanted to pick up a girlfriend, who climbed in with us. The sun was going down, and we settled into a beautiful evening, speeding down the Pacific Coast Highway with the sunroof open and the clear sky above us, the flat sparkling ocean to our right and the steep hills to the left.

We pulled into a sushi restaurant for dinner. I figured we better eat something because the limo bar already had been open for quite some time. Melanie was a little weepy, lying down on the seat with her head in my lap. As great as she was about treating me like a normal person, she kept her sadness bottled up so tightly that it occasionally overflowed, especially after a few drinks. I knew she'd feel better if we stopped to eat.

"Don't worry about me, Melanie. You know I'm going to be fine. I'm fine already. Don't I look fine, or what?"

"You look great, Buddess," she said, her tears wetting my good dress. "It's just that it makes me so sad what happened. It just doesn't seem fair."

I just smiled at her. "Lighten up, Melanie."

We were regulars at the restaurant, so when the limo pulled into the parking lot, a waiter trotted out to take our order. We always stayed in the car, just because it was such a production to go inside. Anyway, the limo was so big that it was like having a private dining room. The waiter soon returned with a giant tray of sushi and Perrier bottles filled with sake, which we didn't really need but seemed appropriate with the sushi.

Melanie and I dove into the sushi. Christy was standing up with her head out the sunroof, leaning on the roof to flirt with the guys who had gathered around the limo. She passed them cups of sake, and we toasted our good fortune. We cranked up the stereo and rolled all night long.

Despite these regular forays into the nightlife, I still wanted to do something special to announce my formal return to society. I felt strong and healthy, but other people still needed to be convinced. The perfect opportunity would be the screening of *The Cannonball Run*, which Bobby said was just a week away. Bobby and I were still going through the motions of a relationship, but frankly I was too busy trying to get better, and he just wasn't that interested anymore.

Bobby was heartbroken by the crash. He always had imagined that someday we would get married and have kids, and that I'd be home fixing dinner when he came back from a hard day of crashing cars and jumping out of airplanes. He was sweet and consoling while I was in the hospital, but now that I was home, his love was growing fainter as he put me out of his mind and out of his future. In his eyes, I was the one who had left; I would not be coming back to him.

Officially we still were together, though, and I had many good friends from the movie. It would be great to see the old gang and to celebrate the release of the film. What better place to show everyone that Heidi was back and ready to jump into the scene again. Stuntgirl rides again! I would need a new dress, something understated but elegant, and Christy could help fix my hair. I imagined all the good friends who would be there, the flashbulbs popping and the champagne flowing. It was going to be great!

I realized it might be a little uncomfortable to see Hal and Burt and some of the others, but I had no hard feelings and I didn't blame anyone for what had happened. I was thinking about the future, not the past. Some people had written me off, a casualty of the "tragedy," so I knew that the first impression would be important, if only to jolt people out of their expectations. For that reason, I hated the idea of making my entrance in a wheelchair. Maybe I could have Brad carry me in and place me on a couch. He looks great in a tuxedo, and I imagined him carrying me proudly into the room, both of us glowing and radiant. Now *that* would be an entrance to remember.

I told my mom about my plan, and she and Joanna raced out to our favorite shops and came back with a dozen beautiful gowns for me to try. I found one that I loved, and we busily prepared for the party. The excitement level was high anyway for the premiere of a new film, but I felt like this night also was going to be the premiere of the new me. I was feeling so confident and strong, and I looked pretty and healthy. I couldn't wait to show myself off and let people see how much progress I was making. I expected to be back in the movie business very soon, probably behind the camera rather than in front, but that's where I had long imagined myself working anyway. I was ready to take on the world.

But as the day of the party approached, one name failed to appear on the guest list: mine. I figured they thought my presence might be a "downer" and set the wrong tone. I was stunned. I probably should have screamed and thrown a fit. Instead, I sat silently, empty of all thought and emotion. Frozen in place. I knew that Bobby and the others hadn't meant to hurt me, but that didn't lessen the hurt or dull the pain. I just wanted this whole thing to end. I just wanted to go to a party like everybody else. I'm the most upbeat person I know; there's nothing "down" about me. I wasn't going to put a damper on their stupid party. They were the ones putting a damper on me. Their attitude steeled me further and gave me another reason to keep fighting: I was going to get up, I was going to make it on my own. Then I'd invite them to my party.

The premiere went on without me, and I heard it was fun. I'm told that the finished version of *The Cannonball Run* is entertaining enough, although it's not exactly required viewing at film schools. I honestly wouldn't know. To this day, I haven't seen it.

Chapter 9

RAY OF SUNSHINE

In the months right after the crash, the last thing on my mind was starting a world-class romance. So naturally fate delivered a gorgeous blue-eyed hunk right to my door. It should happen to everyone.

Early on a brilliant January morning, as we were preparing to take my nieces Allison and Tiffany to the Santa Monica pier for corn dogs and a few turns on the antique carousel, the phone rang. I heard a sexy male voice on my answering machine. I'd heard this voice before. It belonged to Ray Liotta, an actor friend of Melanie's who had attended the University of Miami with Steven "Rocky" Bauer, who was soon to become Melanie's fiancé. In a resourceful move, Melanie and Ray had swapped residences, and Ray was comfortably ensconced in Melanie's beach house, while she occupied his Manhattan flat.

Ray had called several times before to introduce himself, and he hoped we would be able to meet. I took these to be polite queries from a mutual friend and made no firm plans. This time, when I heard his voice on the answering machine, I decided to pick up. I told him we were going to the pier but we'd be back about three in the afternoon. He offered to drive to my place and be there when we got back. I said sure. Even on the phone, the guy had an extraordinary sense of humor and an irresistible appeal. My interest was definitely piqued, although I wasn't expecting anything serious.

Bobby was coming and going at increasingly longer intervals, and while I avoided thinking about it, I could not help but be aware that our bond was largely a product of his guilt. Strangely, this was not painful to me but seemed to go with the territory, and although it remained unspoken, everyone seemed conscious that despite Bobby's chivalry, the shelf life of our relationship had expired.

The drive home from the pier took longer than we expected. The traffic was heavy, and when it got close to three I figured I'd better phone Ray to tell him there was no way we could make it before four. I found a pay phone, but he didn't answer. So he was probably on his way. As we inched along I anxiously watched the traffic for Ray, who was using Rocky's beige BMW, but I didn't spot him.

Jeff was waiting for us when we drove up to the house I shared with my parents. "Some guy came to see you, but I told him you weren't here," Jeff said. "He was pissed."

I felt a little guilty, but I quickly rationalized, Why should someone I don't even know cause me to have an anxiety attack?

I asked Jeff, "How pissed?"

"Pretty pissed."

"What was he like?"

"He was okay."

Jeff's not big on details; it's a guy thing.

"He said to give him a call," Jeff said.

Even though I was sunburned and sandy, I figured I'd better bite the bullet and call to apologize. Christy held the receiver to my ear and dialed. Ray answered on the first ring.

"Are you there now?" he asked.

"Where?"

"At home."

"Yeah. We just walked in."

"How about if I come up right now?"

Oh, no! I thought. What I said was, "Sure."

I wasn't going anywhere. With every minute, I was sinking deeper into the couch. My face was red and shiny from the sun, my tangled hair was fanned out on the cushion, and my clothes looked like I had slept in them. I didn't give my appearance a second thought, though, because really, who cared? I crunched on some potato chips and watched television, my legs spread out in front of me and my feet bare.

I was lost in the TV when the door swung open in slow motion. A figure filled the frame in silence. I glanced over and looked up at a pair of long, firm legs in blue jeans. A faded jean shirt. Dark wavy hair and blue eyes that seemed to have their own source of light behind them. The eyes were brighter than the jean shirt, brighter even than Paul Newman's. He flashed an electric grin, and I wasn't sure if this was a boy dressed as a man or a man with a boy locked inside. There was something else there, too, something fiery behind the coolness of the eyes. I wasn't sure yet what it was. One thing was certain: This was just about the most stunning man I had ever seen.

Ray walked in like he owned the place, navigated over to me, and planted a kiss on my cheek, his lips moist and fresh on my sunburned face. At some point, I closed my gaping mouth and stammered a hello. Luckily, he introduced himself around the room and found a seat. I was speechless and frozen on the couch. I looked over at my mother, who had the expression of someone gazing upon a newborn fawn. Christy was visibly salivating. All three of us sat there, struck dumb by this guy.

"Well," he said. "I'm glad to finally meet you, Heidi."

"Yeah," I said. "Uh, me, too." I was signaling Christy with my eyes, trying to get her to come over and give me a hand, but I couldn't get her to break her eyes away from Ray. By now I had sunk so low on the couch that I was practically lying down and my legs were hardly at their most graceful. I at least wanted to sit up, but I couldn't move anything. All I could think about was what I was going to do to Jeff. I was going to kill him, slowly. "Okay"? Okay, indeed. This guy was a dream.

"Melanie's told me a lot about you," he said.

Little did I know that Melanie had shown him pictures of me taken at a party for her last birthday, which we celebrated at sea. The party boat was shaped like a three-layer wedding cake bobbing on the water, and the skipper was not very excited to see me arrive in a wheelchair. Once they carried me on board, they treated me like some kind of maritime hazard and didn't know what to do with me. The captain ordered me carried to the upper deck, practically in the crow's nest, and they lashed a rope around my chair and tied it to the mast. Most of the other guests were on the lower decks, but I enjoyed my perch with the sun and wind and champagne. By the time someone snapped my picture, I had given new meaning to the expression "three sheets to the wind." My face was red, my eyes were bloodshot, and my hair was whipping around my face. That was the picture Ray had seen. And now I looked even worse, with this incredible guy sitting in front of me.

I smiled like an idiot and tried to figure out a way to get him to leave the room long enough for me to get cleaned up and put on a little makeup. "I'm really sorry to make you come up here twice in one day," I said. "And now I can't even offer you anything to drink because we just got home and I'm out of everything. Maybe Christy could go down and buy some wine. Right, Christy?"

Ray jumped up. "I'll go," he said. "No problem. I'll run down and be right back."

What a relief. When we heard the door close, Christy gushed, "Did you see that guy? Oh my God!"

"He's adorable," my mother said with a long sigh.

I looked at them both, raising my eyebrows. "Just help me throw myself together."

Ray was no sooner out the door than Christy and Mom went into action faster than a pit crew at the Indy 500. My face was washed, blush and gloss were swiftly applied, and I shook out my hair. Thank God my muscle tone was good enough for me to remain curvy, and I was tanned from sitting in the sun. And thanks to Dr. Griner I could at least move my upper body enough to appear animated.

When Ray returned with a nice bottle of wine, he started to say something and did an appreciative double take. "Wow," he said, grinning. "Hello again."

He poured everyone a glass of wine, and soon we were laughing and telling stories. I felt comfortable with him right away, the way old friends can communicate without having to explain everything. Ray's a Sagittarian like my mom: straight to the point and direct, with a killer sense of the absurd. He has a quality that reminds me of Robert De Niro or Al Pacino, or even Tony Bennett or Frank Sinatra. It's a kind of streetwise attitude that's very sexy.

He had grown up in New Jersey in a neighborhood where people were not terribly career-oriented and construction was considered a good, lucrative field. He reluctantly went to college, choosing Florida mostly because a buddy from the neighborhood was going there and they could be roommates. He enrolled in a drama class, where he became friends with Rocky and discovered something he truly loved: acting. He starred in a few college productions, earned a degree in theater arts, and returned east to New York to see if he could make a living as an actor.

Despite the fierce competition, he actually got steady work and landed the part of Joey Perrini on the soap opera *Another World*, which he played for three years. The opportunity and exposure meant a secure future in television, but Ray was impatient. His career was hot and headed in the right direction, fast, but he wanted more. He went under contract with NBC for a series being shot in California called *Casablanca*, which was based on the classic movie, and he moved to the West Coast. The show was going well, he said, but he was almost thirty and he was ready to break into movies. He just needed a shot.

At some point Ray suggested we all go out to a movie. Christy and I caught his enthusiasm and quickly agreed. We suggested that Tom, the local Malibu limo driver, come by and take us all to a drive-in.

"A drive-in? No way," Ray said. "I want to go to a real movie. In a theater with popcorn and everything."

"I've never been to a walk-in," I said, meaning since the crash.

"Never? You're putting me on. Oh, come on, let's do it. This'll be great."

With that the door opened and in walked Bobby! Scratch the limo.

Ray had his back to the door, and Bobby just stood there staring at his broad shoulders. I had been feeling pleasantly light-headed and relaxed, but Bobby's arrival snapped me back to reality.

I introduced them, and Bobby immediately started making proprietary noises. Even if we weren't a hot item anymore, he wasn't sure he liked someone else being with me. I was momentarily disconcerted, but Ray remained resolutely cool. Bobby finally asked him to leave. Ray stubbornly waited for what seemed an endless interval before he walked out, but not before giving me a good-bye kiss. He took my brother with him, and they rolled their eyes like coconspirators on the way to Trancas, a local bar, where they spent the rest of the evening bonding like old brothers from the lodge.

The next day was Super Bowl Sunday, and Bobby never left my side. I could not remember a time when I had been favored with this kind of attention. Instead of welcoming it, I was irritated. Adding to the tension, Ray kept calling with a running commentary on the game—silly and cute and hopelessly annoying to Bobby. Ray and I had a little bet going on the game, and I just wanted Bobby to get lost so I could talk to Ray. I was smitten. My mom spoke to him several times, too, and she burst out laughing when he offered a solution to my dilemma: "Heidi should lose that yutz."

My mother thought this was romantic, if impetuous. My aunt Joanna thought he was "an angel" and still does. I reacted by getting a fever and a roaring headache. The following day when I returned home from my regular bout with Dr. Griner, Bobby said his good-byes. I knew he was relieved to make a graceful exit, and I didn't realize how little we had left until he was gone.

Ray was as delighted as a mischievous imp. "Ahh, he was no good for you," he said, dismissing Bobby with an airy wave of his hand.

So began a relationship that changed the course of my recovery and my life. It was as though we had always known each other; we even looked alike. We did everything together. He became my arms and legs and made me feel I could do anything I wanted. He was a whirlwind of energy, an irresistible force pushing me to do more each day.

We still hadn't made it to that movie. "It'll be great," Ray enthused. "I'll be there with you."

I smiled, unconvinced.

"It's just a movie. No big deal."

When it finally happened, I didn't have time to worry about blocking the theater aisles or getting in and out of the wheelchair. He just pulled up in front of a little Malibu theater, ran in, scoped the situation, and got the tickets. Then he whisked me up in his arms and into the theater before I could object. He was my hero.

We were never separated, and I began to feel a freedom I hadn't felt in a long time. We were a team, and Ray was always either by my side or on my mind. It was a heart-pounding, all-consuming, mad-about-you love. We spent every day together, going to the beach, visiting my therapists, shopping, and seeing friends. I had fun introducing Ray to California and showing him all my favorite spots. We drove around for hours as I pointed out the sights and told him the history of Hollywood. Riding in the car also was therapeutic for me: I concentrated on leaning into the turns, pushing my body against the force of the moving car. I wanted to be exercising or moving all the time, knowing that I had to work my body or lose it forever.

Ray continued to rush off to interviews and auditions, but the truth is, his mind was elsewhere. His principle concern, his most ambitious project, was me. We wanted to be together all the time, and when he wasn't with me he called to see what I was doing. He sent me notes and flowers, bought me pretty things, and showered me with surprises.

The first time we were together as lovers, Ray was slow and patient because I was so scared I was trembling inside. I was more nervous than I had been my very first time years before. When I was younger, I didn't know what to expect and had nothing to compare it to. Now I knew how good love could be, and I worried that I would never experience it the same way again. What if it didn't work? What if I didn't feel anything? How was I going to be able to please him? Ray answered my questions and satisfied my doubts. He made me feel like the sexiest, most desirable woman of all time. He was so tender, so loving, and he pulled me gently with him, awakening my body from a dark sleep.

Every night we went out on the town, often to Trancas, which was a hangout for a lot of stars, including Jack Lemmon, and Woody Allen when he was in California. There was live entertainment every night because members of the Eagles, the Beach Boys, and other bands partied there and often felt like playing.

Ray wheeled me in front of him wherever we went. He made a huge game of everything, navigating stairs like obstacle courses and weaving in and out around crowded tables in busy restaurants. "Excuse me!" he yelled. "Make way! Coming through." Our entrances were always grand, and Ray was so charming and comical that everyone liked him at first sight. I stopped being embarrassed by his extravagances, and I realized that he was drawing attention away from me, causing a scene to protect me from the looks of strangers, much the way a mother bird will squawk and flap to lead predators away from the nest. He was so tender and supportive; no one had ever been so proud of me. He always held my hand or touched my leg, and for no particular reason, he would lean over and kiss me deeply.

Despite all this social activity, my body was not under control by any means; I still was in the process of regaining muscle strength and making the transition from limp to firm. Being paralyzed didn't mean there was no feeling or movement; it was just that I couldn't always control the movement. Sometimes my body, on its own, would get right up and jump out of the chair, which was extremely embarrassing. I called these spontaneous events "waves" because I could feel the energy start tingling my toes, surging up my legs, and then blasting out my shoulders, knocking me back with the force of a wind tunnel.

When a wave began, my feet nailed themselves to the floor and I felt my body snapping straight, almost as if I were going to stand, but once the wave climbed up to my damaged shoulder, the force got derailed. Since my shoulder didn't rotate in the cuff anymore, my whole body twisted instead. My feet tried to flip back over my head, and then they jammed back into the ground, sending my hips thrusting straight up and propelling me out of the chair. The waves were triggered by the slightest vibration, even a bump against the wheelchair. I was so sensitive that I feared being pushed along a sidewalk because I knew that the faintest crack in the pavement could blast me off.

It wasn't until I learned to anticipate the waves that I began to learn how to control them. As soon as I first felt the energy gathering in my legs, I tucked my chin into my chest like a diver in a pike position, and I forced all my power into the seat of the chair. Since I had very little muscle control, some of this effort was "only" psychological, but I was beginning to realize that the barrier between the psychological and the physical was not so much an immovable wall as a living current. In other words, telling my body to move was inextricably related to actually moving it.

Ray, too, began to learn to anticipate the waves. At first I had to tell him, "Grab my shoulders. I feel one coming." Later I could just give him a look, the kind that only the closest friends and lovers share, and he would stand discreetly behind me, as if he just happened to feel like rubbing my shoulders. Between his downward pressure and my tightly held pike position, we usually could keep my butt from popping up out of the chair like a jack-in-the-box.

Ray had his own version of the wave. While mine were physical and triggered by vibration, his were emotional and triggered by certain strong feelings. The thing that our waves had in common was that they were difficult to control and terrifying to witness. Ray's frustrations were many. Living in California, he was far from home and lonely for his friends and family. His career was moving along steadily, but it never moved fast enough. Part of him knew he was going to make it, but as with most actors I knew, another part was convinced that every acting job he had was going to be his last.

I also was a source of frustration, because Ray was ready for me to get up. I looked so normal and healthy that my body appeared to be sleeping instead of paralyzed, and many people, including Ray, expected me to jump up at any second. Ray was feeling more deeply about me with every day that we spent together, and he wanted to share the world with me. But my physical needs were slowing us down. Just getting me dressed and ready to go out took forever. If I wanted a bite to eat, someone else had to prepare it, cut it, and place it in my mouth. Everything I did took longer than it ever had, plus I needed to devote time to my therapy and working out. On top of all that, I tried to think about Ray's needs, too, but my own survival sometimes consumed me.

Ray's deepest insecurity, though, was an emotional wound from his childhood that was so covered in scar tissue that I wasn't sure it ever would disappear completely. Ray had been abandoned by his biological parents and had lived in an orphanage until he was adopted at six months by the Liotta family. A few years later, the Liottas adopted a girl, and Ray remembered going to get his sister. He joked that he always thought that's where babies came from: If you wanted one, you went and picked one up. His new parents couldn't have loved the two babies more, but somewhere inside him, Ray knew that if you could be picked up, you also could be left behind.

Of all the absurd, misguided fears he could have, Ray was terrified that I was going to leave him. How crazy! And I had been thinking it was the other way around. He could have any woman he wanted; if anyone should have been insecure it was me, not him. The closer we became, the more exposed and vulnerable I felt. Evidently he felt the same way.

When we did have an occasional blowup, I always expected Ray to storm out the door for the last time. On one occasion I thought he had done just that. He got only as far as Paradise Cove, a couple of miles from our house, before he stopped to call me from the Sandcastle, a beachfront haunt. He asked me to meet him, and I had Jeff drive me there.

We had been dating for a few passionate months, and I didn't see why I still needed to reassure him about our relationship. No matter what I did or said, he didn't hear. He was convinced that I was going to leave him, that I didn't love him enough. I had things of my own I needed to work out, and I couldn't be holding his hand all the time. I don't mean my paralysis, either. Just because I was stuck in a wheelchair didn't mean that was my only problem. The other problems, the normal insecurities, worries, and fears that everyone has, didn't go away just because I couldn't move. My head was spinning, my heart ached, and I felt torn in five directions.

There was music pounding in the background. We sat at a small table, me in my chair and Ray across from me. "Do we have to go through this again?" I asked him. "I don't feel like dealing with this. I'm having enough problems with my own self, and I'm not really prepared to take on the responsibility of another person."

"I didn't think I was asking for that much," he said, twirling one of several empty shot glasses on the tabletop. "I just need to know you'll always be there for me."

"You have to be who you are," I said. "I need you to be strong enough for both of us."

"Fuck it," he said, in one motion grabbing the shot glass and hurling it up against the wall.

"Whoa, there," the bartender said, moving down the bar toward us and wiping his hands on his apron. "Take it easy."

"Shut up!" Ray yelled at him. "Mind your own business."

"Take it outside," the bartender ordered.

"Yeah, yeah, yeah," Ray said. He stood up, snapped off the locks on my wheels, and started pushing me out the door, banging chairs and tables out of the way as we careened through the room. People stopped talking to stare at us, but no one was stupid enough to block Ray's path.

I tried to look back at Ray and just briefly saw his blue eyes hooded by squinting lids. A cobra. His thin lips were drawn back tight across his frozen mouth in a silent rage.

Great, I thought. I am being pushed by a maniac and there's not a damn thing I can do about it. I started to say something, but he shoved me so hard that my head snapped back against the chair, and it was all I could do to stay in my seat. We blasted through the doors into the cool night air, and for an instant I wondered if he was going to wheel me out into traffic like in an old Keystone Kops comedy.

The fresh air seemed to calm him, though, and eventually we slowed to a reasonable cruising speed. We were still rolling across the darkened parking lot in an unknown direction—at least, it was unknown to me. "Ray?" I said. "Honey?"

"Just a minute," he snapped.

I realized he was pushing me over to Rocky's BMW, which was a relief—as long as he didn't park me in front of the grille and start the engine. He silently opened the door and sat on the runner of the car. He put his head in his hands and kicked at the gravel in the parking lot. "I'm sorry," he said. "I'm sorry. I just feel like you are rejecting me."

"I'm sorry, too," I told him. "I'm not rejecting you. This is not about rejection. I can't believe that you of all people would worry about that. Don't you know that I love you?"

"Yeah, I guess so, but I don't know, I just feel scared sometimes."

"I feel scared, too. I get so caught up in my own problems that I forget about you. I need to focus on getting up. That's what I need to do. Everybody makes it seem like the world revolves around me, and I start believing it after a while. You of all people. You seem so strong and loving and wonderful that I can't possibly imagine that you need any reassurance or anything."

He leaned over and put his head in my lap. He placed my hand on his head and said, "I love you, Heidi. I want to be with you always."

"Me, too," I said. "Me, too."

While our romance was charging forward, so was Melanie and Rocky's. They announced that spring, nearly a year after the crash, that they were going to be married in New York City. Melanie asked me to be her maid of honor, and there was no question I would be there, even if I had to be pushed in a wheelchair all the way from California.

Ray couldn't wait. He was excited about the wedding, but mostly he wanted to take me home to meet his parents in Union Township, New Jersey. I couldn't imagine they would be very pleased to see their son wheeling his girlfriend around, but he insisted they would love me as much as he did.

When we arrived at LAX and headed to the gate, I saw a flight attendant heading toward me with one of those spindly little chairs they use to take people on board. She looked at me, then back at the chair. I just laughed. There was no way they were going to get my big, floppy body into that thing. Ray looked at the chair and grinned at me. He pushed the chair aside, scooped me into his arms, and marched onto the plane, depositing me in a first-class seat. We drank a champagne toast and were on our way.

Ray's dad met us at the airport, and he was a dear. He never treated me differently than he would have treated any other girl; if Ray loved me, that was enough for him. Ray had told them all about me, about the crash and how I was going to be getting up very soon. Ray's mom was waiting for us in their cozy, spotless home decorated with family pictures on the walls—quite different from the house I grew up in, which looked like a museum because Brad was forever bringing home paintings, books, stained-glass windows, and other treasures that he just had to have. Ray's mom greeted us wearing an apron; her hair had been done at the beauty parlor. Compared with my family, the Liottas were Ward and June Cleaver. They bragged about Ray the whole evening and showed me the cutest baby pictures of our boy. Ray squirmed, all the while making plans to take me out on the town.

Ray was dying to show me off to his friends, guys he had grown up with who still were close to him, even though their careers had taken them in different directions. Now we were on Ray's turf, and he showed me the intimate bars and hideaways, the great restaurants and the old haunts of his youth. Ray's parents hoped we would stay at the house, but we moved into a hotel in Manhattan with the rest of the wedding party. I wanted to be near Melanie to help with whatever I could, and I think she appreciated my being there.

On previous visits to New York, I had always enjoyed myself, although being in the city made me feel a little claustrophobic, and I never liked having to look straight up to see the sky. This time I was thrown off by the unfamiliar surroundings. Since the crash, I had stayed close to my family and was surrounded by people who were familiar with my routine. I had created a perfect, comfortable environment, but now I was a long way from home. I shook off my worries, though, knowing that new challenges would help me grow. Whether it was going to the movies or going to New York, Ray was always behind me, pushing.

On rare occasions, Ray pushed too hard, and I had to push back or be run over. One of those times we were having a drink, and a young man came into the lounge passing out flyers. When he got to our table, he extended the flyer to me. I motioned for him to hand it to Ray, but Ray refused.

"Stop," Ray said. "Let her take it." Then he turned to me. "Go ahead, take it."

"What are you trying to prove, Ray?" I asked, my face burning red.

The poor guy was embarrassed, too, and he tried to turn away.

"Give her the flyer," Ray ordered. Ray was not the kind of person you said no to, and he tended to get his way.

Now I was getting mad. "Leave the guy alone, Ray."

Ray wasn't going to give up, though, and the only way to end this stupid scene was to take the flyer. I turned to the young man. "Okay, hand it to me." The guy reached out to me halfway, and I shrugged my shoulder to extend my hand as far as I could in his direction. He shoved the paper between my fingers and quickly ran off to another, less hostile table.

"There," Ray said. "Was that so hard?"

I just sat there, smoldering. I knew he was right, and he was trying to get me to push the envelope, but I hated the fact that I had allowed myself to be provoked.

We had arranged for a nursing service in New York, but when the first of the temporary nurses showed up at the hotel, I felt a little uncomfortable. She was wearing a stiff uniform with a name tag and was very formal, completely different from the casual California staff I was used to. Ray decided we could forgo the day-shift nurse because he was with me anyway and Melanie knew how to help me use the bathroom. Then we got rid of the evening-shift nurse. The last to leave was the overnight nurse, and she was let go when Melanie said she would be there each night to help me pee before I went to sleep. Pretty soon we were on our own in the Big Apple, and it was wonderful. Ray took care of everything, treating me like a princess and trying his hardest to make things fun for me.

For the day of the wedding, Melanie had arranged every little detail for us, down to hair and makeup people for the wedding party. I was going to wear a white tuxedo with a pink bow tie and cummerbund, and Melanie had ordered a crown of roses for my hair. All the other women were busy fussing over Melanie and getting her ready, so Ray volunteered to help me dress.

"I'd rather help you undress," he said lecherously, in his best Groucho Marx impression.

"Later," I promised. He kissed me warmly.

He helped me into the bathtub and soaped me lovingly. He wrapped me, warm and relaxed, in a fluffy white towel and carried me to the bed. I told him where to find everything, starting with a pair of panty hose. Now, it's hard enough to put panty hose on someone else's legs, but it was especially hard with me because my legs were so limp. I tried to explain how to do it, but as usual, Ray had to figure it out himself, which took twice as long. After struggling with the panty hose, he wrestled me into a pair of white stretch pants, a crisply ruffled shirt, and a white jacket. We giggled and played, but Ray also started glancing at his watch, realizing that dressing me was taking more time than we had set aside.

When I was dressed, the hairdresser braided my hair and set the wreath of flowers on top; I felt like a piece of hallway furniture garnished with a vase of roses. I worried the roses weren't attached securely, and I was frustrated that I couldn't reach up and check for myself. I was so nervous about the arrangement falling in my face that I concentrated on not moving my head, which was idiotic because my head was the only part of my body that I could move.

When Ray and company had finished washing, brushing, blushing, buttoning, and tucking me, they said I looked beautiful. I just wanted to get going. We were running late, so Melanie left for the church, and I was to follow close behind.

"Let's do it," Ray said, wheeling me out the door and down the hall to the elevator. He punched the button and stared at the little red light, willing the elevator to come, drumming his fingers on the wheelchair. The tension from his arms was moving through the chair like an electric current, and it was making me buzz.

Finally, the door opened, and Ray reached out one arm to hold open the door while he pushed me onto the elevator with the other arm. The edge of the elevator was too high, though, and he needed both arms to get me over it. But when he released the door to put two hands on the chair, the door rattled closed on my legs. He shot his arm out to slam the door back open, and it clunked against him. Each time he tried to push me, the door closed. Then he tried turning sideways and sticking out his butt to hold the door while he twisted around to push the chair. That didn't work either, because in his contorted position, he didn't have the leverage to get me over the edge. So he began to rock the chair onto the lip, back and forth, bumping into the raised edge, while the door slammed into his butt and the bell chimed insistently.

"Damn it," he said between clenched teeth. "Damn this thing."

"Push," I said.

"I am pushing!"

"I told you we should have kept the nurse."

"Shut up, please. Just shut up."

"Sorry," I said meekly.

The door was banging against Ray, the chair was bumping against the frame, and Ray was rocking me back and forth.

"Ray?"

"What!"

I was tucking my chin into my chest, holding on for dear life. "A wave. I'm getting a wave."

"Jesus, Heidi, not now!"

"I can't help it."

"Hang on, just hang on."

"I can't stop it. It's coming." My feet were pressed onto the pegs of the chair, and I felt my legs tightening. I focused on my butt, trying to imagine it glued to the seat of the chair, but I had more powerful visions of launching onto the floor of the elevator and descending down to the lobby. The door opens, and I'm on the ground in a tattered tuxedo, a rose halo falling off my head.

"Grab my shoulders, Ray."

Ray, however, was focused entirely on getting me inside the elevator. He summoned all his strength, and with a grunt he catapulted us both into the elevator. The entire chair was airborne for a moment, but Ray caught me in midflight before I slammed into the opposite wall.

Ding, the door closed behind us. I had one hip out of the chair, and one hip in. One leg on the peg and one leg off. I was sure my halo was tilting. Ray's face was as red as my roses, and pearls of sweat stood out on his forehead. I stared straight ahead, humming to myself and trying to avoid those chilling blue eyes.

Ding, the door opened onto the lobby. Ray's friends were there waiting for us, and we raced to the ceremony.

Melanie was at the back of the church, ready to walk down the aisle, waiting for her maid of honor. They couldn't start without me because I had the wedding rings. We pulled up in front of the big stone church, but there was no ramp so I could be pushed inside the building. Ray unceremoniously scooped me out of the taxi and carried me up the steps and inside while one of his friends followed with the wheelchair. Once the friend figured out how to unfold the chair (with Ray hissing instructions) Ray dumped me in and pushed me directly down the aisle toward the altar. The music started to catch up with us and the ceremony began.

At the altar, I turned to face the rear of the church, and the sight of beautiful Melanie took my breath away. Ray had left me at the altar and was standing all the way at the back grinning like a proud parent and flashing me thumbs-up signs. As the bride and groom recited their vows, tears coursed down my cheeks. Melanie's mom, Tippi, saw me crying through her own tears. With the instincts of a mother, she reached over and blotted my face with a tissue. The minister took the rings from my fingers and gave one to the bride and one to the groom. They exchanged the golden bands and kissed for the first time as husband and wife.

After the reception at the hotel, the party moved to the disco Studio 54. People came up and introduced themselves and told me what a good job I had done at the wedding. Some of them said they recognized me from television, because the story of my injury had been all over the news, and I had appeared on *Donahue* and a bunch of other programs. Men I had never met danced and gyrated around me, bringing me fresh glasses of champagne and shouting over the thumping music.

It was late when everyone finally said good-bye to Rocky and Melanie as they left for their honeymoon. I don't actually remember seeing them leave because I was distracted by two very cute muscled types with longish hair who were bumping and grinding against my wheelchair and spinning me around the dance floor. I enjoyed every second. I closed my eyes and threw back my head, letting the lights play on my closed eyelids and the music vibrate through my bones. I really was dancing, and it was heavenly.

I was wound up when we finally left the disco, and I still had plenty of energy. Ray stumbled along behind me, leaning on the wheelchair for support as we trundled down Forty-second Street just before dawn. We were laughing and shouting good-byes when an old man with a three-day growth of beard and stained, torn clothes called over to us from where he had been sleeping on the street.

"Hey," he said. "Hey, I know you. I seen you on TV."

Ray puffed up and smiled, bestowing a celebrity wave on this humble fan. "Thank you, sir."

"Not you, man," the old guy said. "Her!"

I laughed. "And how're you this fine night?" I asked.

"I'm great and you doin' great, little lady," he said. "You doin' great!"

"Thanks," I said. "I'm trying."

After a night of dancing and partying and watching me flirt with other men, Ray couldn't wait to get me alone. In all aspects of our relationship, Ray was tender but insistent, and lovemaking was no exception. When he wanted me, he was not likely to take no for an answer. I wasn't so hard to convince anyway, and he could be very, very persuasive.

We loved and we fought with equal intensity. We were two strong personalities, and I imagined two restless seas meeting, waves swelling and crashing against each other. Trying to maintain our love was draining the little energy I had. I knew I should be concentrating on getting my body back, but I was exhausted just being me, and I didn't have the surplus energy to get better. I was idling physically, giving whatever extra energy I could summon to Ray instead of to my recovery.

Ray, however, didn't see it that way. He thought I just wasn't trying hard enough. He was impatient with my lack of progress, and he always thought I could do more. He didn't understand that I was exhausted.

"I love him so much," I told my mom, sobbing. She was sitting on the couch, petting my head in her lap. "I just want it to be normal. I just want a normal relationship. I want to be able to go out like other people and be able to care for myself and take care of Ray and have our babies." I started to cry again.

"It's all right, Heidi," my mom said. "You know I'm crazy about Ray, but that doesn't mean you are right for each other at this particular moment. Both of you have things that you need to accomplish, and you have to decide whether the relationship is helping or hurting. It'll work out one way or another. Whatever is meant to be will happen."

"I already know how I want it to work out," I said. "I want it to be like in the movies. I want a happy ending. With a house and kids and a family and Ray a big star and all of us happy, happy, happy."

"I know, Heidi. I know," my mom said, crying now with me, leaning forward and rocking my head in her lap.

I always had imagined that my future would be in the movie business and I would have that lifestyle, with a big house on a hill and a million projects going at once. I wanted to bring back the old Hollywood with its grandeur and glamour. I wanted to open a nightclub like the Cocoanut Grove where people could go for a fine dinner and a show. I'd have a ranch in the mountains and ski in Aspen. It wasn't the fame or the money that I longed for, it was the business itself, the people and the work. My dreams included dogs and horses, and the big house would be filled with love, like the one in which I had been raised.

A family and a successful career were what my parents wanted for me, too, although they would never say so. They always let us choose our own paths, hoping we would choose correctly. Sometimes they tried to guide us ever so gently, but they knew we had to walk the path alone. My mom was always very independent, and that was how she expected all women to be if they wanted to succeed. She learned to drive when she was twelve years old, and she read voraciously and sucked up all the information she could, realizing that knowledge was power and that a woman needed twice as much as a man to go half as far.

When I was growing up, my mom never once doubted that I would triumph in this life. Even when I was only ten months old, she wrote in her diary that I was "the best coordinated human ever set on the Earth, racing through the house on fat little legs and taking the turn around the coffee table to just miss it, hell bent for leather everywhere." Everything came easily to me—maybe too easily—and my mom remembers being frustrated when I was in second or third grade and arrived at school fifteen minutes late every morning. "Mrs. Borganhagen is going to be mad," my mom said of my teacher. To which I replied, "Mrs. Borganhagen loves me." My mom threw up her hands. End of discussion.

Since we were living in Hollywood, and given my good luck professionally before the crash, my folks assumed that I would become a successful actor. When I was just a girl, Mom thought I was a natural and loved to watch me run lines with Brad and Jimmy Caan. She was so proud when I got my first costar billing on *Charlie's Angels*. She was most distressed that someone who lived for activity, who lived in motion, had been frozen in place. I had raced through life without noticing a single barrier and had lived without a care. Now I had run smack into a wall of adversity.

Part of my dream included kids, and Ray and I talked all the time about having children, even though I wasn't sure it would be physically possible. We loved playing house with Christy's daughter, Allison, and Jeff's, Tiffany. We took them everywhere, and they climbed up in bed to cuddle with us when we watched television. I'm sure on some level we were pretending they were our own daughters. I had never thought very much about having kids before the crash, and now I understood that it was because I had never loved anyone the way I loved Ray.

In the fall, Ray went to Rome to make a film, and we were desolate. He was no sooner out the door than he was calling from LAX and then again from New York. From there, he mailed me a greeting card saying, "Hurry up and get the f—— up so we can get married."

When he arrived in Italy, we hung on the phone endlessly, running up astronomical bills, and he sent me little gifts. I sent him a tape recorder and daily tapes to fill in the gaps between calls. He told me a touching story about walking in the square one afternoon and seeing a young woman pushing her boyfriend in a wheelchair. Ray couldn't resist introducing himself and telling them about me. He encouraged them to never give up and felt a common bond with them.

Back home, I threw myself into a nonstop exercise program and was gratified to find an improvement beyond my expectations. I relized that the distance gave us both an increased objectivity; we could collect our thoughts, gain some perspective, and think about our priorities.

I knew that without Ray I never would have progressed so quickly or had so much fun, and I don't think I would have attempted romance or even considered it with a lesser man. Ray made everything possible. He gave me courage by putting everything within my grasp. His love was unconditional, his support and loyalty complete. Ray did for me what all the doctors and therapists hoped for but couldn't deliver: He gave me back my independence. He taught me how to be me again; not how to be some injured person, but me in a different body.

His absence, however, allowed me to see that I had been stalled physically. We were at crucial points in our lives: If Ray didn't settle down and concentrate on building his promising career, he risked fading into oblivion; I needed to have tunnel vision focused solely on recovery, or risk being paralyzed forever. Together we were like two naughty kids ditching school: much happier going to the beach or into Westwood to a movie than taking care of business.

The decision had to be made, and it almost broke my heart. I easily could have bound Ray to me by using his love, generosity, and compassion against him, but I wouldn't. I had to do what was best for both of us, no matter how painful. I stared endlessly at the card from Ray telling me to hurry and get up, but my mom was right, this was going to take time. My only option was to go it alone and get to work on a serious recovery program—and then run back into Ray's arms.

When Ray returned from Rome, I planned a spectacular evening. I pulled out all the stops: champagne, caviar, a limo, and a friend's penthouse on the Wilshire corridor. I had Beverly Hills' finest boîte cater our homecoming dinner. The only thing missing was strolling minstrels. In typical Ray fashion, he took over the show, hurried the servers through their preparations, and dispatched them back to Jimmy's. Anyway, the food was a total waste because we couldn't keep our hands off each other. The evening was the most romantic rendezvous, and I wanted it to last forever, but I couldn't shake the nagging feeling that things were about to change.

As a kind of test, we decided that Ray should spend the holidays with his family while I began a strenuous program with a Malibu physical therapist, Bill Hunt. Not very festive, but extremely productive. I can't say I was happy; in fact, some days I was miserable missing him so, but I was determined to get the f—— up.

Ray remained in New York for the week following New Year's. Late one afternoon, I had just completed a workout when the door opened. A figure filled the frame in silence. Long legs in faded jeans. I turned to see Ray, just the way I had seen him the very first time in that same doorway a year before. Only now his crystal-blue eyes were red from crying, and his face was puffy from lack of sleep.

Ray fell to his knees in front of me. "Why does it have to be this way?" he asked. "Why can't it just be fun?"

"I don't know, Ray," I said. "I love you so much. I only wish it was different, but it's not and I don't know what to do because it's killing me."

He put his head on my lap, and he lifted my arm to place it on his head. "I love you, Heidi. You know I do."

"I love you, too, Ray. That's not the problem."

He looked up at me and our eyes met. We looked at each other for a long time without speaking. I was filled with sadness and joy, gratitude and longing and regret. In our year together, Ray had given me his strength. I'm not sure what would have happened to me if I had never met him. Maybe I would have emerged slowly from my shell and ventured step by step back into the world, but it would have taken much longer than it did with Ray. He returned my womanhood and gave me a second chance I never dared dream of having. No other love, before or since, can compare with what we had. The hardest thing was to let him go, but I did because I love him.

Chapter 10

THE TRIAL

My year with Ray had been a long, glorious vacation. My love for him was a powerful force that woke me in the morning, kept me strong during the day, and comforted me at night. Ray would not be there physically anymore, but he never was out of my mind—pushing, prodding, luring me forward. It was to him that I ran.

Now, alone again, I faced the reality of my situation. I had escaped from the doctors and the hospitals. I couldn't stand or sit up straight without help, but my broken neck was healed and strong, and I could shrug my shoulders and slightly move both arms. My legs were limp, but I could be pedaled on the bike machine. That much was good. Yes, I was paralyzed, but I was determined not to let my physical condition be the center of my universe. My real struggle was to keep moving forward as a person, even if I needed help moving my arms and legs. Not surprisingly, my major concerns were the same as those of the people around me: personal growth and knowledge, family and friends, and paying the rent. The last one was becoming a problem. We had cardboard boxes stuffed with bills that the insurance company refused to pay, and twenty-four-hour care was draining my bank account.

Money was flowing out, but none was coming in. My parents practically had stopped working. I had been on my own financially for several years before the crash, but my personal wealth consisted of a car, some clothes, and a piggy bank. I hadn't been getting rich as an actress, but I had never worried about money. Just before the crash, I knew I was on the verge of making it in films, first as an actress and later as a producer and director.

I was anxious to get back to work as soon as possible. There was the inevitable talk of making a movie about the crash, and I thought it would be fun to play myself, but a movie, if it ever happened, would be a long-term project. I had immediate financial worries. Everyone around us figured that money was not a problem because they assumed I would be "compensated" for my loss, that the insurance company or the *Cannonball* producers or someone with lots of money was going to support me financially for the rest of my "helpless" life. I never considered that an option, and I fully expected to continue supporting myself.

First I had to pay the costs of getting better. Bit by bit, we began to penetrate the maze of red tape and bureaucracy surrounding the financing of health care. The only thing more complicated and full of jargon than medical care itself is the way you pay for it. Eventually, through repeated questions, phone calls, and letters, we learned that the company insuring the *Cannonball* producers planned to pay for my health care up to the point where I was on my own and my condition was not getting any worse (or better).

That day had arrived about a year after the crash, and the insurance company assumed its responsibility toward me had ended. Just like any other person hurt in a work-related accident, I then was expected to support myself with workmen's compensation. Under the law, I was 100 percent disabled and eligible for the highest benefit, which would have been between $500 and $750 per month. There was no way I could have lived on that, even without the additional expenses caused by my injury.

The obvious solution to the money problem was to sue somebody. Legal action had never occurred to me, though, because there was no way I was going to sue my friends from *Cannonball*. I was the one who had wanted to work on the movie; I had considered it a privilege, and I had loved every second until the moment I stepped into that car. I was an adult, a paid suntwoman, and I knew that stunt work could be dangerous. I had agreed to do the stunt in the Aston Martin mock-up. In fact, I had begged to do it. Maybe I should have asked more questions or insisted on having seat belts in the car. Maybe I should have left the scene to a more experienced stunt-woman. But the stunt coordinator and everybody on the set, the pros, told me the stunt wasn't a big deal and that it certainly wasn't dangerous. I believed them.

Should I sue the stunt coordinator, Bobby Bass, the man who had adored me and wanted to marry me? Would he have deliber-ately endangered my life? No way. When I saw him later being in-terviewed on television for a news report about dangerous stunts, he seemed defensive about the crash, as if I were blaming him, which wasn't true at all. I wasn't blaming anybody, least of all Bobby.

My parents didn't want to blame anyone either, but they did think that everyone in charge should have acted more responsibly. They felt the stunt was not set up properly and should not have been performed, and that someone should shoulder the responsibility for what happened. They also were concerned with the practical reality of how we were going to eat. "We're not going to sue your friends, Heidi," Brad said. "There is an insurance company that charged a lot of money to the production company, just in case something like this happens. That's what it's for." Reluctantly, I agreed that we should at least talk to a lawyer.

We had no trouble finding lawyers. Christy was working as a P.R. person for a celebrity hair salon, and after the crash lawyers started showing up twice a week at the salon. With their wet heads in the sink, the biggest tort lawyers in town would shout to Christy over the sound of whirring hair-dryers, "So how's Heidi? She have represen-tation yet?"

Christy arranged for one of the lawyers, an expert in workmen's compensation (and who now was impeccably coiffed), to meet with my parents. The lawyer was confident that we had a case, but he explained that workmen's compensation was based on actual income earned before the injury and on an estimate of the future income that would be lost. My actual income had been modest to that point, and my potential income was unknown. I fully expected to make it in the business, and I knew that my eventual income would have been good, but who's to say how my life would have evolved without the crash?

After considering my case and looking at the figures, the lawyer scratched some numbers on a piece of paper. He looked up and said, "You easily could get two hundred fifty to four hundred thousand dollars."

"You've got to be kidding," Brad said.

"No, I think you could get that."

"What I'm saying is that's nothing," Brad said. "That won't pay for anything. We're talking about this girl's life."

My parents were astounded and dismayed by the modest and unrealistic numbers, but Christy refused to be down about anything. "Mom," she said, "if you could get any lawyer, anybody in the world, who would you want?"

"Well," my mom said, "Melvin Belli is the best. He's good, and he's certainly famous. And he's so handsome."

"Okay," Christy said. "We'll get Mel Belli."

And she did. Melvin Belli, the man known as the King of Torts, arrived at the hospital a few days later. He had a mane of white hair and wore a dark suit with a fire-engine red lining that he flashed like a matador's cape. On his feet he wore a pair of handmade, finely tooled cowboy boots, which helped convince Brad that Belli was a good guy. Belli said he had followed my case in the press and was very pleased that we had called. He certainly wasn't interested in me because he needed any more money, but he said mine was going to be a high-profile case; it would set an important precedent for the film industry, and he believed my cause was just. After several months of investigating the circumstances of the crash and deposing the participants, Belli filed a multimillion-dollar lawsuit against Cannonball Productions.

The lawsuit was big news and became the talk of Hollywood. People in the business were concerned about me as a person, and I received baskets of cards and letters, but the reason the studios' followed the case so closely was out of concern for their own profits. Traditionally, injuries on a set were taken care of quietly and with little cost to the studios. Many accidents were never reported at all. If the *Cannonball* producers were found liable for my injuries and I won a major award, that would have a lasting impact on the bottom line of all the studios.

The press focused more on my personal story—"The Brave Stuntgirl"—and I was swamped with interview requests from reporters, including Christy's boyfriend at the time. Robin Leach, a whimsical, charming fellow and an enterprising reporter, then was working for a newspaper and still managed to approach his own lifestyle of the rich and famous. Robin had lived through the crash and the long hospital experience with Christy crying on his shoulder, and he insisted on doing a story about me. The first piece pointedly noted that Farrah Fawcett, one of the stars of the film, hadn't bothered to visit me or even call. I never expected her to visit, but soon after Robin's story appeared, she did call me. Then a woman who worked for Farrah stopped by and gave me a cute pillow shaped like a pair of red lips. Robin was satisfied, and he wrote a follow-up story with a photograph showing me holding the pillow.

When my lawsuit finally made it to trial in 1986, six years after the crash, reporters mobbed the courtroom, and the intense interest continued during the long days of testimony and cross-examination. There were stand-ups from the courthouse steps and live shots from the lawn. News departments produced entire programs on the issue of stunt safety, which I was glad to see. What made my lawsuit even more newsworthy was that the *Twilight Zone—The Movie* case also was coming to trial after a helicopter crashed on location in 1982 and killed actor Vic Morrow and two young children.

After all the witnesses had been heard, after my lawyers and the lawyers for *Cannonball* had made their closing arguments, the judge sent the jury out to decide if I should be compensated and for how much. We thought the trial had gone very well, and that the evidence clearly showed that I deserved a substantial award. Most of the reporters covering the trial seemed to agree, and everyone assumed we would be celebrating very soon.

After an alarmingly long time in deliberations—five days—the members of the jury walked back into the courtroom. The judge asked them if they had reached a verdict. The weary foreman shook his head and replied that, no, they were not able to agree on a verdict. The jury was deadlocked, with eight jurors ruling in my favor and four against. My heart sank. We had worked so hard to prepare. How could this have happened? How could they not decide? The judge declared a mistrial and said the suit would be heard by another jury.

I was curious about what had gone wrong. We interviewed the jurors after the trial, and two of the women revealed that they had voted against me because they opposed me "living in sin" with Bobby. Aside from the fact that this wasn't true, that we always had separate apartments, it didn't seem to me to be relevant to the issue. We were frustrated and angered by the lack of a verdict, but there wasn't anything we could do except get ready for another trial.

The trial had been exhausting, and many times during the testimony we were made to feel like we were the ones being judged, that we were the ones who had done something wrong. I felt as if I were the one who had to explain just what I was doing out there in the desert rather than the producers having to explain how a "simple" stunt could have gone so badly. The ordeal was hardest on my parents, and to this day my mother can't talk about the trial without becoming emotional. She felt violated and abused by the entire process, even though she was guilty only of being my mother. Brad was terribly frustrated that fair-minded people couldn't see clearly. It seemed so obvious to him that I had been wronged, and he couldn't imagine why the whole thing had to be all tangled up in legal mumbo-jumbo.

We had no choice but to slog through the whole lengthy and costly process a second time. David Sabih, a brilliant lawyer who took the case from his partner, Belli, handled the opening arguments for our side. A craggy-faced renegade with a sterling academic background, Sabih paced in front of the courtroom and told the jury with great confidence—and some dramatic hyperbole—why director Hal Needham should be held accountable for my injuries.

"We will prove to you that Mr. Needham was grossly negligent in the happening of this accident. He did not care about the safety of the people involved because he wanted to save money," Sabih said. Why else, he asked the jury, would Needham do the stunt with a cheap mock-up instead of the original, and very expensive, car? If he was sure that nothing could go wrong, why not use the original car?

Sabih told me to stay out of the courtroom that first week, but he promised the jurors they would meet me in person and also learn about my life from a videotape. "You will see a blue-eyed blond, attractive girl sitting. You will see that she is eating, but as you look around, you will see it is not through her hand. There is somebody else feeding her. You will see that somebody has to comb her hair, someone has to brush her teeth. You will see a roomful of trophies where she was a champion skier. You will see photographs of her modeling career, and her movie career. And then you will know that at the present time she can do nothing for herself, but she requires around-the-clock care.

"How did this happen?" Sabih asked the jury.

Sabih answered his own question: Hal Needham knew the Aston Martin mockup was barely driveable and sent it out for repairs. Even when the car was more or less repaired and able to run under its own power, the flimsy mock-up didn't have seat belts, the lawyer told the jury, adopting an emotional tone of dramatic disgust.

Sabih concluded: "It is going to be hard not to give us a verdict because of the facts. And the law is on our side."

Next, the lawyer for Cannonball Productions, whose name was Jack Daniels, faced the jury. The cool and polished Daniels had a style that contrasted sharply with the emotional and excitable Sabih. Instead of the European silk suits favored by Sabih, Daniels's clothes were 100 percent Brooks Brothers, from the button-down collar of his broadcloth shirt to the buffed toes of his wingtips. He introduced himself to the jury and told a little joke about not being the same Jack Daniels who owned the liquor company. The women on the jury chuckled and clucked appreciatively.

Then Daniels launched a merciless counterattack. "In doing a stunt, there is always some element of danger, no matter how simple the stunt is," Daniels said. That's why there are doubles and stuntmen and why Hal Needham used a modified stunt car instead of the real Aston Martin.

"It does not make any sense to take any chances at all with that Aston Martin. So in a stunt scene, it makes good business sense to use a duplicate Aston Martin," Daniels said, according to the trial transcripts.

The director is the boss on the picture, Daniels continued, but he can't be aware of every detail, so he delegates that responsibility to the camera crews, to the transportation experts, and to the stunt-people. "Within the stunt industry, the stunt person is the one who has the responsibility for his or her own safety. The evidence will be that this makes good sense. They are the ones who are at risk, and whatever they want for a particular stunt, be it seat belts or helmets or roll bars . . . it is up to the stuntpeople to say what they want."

Referring to the mock-up of the Aston Martin that crashed, the *Cannonball* lawyer conceded that "the evidence will be that the vehicle was sent out for repairs, and the evidence is uncontroverted that on the day of this particular accident, there were no complaints, no requests or anything about this particular vehicle. There were no requests for seat belts."

Wrapping up his tight opening remarks to the jury, the lawyer opposing me blamed the crash not on Cannonball Productions or on director Hal Needham but on "driver error" by Jimmy Nickerson, who was at the wheel of the mock-up.

Sabih deliberately kept me out of the courtroom until the final day of testimony. He was afraid that if I spent too much time there, the jurors would become accustomed to seeing me in a wheelchair and not think anything was wrong. Sabih first showed the court a video. During the shooting of this day-in-the-life video, we had some creative disagreements about the tone: Basically, the lawyers wanted me to drool and look pathetic, and I refused. I went on camera as I always did, which was looking my very best. I wasn't trying to mislead anybody about my condition or trying to look better or worse than I actually was. No amount of makeup or working on my hair was going to restore the use of my body.

The first witness for our side was a neurosurgeon named J. Dewitt Fox, who had examined me several times and was asked to explain my injuries to the jury. Dr. Fox and I didn't agree about my prognosis, but he certainly gave good testimony. When people asked me about my injuries, I described them as a minor setback, a slight blemish on the canvas of my life that soon would be wiped clean. Dr. Fox was not so optimistic. He told the jury, in words that still make me wince, "The patient is in essence a neck and head."

My lawyer, Sabih, pressed on: "Is her condition reversible? Can we get some improvements? Can we get her to walk or move her hands?"

I would have answered, "Of course. I'm getting better every day." The gloomy Dr. Fox, however, told the jury the same thing that every doctor had told me since the day of the crash: "No. In my opinion, she is permanent and stationary. She has no sensation below the shoulder level. If you were to put a cigarette on her abdomen, leg, anywhere, she would not feel it."

The next witness was an expert in car crashes. Louis Piziali, a handsome young biomechanical engineer, used film of the crash and computer simulations to estimate that we were going about fifty-one miles per hour when we slammed into the van. During the impact, which lasted one tenth of one second, the force released was twenty-four G's, which means a force twenty-four times the rate of gravity. By comparison, the fastest jet fighters in the U.S. Air Force are designed to subject the pilots to fewer than nine G's on takeoff—otherwise they black out.

"The body basically goes forward as a projectile until it hits something," Piziali testified. "So the car is stopping, but the body is just traveling straight ahead until something stops it. And what stops it is the impact between the head, chest, neck, feet, knees, and arms, you know, against the dash and roof and windshield. So if you are in an accident without a belt, basically you just run into the interior of the car."

Using a computer simulation, Piziali ran the crash again, but this time he gave all of us seat belts. Referring to me, Piziali said, "With a seat belt, her body would not have impacted the interior of the vehicle. I don't believe she would have been a quadriplegic today. The really only injury that she might have sustained would be the fracture of some ribs." In fact, the man driving the van that hit us was wearing a seat belt and suffered only a broken rib, just as Piziali's simulation predicted.

Cliff Wenger, who was working the smoke machine until the impact shot him out of the backseat of our car, was next to testify. He remembered that Hal was unhappy with the first take of the scene and wanted to do it again. "It just didn't look . . . it looked too lazy. That is I think the words I heard said," Cliff recalled. "And he said if we would just 'Pick it up, boys, a little bit.' "

Cliff said he couldn't see much from his position on the floor in the back of the car, but that the first take felt smooth. The second time we did the scene, however, "the sensation that I would sense from where I was sitting seemed to be a lot more of violent turning. Like we made the first turn, and I had to brace myself into the car. It was like being tossed almost across the back of the seat. We made the first turn, and I believe we started to make a second, and I heard tires squealing, and that was all I remember."

Our driver, Jimmy Nickerson, testified that the very first time he drove the mock-up several days before the crash, he needed a push from another car just to get it moving. Then the car would only go about eight miles per hour. Jimmy testified, "I don't know if you have ever driven an old car with a bad chassis, all right? And the body is up on the chassis, and you go down and make the turn and your body stays and your chassis goes on and your body slingshots back to your car." Jimmy said that he was following Hal's instructions to get the car in position for the shot. "By the time I got down to the spot, Hal was out in the middle of the road yelling at me, saying why I wasn't—I don't know if I can use the words—but he was out there saying why didn't I get the car there.

"I got out of the car, and I says I am not going to drive the car until the front end is fixed, until you time the clutch in it and put some safety belts in it because I can't get this damn thing to even start on the spot. I said, 'Hal, look at the car. The clutch is out of the goddamn thing, the front end—the thing is all over the damn place. I can't get the thing up to speed. They ain't got no seat belts, and look at the goddamn tires.'

"Well, right then he started yelling," Jimmy said. Jimmy was asked how he responded: "Well, I walked away." Hal immediately ordered that the car be sent out for repairs, and it came back from the shop in much better condition—but still without seat belts.

The lawyers carefully established Jimmy's top professional credentials as a stuntman who had worked for more than one hundred directors during his twenty-year career. He said that he had performed driving stunts like this one, with the same serpentine motions, as many as sixty times in different pictures. This particular stunt routine is an action-film staple. Like a typical barroom-brawl scene, a good car chase is choreographed to appear violent and chaotic when in fact it's nothing more than a fast-moving ballet.

Jimmy told the court exactly what he was ordered to do in the shot and how Hal's concept of the scene changed after the first take. "Take one required just to go down and bypass one car, get on the off-side shoulder of the road, pass all the cars going by me, get back on the road, and continue. The second take I was requested to serpentine through all the cars in this motion," Jimmy said, weaving his hand in and out of the imaginary cars.

"Who requested that?"

"Mr. Needham," Jimmy said.

Sabih pressed on. "Did anyone ask you when you were doing the sequence after take one to double the speed?"

"Yes, I was."

"Who asked you to double the speed?"

"Mr. Needham."

Then Jimmy was asked to describe the accident itself. He explained that we had done the first take and we now were trying the scene again, this time weaving in and out of the oncoming cars, releasing more smoke, and driving faster than we had the first time.

"I remember the terrifying thing is that when I brought the car back to the right in this motion, the body of the car floated over so severely that the car was starting to bite," Jimmy said. "From my past experience from rolling cars, I felt the car had a very, very good chance of maybe turning over, rolling, whatever, or something drastic, because I knew this car was not capable of handling a lot of stress. I felt if I just stayed on that line over there that this car was in such bad shape it could have possibly went out of control, rolled into the camera crew or the crew itself."

"So what did you do?"

"I tried to abort the situation and go back to the left and deal with my chances over on the left side." Unfortunately, Jimmy said, the driver of the oncoming van tried to bail out of the shot in the same direction, and the two vehicles crashed.

Bobby Bass testified that after the mock-up came back from repairs, he took it on a test drive with Jimmy. "I was the passenger, and he was driving," Bobby said. "I asked him if he would weave back and forth going up into the gears. We swerved from lane to lane. I think probably the highest speed we came up to was approximately seventy miles an hour.

"I asked him if he was satisfied, and he said yes," Bobby testified.

"Did you have a seat belt on?"

"No. I didn't have a seat belt on."

Mr. Daniels, the lawyer for Cannonball, stepped up to cross-examine Bobby. "Did anyone ask you to install seat belts in the double Aston Martin?"

"No."

"Whose responsibility was it to check for seat belts?"

"In my opinion, the responsibility is the person who is in charge of the car. That would be the wheel man."

"And the one who was in charge of the double Aston Martin was Mr. Nickerson," Daniels said. "Isn't that correct?"

"That is correct."

Attorney Laurence Corcoran, who was defending Hal Needham, pressed the point with Bobby. "At no time did Heidi von Beltz say to you, 'This vehicle doesn't have seat belts. I need seat belts in this vehicle?' "

"No, she did not."

"If Heidi had said such a thing, would they have been installed, sir?"

"Yes, they would have," Bobby said.

"If you talk about the installation time itself (for seat belts), it is only fifteen or twenty minutes?"

"That is correct."

After laying down the technical details of the crash and my injuries, my lawyers changed tacks and called my mother to the stand. Even though we were the ones suing, the case put all of us on trial, and my mother and father were not spared. The insurance-company lawyers wanted to make an issue of our behavior and even our character, which was infuriating, but I guess we shouldn't have been surprised. We could only respond by defending ourselves on the stand.

Sabih began the questioning of my mother by asking her to describe me and my career.

"My daughter is—is and was—a beautiful girl, fabulous personality and very bright and athletic. She was good with horses. She ice-skates, skis. She modeled for all the top photographers, I would say the biggest photographers in the country. Just before she finished high school, she did two commercials, for the Hollywood Bowl and one for Pepsi.

"She was not interested in modeling per se, because it is not very challenging, but she was called for by Bob Hope on a number of occasions to do pretty-girl atmosphere stuff and for the Muhammad

Ali special. Heidi was a model her whole life. From the age of ten months on. She did episodic television, *Nancy Drew*, *Starsky and Hutch*. She had reached costar status, which is not easy to do in this business."

Then Sabih led my mother through the day of the crash, her arrival at the hospital in Las Vegas, and finally my transfer to Long Beach. My mom talked about the frustration with the doctors and the need to be with me all the time. Even though she was testifying on my behalf, she refused to be maudlin or weepy. She wouldn't bite on Sabih's question, "Could you tell us what has your daughter missed the most as a result of the accident?"

"Well, I'm not in her head, so I really don't know and she is a very private girl," my mother replied truthfully. "But I think what she misses the most, from what she says, is the fact that she has to have someone at her elbow at all times. And she also misses having a husband like her girlfriends and babies like her girlfriends."

Phil Gerard testified about how he taught me skiing when I was a teenager. "She was the best woman skier I ever trained. I trained all the top champions in the world," he said, which made me feel proud. Comparing me with another of his students, the 1966 U.S. Olympic Team captain, Suzy Chaffee, Gerard said, "She was better than Suzy. She was far better, far. She was more athletic. She was the best aerialist I ever had."

Phil's daughter, Michelle, who had just made the U.S. Olympic ski team, testified. "I have known Heidi since I was eleven years old. Heidi to me was one of my idols. There are a few people who really excel in sports, and in order to do what I do now, it takes a lot of hard training, and for me to be able to have watched a woman like Heidi train as hard as she did to get as good as she did, that is what it takes to be the best in anything you do. With that attitude, you carry that wherever you go, no matter what you are doing, whether it is dancing, skiing, skating, acting. That is the type of person she was."

All this glowing testimony was making my ears burn; the trial was beginning to sound like the old *This Is Your Life*. Only in this case, the prize was not a trip to Hawaii but enough money for me to stay alive and to continue my therapy.

Tippi Hedren testified about my work with her as second assistant director on the movie *Roar*. Tippi was in a good position to judge my potential because she herself had started as a top Eileen Ford cover girl. She starred in many films and went on to produce them and to manage her own game preserve, among many accomplishments.

"Heidi was a very bright, alert, interested woman that really made an effect on you. You couldn't forget Heidi. She was not only vivacious, she wanted to learn. She was active, her vitality, her energy level was high," Tippi said. "She was totally capable of really doing whatever she wanted to do or whatever we asked of her to do. This was not an easy film to do. There was a great deal required of Heidi in this."

Other witnesses talked about the nature of my disability, the kind of care I would need and what it would cost. They said I would need nurses and special equipment and even modifications to my house to be able to get around in a wheelchair and to use some of the appliances.

So far, most of the testimony had been on my behalf and in my favor. I admit that I am biased, but after learning about the law and understanding what I was entitled to, I was starting to accept the idea that the injured party deserved a break. The case was hardly open-and-shut, though, and I was very interested to hear what Hal Needham would have to say in his defense. Hal was in a bind because even if he personally thought I should be compensated, a victory for me would come at some cost to him and could possibly hurt his future in the business, despite his ample insurance coverage.

When Hal took the stand, my lawyer asked him about a conversation between Hal and Bobby a few days before the crash. Hal said that Bobby had indeed informed him about the car. "He said there was some kind of problem with the Aston Martin and that we need to have it repaired," Hal said. "We sent the car to the shop. My instructions were to send it in, have it fixed, and we would move and do something else."

Asked to think back to the day of the crash, Hal was told to recall his instructions to Jimmy and the drivers of the other cars after the first take. My lawyer asked, "Did you tell the other drivers, after take one, 'Pick it up, boys'?"

Hal testified, "No, I don't think so."

"Did you tell Mr. Nickerson to double up the speed between take one and take two?"

"No."

"Now, Mr. Needham, regarding seat belts, do you have an opinion whether or not seat belts—is it good to use them in this kind of sequence for the purpose of safety?"

"I would say seat belts are good to use anytime, anywhere you are in an automobile, so the answer would be yes," Hal said.

Sabih pressed Hal on the way the stunt was designed and executed. Hal contended that he had prepared the stunt properly but that it wasn't carried out the way he had intended, and that's why we crashed.

"The way I lined up the sequence," Hal testified, "if it were executed the way that I lined it up, it would have been safe."

Hal's lawyer asked him to explain the roles and responsibilities of key crew members on a set. Hal talked about how the cameraman is expected to have film in the camera and how the soundman is expected to tell the director if a noisy airplane is passing overhead. When it comes to stunts, Hal said, the stuntman ultimately decides what he's going to do and how he's going to do it. If a stunt isn't planned correctly or if a director wants the cars to go too fast, then it's up to the stuntman to object. "The stuntman becomes the boss," Hal declared.

Hal's lawyer continued: "So are you saying then it is the stuntman sitting in the car who will determine the outer limit of the speed, and not you as the director?"

"Absolutely. He has his foot on the gas. I don't control that car. He does."

The Cannonball attorney took up the same line of questioning with Hal. "Does the stuntperson have any responsibility for their own safety and in performing a stunt?"

"Yes," Hal said. "I think you have to judge by your ability what you think or know you are capable of with the equipment that you are supposed to work with."

And if certain equipment is not available for the stuntperson, whose responsibility is it to ask for it?

"Well, it would be the stuntperson's responsibility to ask for it. And I would say they should go probably to the stunt coordinator."

"Was it your job as the director of the movie to see that the double Aston Martin had seat belts?"

"No."

"Did you receive any complaints, you personally, on the day of the shoot from anybody about the double Aston Martin?"

"None whatsoever," Hal said.

"Did you receive any requests from anybody requesting seat belts be put in that vehicle?"

"No."

When my lawyer had a chance to question Hal again, he tried to re-create the scene in the hospital on the night of the crash, when Hal and Brad saw each other for the first time. The way we remember that encounter, Hal sheepishly suggested that Brad "beat the shit" out of him.

Sabih asked Hal, "Did you tell him about anyone that in your opinion was responsible for that accident?"

"I don't recall if I did or not."

Sabih next confronted Bobby to establish that the crash had caused me mental as well as physical pain. Sabih tried to show the jury that after the accident I became an embarrassment to the Cannonball producers, that they regarded me as a mistake to be pushed aside. Sabih wanted the jury to know how excited I was to attend the screening of *Cannonball*, how I had picked out a beautiful new dress, only to be "disinvited" just before the party.

Asked about me going to the party, Bobby replied, "Um, I have to say to my best recollection, I don't recall that."

I was crushed that my friends had such bad memories. Could it be possible that they really didn't remember what had happened? Could events that changed my life completely have been so inconsequential to them that they forgot? I was proud to hear the testimony of the many people who spoke so fondly of me, but Hal and Bobby were not making the trial any easier.

Many hours of testimony followed about what actually happened on the day of the crash and who said what to whom. The lawyers argued about whether I should have done the stunt, about whether the car was safe, and about whether we should have been told to perform the stunt a second time after we already had done it once. There was an entire, unrelated discussion of how movie deals were structured financially and who can be held liable for an accident. Then the lawyers for both sides stood before the jury and debated how to put a monetary value on my ability to move. The complicated calculation was based on an estimate of how much money I would have earned if my career had continued, which was a difficult number to determine, especially in show business.

Finally, the arguments for both sides were wrapped up, and the jury began its deliberations. While this second jury was sequestered, Brad received a strange telephone call at home. An anonymous voice whispered that our jury was being tampered with and that it wasn't right what was going to happen in my case. We were frightened that something had gone wrong, so we called Belli and Sabih. There was nothing we could do now, the lawyers said, except sit tight. Brad was worried. The whole trial smelled fishy, and Brad felt helpless to stop what he feared was going to be a disaster. He was blind with rage at the lies he heard on the stand and sickened that my character had been questioned. He is a person who likes to be in control, always, and the trial was agony for him.

On June 13, 1986, the members of the second jury marched back into the courtroom. They told the judge that they had reached a decision. The foreman stood at attention, and the judge asked for the verdict. We rule in favor of the plaintiff, Heidi von Beltz, the foreman announced. I let out a sigh, not an expression of victory but one of relief. The foreman quickly added that I was not guilt-free in this case. The jury had decided that I shared part of the blame for the accident because I had willingly gotten into the car to perform the stunt.

I wasn't surprised by the jury's finding in my favor or even that they put part of the blame on me. I'd always taken responsibility for my actions. I was, however, surprised by what came next.

The foreman was asked to reveal the jury's decision about a monetary award. The foreman said that he and the other jurors agreed that I should be compensated for my injuries, and that I was to be awarded $7 million. A wave of murmurs and muffled whispers washed over the courtroom, and a few people clapped.

There was a catch, however. Since the jury considered me to be 35 percent responsible for what had happened, the judge explained, the award would be reduced by that much. So the final amount awarded to me was not $7 million but $4.5 million. By the time the money actually got into my bank account, legal fees had shrunk it down to $3.2 million, plus another $1 million from a workmen's compensation settlement.

We celebrated the award as a victory, although the reduced amount did not prove to be as large as it sounded at the time. We never actually got a check until many years after the crash, and by then much of the money already had been spent on legal fees and a stack of medical bills with big red PAST DUE warnings. The rest was invested to generate enough income for me to live on and to hire a person to stay with me around the clock. To keep inflation from eating up big chunks of the money, we bought a little shack for my parents on the beach in Malibu, which we never dreamed would prove to be our best investment.

Even with the award money, we were not well off financially, and the interest earnings alone were not enough. We were forced to dip into the capital as well, which meant that this money would not last forever. At the time, the only money-making project we had going was a film that Brad wrote and produced called *Kill the Golden Goose*. The picture was nearly completed at the time of the crash, and somehow Brad managed to find time to finish it. This was the Hollywood version of a mom-and-pop operation: Christy and I appeared in the film, and my mom and Joanna handled elements of the production ranging from transportation to making sandwiches on location. Brad did just about everything else. Even the sets were decorated with furniture from our house.

Kill the Golden Goose premiered in Las Vegas to decent reviews while I was still in the hospital, and my parents, Joanna, and Christy flew out for the big night. The picture opened well, about as well as Bruce Lee's *Enter the Dragon*, and it still has a cult following. Brad was getting ready to do another picture when I was hurt, but that project, like many others, was put on hold indefinitely. Brad normally had five or six balls in the air at a time, but after the crash he had so much to manage just to keep my head above water: hospitals, doctors, therapists, insurance, lawyers, the trial. There was no way he could dedicate sufficient time to his work, especially writing, which requires absolute concentration.

The only thing Brad was able to concentrate on was getting me better. I didn't want him hovering over me; I wanted him to return to work and to get on with his life. I definitely needed his help, but I didn't want to be a total burden to him or to the rest of the family. Despite my efforts to keep things as normal as possible, the emotional shock waves of the crash were felt not only by my parents, but also by Christy and Jeff and their families. Even Brad was knocked off his normally steady course. I think of Brad as strong and disciplined, and he is, but when it comes to me, he's not as tough as he should be. For the first few years after the crash, his mind couldn't close around anything except me. He worried, he fretted, he wanted to be with me all the time.

He always kept up a strong front with me because he knew that I was watching him for guidance. He was my rock and always had been. It wasn't until the trial that I appreciated how deeply he had been hurt, perhaps even more hurt than I had been.

On the day Brad was to testify, he wore a tie for the first time in years. He looked ruggedly handsome and serious, a sunburned cowboy dressed in his Sunday best. He had sat through the proceedings quietly, listening closely to the testimony and making notes to himself. As the days dragged on and the lies and the obfuscation began to stink to high heaven, he stopped taking notes. By the end he sat stonily, barely able to restrain the overwhelming impulse to stand up and shout and send everyone scurrying.

When Brad's name was called to testify, he walked forward, head high and back straight, and took his place on the stand. I smiled up at him, and he smiled back at me and my mom. He raised his right hand and took the oath and was asked to spell his name for the record. He did, and then he asked for a glass of water. Someone handed him the water, and he took a deep drink. He set the glass down carefully in front of him. When he spoke again, I heard an almost imperceptible crack in his voice. It was so faint that I thought I was imagining it. I stared up at him and tried to read the emotion behind his solemn face. He spoke again, and this time his voice cracked deeply. I jumped, startled. I had never heard from Brad, my father, the sound of fear and sadness; this was the first outward sign of the corrosive frustration eating at his insides.

I bit my lip and looked anxiously at my mother. She had realized what was happening before I did. She squeezed my leg and focused on Brad to shore him up with her inner strength. I tried to help him, too, but I was truly frightened. I could see him alert and erect on the stand but trembling ever so slightly. No one else in the courtroom knew, but my mother and I could see that Brad was teetering dangerously close to the edge of his self-control.

My lawyer saw only the mask of Brad's calm exterior, and he confidently began to lead him through a series of routine questions about our family and the effects of the accident. "So, Mr. von Beltz, please tell the court about how you found Heidi when you arrived at the hospital."

Brad began to answer and stopped. How could he possibly express his feelings in mere words? How could anyone understand what he had felt that night? He thought to himself: The whole trial is a farce—a poorly acted, poorly written play. This girl is hurt and needs care. End of story. If only people could just brush aside all the legal jargon and the garbage and see the truth. Isn't justice what all of us want? He opened his mouth and tried a second time to speak. Swollen emotion, no longer held in check, burst through and shattered his voice. Brad's words crashed at his feet in a pile of shards, and he began to cry and to shudder. He shook his head of shaggy blond hair and pawed at his eyes, and big tears poured through his calloused hands and down his face. He tried to speak and choked. He coughed and cleared his throat. The courtroom was hushed and silent, suffering with him. Brad mumbled an apology to the judge.

"Are you able to continue, Mr. von Beltz?"

Brad shook his head no. The judge excused him. With a nod, Brad stepped down from the witness stand, searching for his seat among us.

And my pounding heart was torn from my chest.

Chapter 11

THE KEY

I felt like I had been failed and abandoned twice: first by the medical system and then by the legal system. After the crash I was left lying in a hospital bed for sixteen days before anybody did anything for me. I tried to get better, but I couldn't convince anyone to help me. Then I was put on trial. I always considered myself a good, dependable worker who was injured while performing her job to the best of her ability. According to the law, I was entitled to compensation. Instead, the trial made me feel like I had screwed up, that I was irresponsible and deserved what I got.

My life had been moving so fast since the crash that I hadn't had time to think. First there was all the effort to recover and regain independence. Then the whirlwind year with Ray, all my therapy, and finally the trial. Now my feelings had a chance to catch up to the reality, and they slammed into me. The best analogy I can think of is the time my friend Pam and I feared we were being abducted and we jumped from a speeding car: When I put my foot down on the pavement, I instantly had to adjust my body to the momentum of the vehicle. To go from speeding motion to dead stop took a frantic readjustment, and there was no time to think about anything except keeping my balance. That's how I felt during the first years after the crash. But now time stopped short and reality caught up to me. It was like being spit out of a chute into a mud bath. And there I was.

I turned to books, not for solace or to escape, but for answers, some way to explain my situation. I read the Bible, metaphysics, philosophy, and the works of Mary Baker Eddy, the discoverer and founder of Christian Science, and the theme I saw over and over was that all the suffering, indecision, and ignorance that we endure is meant to force us to go higher. The pain is supposed to push us to find the key to open the door to understanding, to find our purpose, in order to get to the next level of our spiritual selves—our real selves. Adversity is supposed to make us think and work on this inner being. I knew that I had a choice: I could give up or go forward. If those were my only two options in life—to be a victim or a victor—the decision was easy.

Exactly how to become victorious was harder to know, but somehow I suspected that the answer was in front of me all along. I had been exposed to the basic spiritual truths since childhood. Only now, for the first time in a charmed life, I really needed them. I remembered how every Sunday when I was a girl, we trooped down to the Ebell Theatre on Wilshire Boulevard to see Joseph Murphy, a great author and metaphysician. I still love the doxology we sang every week:

> Open mine eyes that I may see;
> Fullness of truth Thou hast for me.
> Place in my hand that wonderful key,
> That shall unclasp and set me free.
> Silently now I wait for Thee,
> Ready my God thy will to see.
> Open mine eyes, illumine me,
> Spirit Divine.

This taught us that we alone hold the keys to unclasp our bonds and set ourselves free. In Sunday school our teacher Billie Burke taught us that God is everywhere, not a distant figure but a force, a presence that is part of the world and part of us.

To find my way back to these old truths, I needed a helping hand. Just as I sought out therapists for my physical recovery, I turned to a professional for my spiritual recovery. I wanted to start in again with Mrs. S., the Christian Science practitioner who had helped us by telephone in the Las Vegas hospital. My mom thought Mrs. S. might be too intense for me, but I insisted; I didn't want decaf if I could have espresso.

My mom and I drove to her well-kept little home, with its closely trimmed lawn and evenly spaced roses. Inside, the house was immaculate, and Mrs. S. led us into her meticulous office, where nothing was ever out of place. Mrs. S. herself was as neat and proper as her surroundings, and I would have been shocked to see her gray hair in anything but a tight marcel. My mom hissed to me in a stage whisper, "She's as old as God." I shushed her, afraid of appearing less than respectful.

We visited every Friday, and Mrs. S. walked me through the Christian Science weekly lesson, which made me one of millions focusing on the same idea, a collective force strong enough to change the world. She also introduced me to additional works by the founder of Christian Science. I became fascinated with Mary Baker Eddy, who not only wrote columns for the *Boston Herald, Cosmopolitan,* and *Harper's Weekly* but managed to found the Pulitzer Prize–winning newspaper *The Christian Science Monitor* as well as the church, whose members today number in the millions. Among this remarkable woman's staunch admirers were Clara Barton, first president of the American Red Cross, and Florence Nightingale.

For me, today's science validates Mrs. Eddy's premise that every cell of the body has intelligence. If you hold a picture of yourself in your mind, every cell reflects it like a mirror image, just as every cell contains all the genetic material needed to build you. The more you are able to focus your mind toward perfection, the faster you heal.

The teachings of Christian Science confirmed things I had felt intuitively, and put words to beliefs I already held. I'm the key. God is in me, not out there. God is not an old guy on a throne but a power, an intelligence available to everyone. These are not ideas limited to Christian Scientists—and I've never been doctrinaire about anything, including religion. These concepts can be used by people of all beliefs.

I am responsible for what happens to me; I can't blame an injury or use it as an excuse for not acting. The more I understood, the more I saw connections between my physical condition and my spiritual growth. Mrs. S. was giving me the tools to heal myself—my body and my soul. I took her information, added my own, and combined it with medical science to design my own healing program.

This was truth and it was beauty. It was illumination and joy. It wasn't complicated or difficult to understand. Everything I needed was contained in a simple, lovely childhood rhyme that finally revealed to me its many layers of meaning:

> I am the place where God shines through,
> For He and I are one not two.
> He wants me where and how I am,
> I need not fret nor will nor plan.
> If I'll just be relaxed and free,
> He'll carry out his plan through me.

I didn't stop with the Bible and the classic texts of Christian Science. I discovered so many people, from so many different cultures and times, who had made their own journeys and had recorded what they learned. Every book sent me looking for new books. Everything I learned opened another door, and I couldn't help but race through the doors into new, wondrous rooms filled with treasures. I gave Brad long lists of books to get from the library. Impatient with other people reading to me or struggling to turn the pages myself, I had Brad make me a long stick to turn the pages. One end of the stick was as flat as a tongue depressor, which went in my mouth, and the other end had a stubby pencil eraser to grip the page enough to turn it. I read so much that the stick was soggy by the end of the day.

Everything dealing with the body and the mind was of interest to me. I was especially fascinated by miraculous healings. I read about hundreds of people who were suffering from horrible diseases who suddenly and miraculously were cured. The blind opened their eyes and could see, and the deaf could hear. There were biblical tales, and the laying on of hands, and modern stories of people just like me who were healed overnight.

I knew of one case personally. I had been making the rounds of the studios to see if anyone had any acting parts for me. All the studios keep lists of "disabled" actors, categorized by what is missing or what the actors can't do. Not a great list to be on, but I wanted to work, even if it meant being typecast. I visited Fox and saw Elaine Rich, who was producing *Dynasty*. "Call me," I urged. "You know I used to do stunts. I'm there for you if you need someone to drive a wheelchair off a pier or something." Nice try, but no luck. One person did notice me, though. A producer named Steve Reuther called my friend Linda Meyers to say that he had seen me that day at Fox. He wanted to meet me because he had something important to tell me.

Steve came to the house and told me his story. Many years before, he had been in an accident and had broken his neck. For ten years he was paralyzed. I looked at him while he was telling me this and couldn't believe it. There was absolutely nothing wrong with him. For the entire ten years, he said, he had someone move him every single waking moment. When he got the first flicker of movement back, he jumped on it and worked it until he couldn't keep his eyes open. The next day he worked on it again, and the movement spread. Muscle by muscle, he came back. At this point in his life, he was swimming three miles a day and pushing a rigorous shooting schedule. Just a few days before we met he had taken a helicopter into the mountains to ski with Barbra Streisand and Richard Baskin.

Steve visited me every day. He listened to my tales of recovery and massaged my hands, pulling my fingers, rubbing my palms. "Keep moving," he said. "Don't stop moving." He followed his own advice and kept moving himself, right up to the heights of show business, producing a string of hit movies, including *Pretty Woman* with

Richard Gere and Julia Roberts. Recently Steve and Michael Douglas formed a partnership and raised $500 million to finance twelve new films. Steve is a good friend and a living inspiration. I dreamed I would recover just like he did—and turn Hollywood on its ear.

Risking the dismay of Mrs. S., I sought out new therapists, healers, and hypnotists; anyone who might be able to help me. Griner retired three years after the crash, but by then I had discovered a whole world of progressive people like him. I spent the entire decade of the 1980s in study and exercise—and having fun.

Each new piece of knowledge, each therapy or technique, was part of a process or a stepping stone on a longer journey. Each therapy had its own promise and kernel of reward, that I collected and used to correlate the principles involved. Mostly they involved different facets of the same idea, and the experimenting was like developing a taste for good food: The more you try, the more discriminating you become. The same is true for the mind and body. I just had to find the right person, the right technique. Somehow I had to tap in to the power, the force that was out there and available. If only I could find the way to connect myself.

Then, like a vision of clear light in a shadowy dream, Maharishi appeared before me. If the truth be known, the light came from the television set, but I was impressed. The hour was late, and I was waging the nightly battle to fall asleep. As usual, the television was on with the sound turned low, flickering silently. From the corner of my eye, I noticed the harsh blue light change to a warm saffron color, pulling my glance toward the screen. I moved my head to the highest point on the mound of pillows and focused my eyes in the darkness.

A man in a robe was sitting on a couch surrounded by flowers. Other men were dressed in suits. I realized that I had no trouble hearing what they were saying, even with the volume turned low. The program was something on PBS, a science or discovery show. The men in suits were scientists talking with Maharishi Mahesh Yogi, the founder of transcendental meditation (TM) and the 1960s guru to the Beatles, Mia Farrow, and many others. The scientists were explaining the teachings of Maharishi, showing how thought waves behave exactly like sound waves or light waves. Thought waves also have a physical effect on the world and can be measured with the proper instruments, the scientists said. This concept, of course, was obvious to Maharishi, but it was my first introduction to the science behind visualization techniques that can change reality.

The scientists explained how holograms are made by photographing an object with a laser so the image appears suspended in space. The image appears to be three-dimensional and absolutely real, but it's an illusion. The holograms reminded me of what Mrs. S. said about the distinction between illusion and reality. Maybe this was what she meant by the tendency of the eye to be fooled by appearance. The five senses are unreliable, she always said, reminding me that a straight stick of wood thrust into a stream appears bent, and that a man walking away appears to grow smaller. An echo puts sound where it's not; sometimes it's impossible to tell a taste from a smell, and a very cold object can feel hot. All sensory impressions are affected by perception and the emotions.

Mrs. S. took this understanding to the limit. I remember very well complaining to her about not being able to sleep more than a few hours each night. I was so tired that I had trouble concentrating on my weekly lesson.

"Heidi!" she yelled, slamming her palm on the desk. "Fatigue is simply an idea, it is a belief, another illusion of the senses. You are getting as much sleep as you need."

That night, sleepless, my head spinning with the idea of thought waves being able to shape the physical world, I imagined myself as a hologram. I project thoughts that create an image for others to see. There is the real me and the image that others see. What exactly is the relationship between the image and the reality? Why can't I just imagine a perfect me and shape my body accordingly?

Could all reality be changed in this way? Could I, by closing my eyes and imagining the picture of how my body should be, pull all the atoms and molecules into line and bring that picture to fruition? If thought waves really change the physical world, then I could use thought to sculpt and mold my body, to repair the damaged nerves and restore severed connections. Maybe I could focus so hard on my perfection, a perfection that still existed somewhere but was buried under my injury, and bring it to reality.

I did an exercise where I focused on each muscle group and imagined it working properly. The idea was to repeat patterns of thought until the mind and body were programmed. I would imagine all my nerve cells lined up to run a relay race, passing the signals like a baton. I used my conscious mind to give them the baton and help it along. Through my reading I realized that scientists already had documented the positive effects of this exercise called "patterning."

The more I read and practiced visualization, the more I saw it was not just wishful thinking but scientific therapy. What began for me as religious belief was evolving into scientific understanding. I was going from religion to biology and anatomy. Most doctors accept that a patient won't get better unless he wants to. This was just taking the theory one step farther and using it for positive effect.

I started visualizing individual muscle fibers, sometimes even individual cells. I studied anatomy books and biology texts until I understood how the nerves work, and how the spinal cord is just a downward extension of the brain. I tried to imagine my central nervous system like a giant computer: collecting information from the outside world and my body, storing the information as memory, and then acting to keep me alive and happy. I had pinched the main cable, but that didn't seem like a terminal problem to me. If you twist a garden hose, the water stops flowing, but as soon as you straighten the hose, the flow resumes.

I imagined whole areas of my body working in synchronization. I studied the mechanisms that control body temperature and tried to imagine their perfection. I imagined food entering my system, being digested and converted to energy, right down to the tiniest cell taking on nutrition. I repeated to myself: My nervous system is a high-speed supercomputer, not an old laptop that fell onto the floor. My stomach is a smoothly pumping machine, not a pocked, bloody bag of acid. My lungs are blacksmith's bellows, not limp sacks of mucus. My blood is a cool, clean stream, and my white cells are fearless infection fighters. I tried to picture all the parts and subsystems of my body working together in harmony, in perfection. I dreamed of myself as Gulliver, and the Lilliputians were a team of medical specialists swarming over my prone body to make me well.

When I was in the hospital, I kept looking at my body, wondering why it wouldn't move. I could see my chest rise when I breathed, and I could feel the pounding of my heart. My hair grew and my nails needed to be trimmed. My skin glowed and my muscles were toned. The complex functions of the peripheral nervous system were working normally, but I couldn't make the whole thing get up and move. How could I make it move? The doctors didn't have a clue how to help me, but I didn't know what I could do by myself. I didn't have any fancy degrees, and I could barely understand the medical texts. How was I going to fix myself?

I closed my eyes and pretended I was an X-ray machine, able to see the hidden, inner reality around me. I saw that the world is composed not of dormant things or lumps of stuff but of atoms vibrating at different frequencies. The same is true for people: We are works in progress, vibrating, humming, buzzing bundles of energy. It is the intelligence or creative force, or God, that composes these vibrating atoms into molecules, and the molecules into cells, and the cells into tissues, and the tissues into organs and the organs into our systems.

The secret of working with this force is understanding, not belief. This is not something I *believe* in, it is something I *know*. And I know because it has delivered results: the transformation of the physical body. This message of self-healing is familiar, and it permeates our culture. Today this old concept of self-reliance is joining up with science and technology to enhance medicine, taking scientific tools and using them to our advantage.

I don't mean to suggest this is easy. If it were easy to live well and to have absolute dominion over our minds and bodies, everyone would do it. The beauty of our human condition is that we are given the option to change our minds, to turn our attention in a new direction and to work with the creative principal, with the power of the seasons and the tides and the rotation of the earth. Imagine tapping into that source! I put my head down and went to work, for this is a process that takes conscious, continuous effort.

My friend Jess Stearn, a great author and thinker, was working on these techniques long before I was. Jess was an inspiration, and he referred me to a noted neurologist, Dr. Eugene Jusseck, who commandeered my voluminous medical records from the archives of Long Beach Memorial Island. Fortunately he agreed to see me before the records arrived because he swore that if he had read the records first he would have assumed I was dead. To his amazement, he verified the very much alive condition of my deep reflexes and all my other systems. This meant my spinal cord was sending messages, both from the brain to the muscle and back again, which most of my doctors had said was impossible. Dr. Jusseck's conclusion was that I should be walking.

Jess, who never has doubted that I'll get up, compares the mind's role in healing to a carpenter in a workshop. In his book *The Power of Alpha Thinking* he says that anyone can build a new body in a mental workshop. He urges us to imagine that the workshop contains a screen, upon which we float the problems to be solved. In the workshop all things are possible simply by allowing the brain to enter the "alpha" state, which lies between conscious thought and the subconscious. With Jess's technique it's possible to take charge of your life and change your circumstances. No need to continue the daily exercise in futility that traps most of us: get up, go to school, go to work, come home, watch TV, go to bed, and get up in the morning and do it again. Instead, take a page from one of my favorite books, *Jonathan Livingston Seagull*, and fly high for the adventure of perfection.

I tore through my new reading like a starving person, absorbing information as fast as I possibly could. Now I was learning for survival. There's nothing like a bad spinal injury to focus your attention. Studying was actually fun now, and empowering. Not content with the printed page, I bought a computer and became a junkie. I immediately spotted a parallel between the science of the mind that I was studying and the science that built my computer. It seemed to me that the computer was man's first attempt to simulate God's creation—mind.

I was fascinated to read about William Gibson, the sci-fi writer who coined the word *cyberspace*. In *Time* magazine, his observations on watching kids playing video games were later quoted: "I could see in the physical intensity of their postures how rapt the kids were. It was like a feedback loop, with photons coming off the screens into the kids' eyes, neurons moving through their bodies and electrons moving through the video game. These kids clearly believed in the space the games projected. . . . They develop a belief that there's some kind of *actual space* behind the screen, some place that you can't see but you know is there."

Gibson called the place cyberspace. He was describing virtual reality, a kind of holographic representation that the characters in his novels enter by "jacking in." In effect, this is what we're doing when we pray, meditate, or visualize. We are turning virtual reality into actual reality through the knowledge that what we're looking for actually *is*.

Cyberspace—or the net, the web, the datasphere—is similar to my interpretation of the next dimension or the spiritual realm. I see Christian Science as the cyberspace of Christianity; call it cyberspirit. Easy access to the Internet of the spirit with no cumbersome wires, no physical reality. The built-in computers we are born with are far superior to the ones in stores. Once you "jack into" this realm, you can't relax into a passive mode again. You are constantly on-line with the "supplier," constantly transmitting images that form the matrix of your reality, your life. To some, this may seem like a quantum leap, but to me the "key" was the computer key marked "Enter." I was going on-line, onto the spiritual superhighway, the Healing Internet, the web of consciousness.

My parents, who were on-line even before computers were invented, gave me their favorite works of inspiration, such as *The*

Awakened Imagination by Neville Goddard. This book helped tie together some of the disparate threads I had been collecting, and more important, it helped me realize that I was trying so hard to understand the words, the text, that I wasn't letting the spirit happen. When Brad explained to me that I should think of spirit as a feeling, that was the first time it really registered. Words are mere symbols used to communicate ideas, thoughts, and emotions. The feelings they trigger create our reality.

Goddard's argument is that "feeling is the secret." For him, our thoughts and imagination determine everything and shape our world. Healthy thoughts build healthy bodies. "Imagination travels according to habit," he writes. "Awake or asleep Man's imagination is constrained to follow certain definite patterns. It is this benumbing influence of habit that Man must change. If he does not, his dreams will fade under the paralysis of custom."

Goddard continues, "Any change in the behavior of the inner self will result in corresponding outer changes."

That message fell on receptive ears, and I consciously tried to build myself up with positive, helpful thoughts and attitudes. When self-doubt and fear tried to invade my mind, I remembered Mrs. S.'s constant admonition to "turn away."

Our perceptions of things outside our bodies cause real, measurable physical changes inside our bodies. Just imagine a ripe, cut lemon, and your mouth starts to water. A more powerful example is what is known as the stress response, which is a cascade of physical and chemical changes set off by the perception of a threat to the body. This is why a sudden bang makes your heart pound and your palms sweat. When a person consciously and deliberately changes perceptions through knowledge and understanding, then the physical body and worldly experiences change as well. The chain of action begins inside: the thought to the thing.

During the decade after the crash, almost without realizing it, I was moving forward. I was learning so much about myself, my body, about science and biology, about my spirit and my soul. I was taking long intellectual journeys without ever leaving my room, branching off into obscure corners of learning until I lost interest and then heading off in another direction. The more I learned, the more I realized how much was out there waiting for me to discover.

As my grand plan for recovery was taking shape in my mind, I began to blend knowledge gleaned from technical medical journals with ancient remedies and folklore. I adapted some cures to my own use, and others I rejected as not right for me. Some of the techniques were "mental" and some were "physical," but I always knew this was a false dichotomy. It seems obvious now, but it took time for me to realize that the body and the mind are on the physical plane while the spirit is in charge on a higher plane. While I worked my mind and body, I always remembered to let the spirit happen. Word got out about what I was doing, and I got calls from interesting people asking for information. Even the great Norman Cousins wanted to hear about my progress for a documentary on healing.

Others had a better understanding of holistic therapy than I did, thank goodness, and from the beginning I tapped into a network of gifted people living nearby. One of them was David Bressler, who started the Bressler Center in Los Angeles. Bressler was at UCLA and built his own practice using a combination of recovery techniques ranging from visualization to pain management to physical therapy and massage. The idea is that integrating the therapies creates a force greater than the sum of the individual techniques. That made sense to me, and I was excited to meet Bressler. He was excited to meet me, too, although he was a lot more excited when I introduced him to my girlfriend Loretta, whom he married practically the next day.

Some of Bressler's techniques proved to be slightly unorthodox, even for me. For example, it wasn't until I got to the center that I learned my aura needed cleaning. I hadn't thought much about my aura before, and I certainly wasn't aware that it needed to be cleaned. You know how it is: You lead a busy life, you don't have a lot of time, and pretty soon there are dust balls under the sofa and gunk on your aura. This aura, I was told, was not something I could send out and get back the same day, on a hanger/no starch. Aura cleansing was a hands-on therapy like any other, and I had to sit through it with a straight face.

The aura cleanser positioned himself in front of me and told me to relax and be still. *Aura*, he said, is just an esoteric term for electromagnetic field. He faced me and began to move his hands like wands about four inches from my body. He brushed and burnished the areas with heavy grime, flicking away little bits of aura lint. Despite my initial skepticism, this was by no means my first visit to the Twilight Zone, and I allowed myself to relax. The aura cleaner, who turned out to be a very interesting fellow, spoke knowledgeably about his work. I had seen photographs that purported to show people surrounded by real, physical auras, so I didn't dismiss the possibility that they exist. In fact, I did "feel" his hands as they passed near me, even with my eyes closed tight, and the treatment was a soothing air massage. I was willing to try anything that appeared to be a part of the bigger picture that I envisioned. If a dirty aura was holding me back, well then, hose it down.

The greatest discovery I made at the center was biofeedback. Dianne, the technician, hooked me up to a machine that measures the energy levels in different parts of the body. The theory is that by monitoring your heart rate, breathing levels, and other bodily indicators, you can begin to control them mentally. Dianne showed me how to concentrate my energy on my hands and actually heat them up with the power of thought. I always had sensed this happening, but I couldn't be sure if it was just my imagination. Dianne insisted that the energy is real. To prove it, she touched the end of the biofeedback machine to my hand. The gauge hovered near the bottom of the scale, a normal reading for the body at rest.

"Okay," she said. "Now heat up your hand like before."

I focused my energy.

"Harder," she said.

I closed my eyes and concentrated. The dial crackled like a Geiger counter, and I opened my eyes to see a little needle sweeping across the dial.

"Is that cool!" I said. "I'm connected."

"Of course you are," Dianne said.

I was connected—I never doubted that—and I had more encouraging signs of recovery as the years passed. I started using the biofeedback machine regularly, combining this with exercise, massage, and anything else that seemed at all useful. I filled my room with hundreds of books about spirituality and deepened my search for the key that would set me free—and get me up.

The years were passing. My life was good, but my physical progress was too slow. I was impatient, and I fantasized about jumping up one day and running down the beach. I was ready, so ready. There must be some machine that could energize me, some therapy that would wake up my body. I just wanted to plug in, or get on, or be "jacked into" something that would fix me. I was burning daylight.

Then, in 1989, after nearly a decade of daily effort, of exercise machines and visualization and prayer, of science books and study, I finally had a breakthrough.

The sun was rising and lightening the cloudless sky of another perfect California day. I was awake and ready to get out of bed, just as I had done hundreds of mornings before.

"Reina!" I called to my veteran helper. "Could you come here, please?"

Reina came into the room with a smile as bright as the new day. "Good morning," she said. "How was your night?"

"Fine," I said. "How are you today?"

"Fine, too."

"I'm ready to get up," I said. "Could you pull me down to the edge, please?"

Reina peeled away the sheet and blankets, grabbed my ankles, and slid me on my back to the foot of the bed. She is compact rather than small, and surprisingly strong, partly from lifting and adjusting my long body every day. Next she positioned the chair against the bed.

"Okay," I said, "put my legs down."

Reina pushed my legs over the side of the bed so my feet were on the floor next to the chair, while the rest of me remained flat on my back on the bed. In our well-honed routine, the next step was for her to straighten me into a sitting position, which was difficult because I am twice her size and my upper body was completely, heavily limp. The final trick in the process was for Reina to hold me up in a sitting position, angle me just so, and swiftly transfer my butt from the edge of the bed to the chair.

On this particular morning, sitting on the edge of the bed with Reina supporting my shoulders, I felt strange. Good strange. I was overcome by an awareness of muscles in my torso. I hadn't felt anything like this since the crash. I should say before the crash as well, because I don't remember ever thinking very much about the muscles in my torso. Before I was injured, the torso muscles held me up like they were supposed to, and I didn't worry about them one way or another. But on this particular sunny day, I noticed them.

"This feels different," I told Reina.

She was balancing me on the bed by holding my shoulders and getting ready to whisk me onto the chair. She mumbled something but was concentrating on the next step.

"Let me go," I said.

"What?"

"Let go."

"Are you sure?"

I made an impatient face. "Just let go."

She pulled away her hands. I sat on the edge of the bed, perfectly still, without anything or anyone supporting my body. Just me. I was almost afraid to move my head, afraid I would topple, but then slowly I glanced side to side. I didn't fall. I shrugged my shoulders. Steady as she goes. I shrugged a little harder and started to teeter. Reina grabbed me and held me up, laughing and hugging me.

"You did it!" she said.

"Yeah, I did," I said, astonished and joining her in laughter.

"Let me go again," I said.

She released me, and I balanced on the edge of the bed. I was sitting up on my own again, supported only by my own muscles, for the first time since the crash.

We practiced for a week. She pulled me up to a sitting position and then released me, only grabbing me when I started to topple. I balanced by myself for two minutes, then five. This is too easy, I thought. Something's wrong. I worried every night when I went to bed that the power would leave me during my sleep. When Reina came for me in the morning, I hesitated, fearing a little more each day that this would be the time when I wouldn't be able to hold myself up anymore.

"If it doesn't happen," I told her, lying in bed and not daring to budge, "I'm going to be so disappointed."

"It'll happen," she said. "You're doing it."

She was right. Not only did I manage to sit up every morning, I was holding it longer as the days progressed. We built up to ten minutes, then thirty. Humans are designed to function erect, not lying down, and I felt that at last I was resuming my natural position.

Reina and I agreed to keep our project top secret until we were sure it wasn't a fluke. I couldn't bear to tell everyone and raise the hopes of my parents, only to fall back into a heap. I could trust Reina with my secret because we have been through the worst together. She has seen me in positions and moods that are best kept to ourselves. She was, and is, my constant companion, my steady hand and patient friend. Finally, after a week or so when I could sit up for an hour, we were ready for the premiere of our show. I told my mom and Brad to bring Jeff and Christy and Joanna, the dogs, the neighbors, anybody who wanted to see something truly amazing.

"What's going on?" my mother asked.

"Just get everybody, please," I insisted.

"Okay. Okay."

I was in bed, assuming a familiar, reclined pose. My mom, Brad, Jeff, Christy, and Joanna filed into my bedroom and stood around the foot of the bed.

"So what's this all about, Heidi?" Brad asked, unable to restrain his curiosity.

"You'll see," I told him.

"Reina," I said. "Could you pull me down to the edge of the bed, please?"

She pulled my legs over the foot of the bed so my feet were on the floor. Then she helped me sit straight, leaving her two hands supporting my shoulders. So far, this was the normal procedure, nothing unusual. My mother's arms were crossed in front of her, her foot tapping on the creaky wooden floor. Jeff leafed through my stack of magazines. Brad looked only at me, expectant as a kid at Christmas.

I dragged out the moment as long as I could. "Ready?"

"Yes, already," my mother sighed. "We've been ready all morning."

Reina let go. I sat on the edge of the bed, beaming.

My mother and Joanna shrieked with joy and crushed me in a bear hug, almost knocking me onto the floor. Brad and Jeff let out whoops. There were more hugs, and Reina ran to the kitchen for a bottle of champagne. This was a triumph to celebrate. I couldn't have felt more free if chains had been cut from my body.

Chapter 12

HITTING THE GROUND RUNNING

Being able to sit up by myself meant the transmissions were being received; almost a decade of studying and exercising was paying off. But I had always found that living the life of an ascetic did not suit me. I never wanted to put my life on hold while I got better or sit around and wait to be healed. So during the same time I was learning about the spirit, I had never forgotten to be social. As the character in Somerset Maugham's *The Razor's Edge* learns, you need to take your wisdom and live it in the real world. Or, as my old friend Jack Nicholson put it in *The Shining*, "All work and no play makes Jack a dull boy."

Being spiritual doesn't mean leaving the fun out of your life. On the contrary, life should be more fun with an infusion of spirit. Ever since the crash I've been busy with my new job—which is how I regard my study and exercise program—but why risk burnout by working too hard? Because I saw the importance of balancing work and fun, I incorporated into my rigorous schedule a plan to maintain my social life. To use an old paratrooper's expression, I hit the ground running.

So there were parties, lots of parties. During the 1980s the house was filled most weekends with dozens of fascinating people. Some were famous, powerful, and rich, but all were bright and witty—a requisite. I'm fortunate to have the kind of friends who make for a terrific mix: stimulating groups who gathered for good conversation and fun.

To help with all this entertaining, and with my recovery program, I've been lucky to have an excellent staff, headed by Reina, who has an impish sense of humor and a real talent for organizing. Reina is the essence of consistency and loyalty. Much more than an employee, she is my friend and part of our family.

The oldest child in a large family originally from El Salvador, Reina helped her mother by cooking and cleaning, and taking outside work for extra money. Reina deeply empathized with my struggle to be independent again after the crash. She followed my lead, and with my encouragement she gathered the strength to tell her family that she needed her own life. I supported her the best I could, trying to convince her that she was doing the right thing for everyone by moving out of her mother's house. We shared a profound sense of triumph when she got her own apartment and a new car.

My other great helpers included Jeff and his wife, Saundra. They had been living in Carmel, but after their daughter Chelsea was born they came to Malibu, where my parents and I had moved from downtown to be near the ocean and to breathe clean air. My mom, Brad, Joanna, and I shared a house because I still wasn't able to live alone. Saundra became one of my most entertaining friends and served as my, shall we say, social secretary without portfolio. She often drove my black Corvette convertible, with me as copilot, as we zipped into town, visited friends, or had lunch and shopped. As a bonus, Saundra has an IQ that is clear off the charts.

At the same time Saundra was pregnant, Melanie was carrying the boy she would name Alexander. I was honored to be chosen to be one of his three godmothers, along with Jamie Lee Curtis and Kathleen Quinlan. Warren Beatty had the distinction of being the sole godfather. Kathleen, Jamie Lee, and I got together to plan a huge baby shower at my house. We were excited because the three godmothers-elect were performing our first official act on behalf of the soon-to-arrive baby prince, and we intended to do it right.

We started with the basics: engraved invitations and a top-of-the-line caterer, Malibu's own godmother, Dolores. A jazz group was assembled by Ron Anthony, Frank Sinatra's guitar man. Hansen's Bakery built a monumental, many-tiered cake, which was ensconced in the center atrium, along with a silver fountain flowing with champagne. Jamie Lee and Kathleen bustled around in shorts, supervising the deliveries, placing massive flower arrangements from Cosentino's, and piling up the artfully wrapped gifts that were arriving from everywhere and soon filled the house to bursting. I fell in love with my co-godmothers. Jamie Lee was a new friend, but I had met Kathleen before, when Melanie was playing matchmaker for her and Al Pacino. This began a torrid, four-year romance, the details of which I'll leave for Kathleen's book. The first time I met Kathleen she looked into my eyes in a special, powerful way, a look that validated everything I was doing and gave me such a boost of energy. I knew she would be an important friend.

Only Melanie would have a baby shower with more men than women. A guest list that looked like a show-biz award show was headed by Tatum O'Neal, Diane Lane, and Betty Buckley. I guess there's no doubt that before his marriage, Alexander's godfather was a world-class ladies' man. In fact, it was rumored that when a hostess sent an invitation to Warren, it was de rigueur to include a list of the beautiful women who would be attending. This story is probably apocryphal, but I remembered it when we sat down to open presents and he was nowhere to be seen. I thought it told a lot about Warren the rogue when he turned up in my parents' room, a crow's nest overlooking the water. He was stretched out on their big brass bed, talking business on the phone. Lying happily at his side was the huge Harvey, a mix of Saint Bernard and Rhodesian Ridgeback. So much for Hollywood's playboy.

There were many new friends in those days, and high on the list of those stalwarts who never doubted my full recovery was Bruce Willis. The moment I spied that face on *Moonlighting*, I announced to anyone who would listen, "This guy is going to be big!" If I had been walking around, I would have run right over to the studio and claimed him. Instead, I decided to write him a little note. What the heck. I pulled out all the stops and included a couple dozen roses and a picture of myself. For good measure, I sent it all by messenger.

The ball was in motion. I had all my players in place: Linda Meyers was at the studio where Bruce was working, Christy was in charge of delivery service, and Saundra coordinated the care package. When my spies confirmed that the "eagle had landed," I had no choice but to leave everything to the gods.

Two hours later, I was busily reading. The phone rang. The machine picked up and filled the room with that now famous chuckle. "Heh, heh, heh. You're pretty funny. This is Bruce Willis." Saundra burst into the room, her mouth agape. We stared at each other grinning, our eyes like saucers while we listened. Saundra gave me five, and I began a year of intense communication with a very intense man.

Bruno, as he's known, was dealing with a punishing fourteen-hour schedule that required him to be in almost every shot of *Moonlighting*. In addition to the hard work, he was learning to live with the demands of monster celebrity and the loss of privacy that comes with it. He found much of the daily grind exhausting and downright unpleasant. (Be careful what you wish for; you just might get it.)

Beneath Bruno's cocky demeanor, I sensed a slight insecurity, a vulnerability, that was irresistible. Because I grew up in this town and was a veteran, while Bruce was still a show-biz virgin, I advised him along these lines, repeated again and again: "Don't let the suits get to you. Don't kick against them. You're in the driver's seat. *Carpe diem*, as they say in Latin; seize the day!" He was a quick study and soon became one of the toughest businessmen in films.

We talked often on the phone and challenged each other to leave the most clever messages on our answering machines. I sent him silly packages I knew would amuse him: toys, radio-controlled cars, programmable robots, neon signs, and during the holidays when he couldn't get off the set, a Christmas tree. One morning my machine answered and I heard the voice: "Pick up, von B. Pick up the phone. I've got somebody here who wants to talk to you." Then my bud Kathleen Quinlan came on to say hi. They were starring together in a Blake Edwards film, *Sunset*, and had big news: Bruno had been nominated for an Emmy.

I had been nagging him for a photo, and on the day of the Emmys his car arrived with not just one picture, but a bunch of his own personal candids, Polaroids and other casual snapshots. He must have just ripped them off the wall because they still had thumbtack holes. Bruno's driver handed me the package and said, "Bruce says to keep your fingers crossed and wish us good luck." Of course, he won the award.

The following day Kathleen called and said, "I don't know what the deal is, but Bruce keeps saying he has a surprise for you, and he won't say what." We speculated fruitlessly on what it might be until he called and told me to pick up *The Hollywood Reporter*. I opened the daily to see that he had taken the obligatory double-page ad to thank his managers, producers, directors, writers, and everyone for helping to win the Emmy. High up on the list, in a prominent place between his agent and publicist, he had placed my name. What a guy!

It may sound a bit strange, but for the longest time we never actually met in person. Our relationship was entirely in the form of phone calls, messages, and notes. We could have met anytime—we lived just down the beach from each other in Malibu and had many common friends—but perhaps unconsciously we decided not to because it would have ruined the game. I still missed the strong support of Ray, and this cyberchat with Bruno kept me endlessly entertained. It was rewarding precisely because it was without the pressure of a physical relationship. I can see how George Bernard Shaw and Mrs. Patrick Campbell found it exciting to remain at a distance and "merely" exchange letters. And what about Cyrano and Roxanne? That safe sense of distance is liberating; I recommend it enthusiastically.

We finally met at Melanie and Don's, long after Bruno and that lucky Demi Moore got married. He had brought his cute little girl,

Rumer, to Alexander's birthday party. The first time we saw each other "live," I felt like we were old friends being reunited.

I found that my closest friends were sharing the spiritual journey, and part of our fun was observing one another's progress. Kathleen is totally focused on her goals and makes a clear distinction between who she is and her "work." Along the way she has become more conscious of her spiritual nature. Her world has evolved into that of a gifted actress who is as comfortable in the theater as she is on-screen, starring recently with Tom Hanks in Ron Howard's *Apollo 13*. Despite her nonstop high-pressure schedule and glowing spiritual life, something was missing—until she met that fascinating hunk, actor Bruce Abbott. Kathleen has great taste in men, and I would have settled for any of her choices over the years, but she made the romantic score of a lifetime when she found herself starring opposite the tall, dark, and gorgeous Bruce in a movie called *Trapped*, a female knockoff of the *Die Hard* films. Together they have a beautiful son, Tyler.

My life was moving at the old quick pace, my recovery was on track, and now it was time to strike out on my own. I left my mom, Brad, and Joanna and moved into a great place of my own just up the Malibu coast near the Holiday House, which was famous in its day for being a weekend getaway for those in Hollywood who weren't already residing on the sand. The house was perfect for one person, with a large living room, bar, and kitchen as well as two bedrooms, bath, and den. It was my pad. I felt I was back in control again for the first time since the accident. I also felt like I was coming home. This section of beach, Malibu Cove Colony, is next to a beach called Escondido, which is where I had my very first apartment.

Malibu is a nineteen-mile stretch of separate beaches north of Santa Monica Bay. Going up the coast, there is Will Rogers State Beach, where they film *Baywatch*; then Las Tunas; Big Rock, where all the mud slides are; Dog Beach; Le Costa; Carbon Beach; and Surf Rider Beach, home of the surf contests. Farther up the coast are Latigo; Malibu Cove Colony; Escondido; Paradise Cove; Point Dume, which is a cliff that juts into the ocean; then Zuma and the star-studded Broad Beach, followed by state parks all the way up to the L.A. county line.

I've always felt that Paradise Cove is the most beautiful section of Malibu, with Malibu Cove and Escondido tucked in next to it. The water there is blue and placid, perfect for water-skiing. I had a speedboat with a 275-horsepower Cobra engine anchored beyond the breakers off the front of the house. We used a Sea Eagle dinghy to reach the boat, which was a thrilling ride in itself because our timing had to be precise between sets of waves to avoid getting nailed. My family and I spent weekends roaring up and down the coast, calling friends on the cellular phone and urging them to run out onto the beach and join us.

One sunny weekend I was busily doing the hostess number when I noticed that Christy had paused in her usual party surfing—a skill-ful maneuvering through a sea of former beaus and prospective beaus. She was huddled in a corner with Buck Henry and talking so intently that I was sure they were solving some international crisis. When I finally got in a word with her, she said that Buck wanted to know what I was doing for exercise. He had listened very carefully to Christy's description of my workout program, paying close attention to what I could and couldn't do. Buck got energized and told Christy he had an idea for a piece of equipment that could help. Buck knows gadgets; remember, he was the cocreator of *Get Smart*.

He began to describe a harness suspended from the ceiling to form an adult-sized jumper, like the kind toddlers use to bounce up and down and build strong legs. Buck thought we could make a large one with a parachute harness and a pulley to raise me off the ground. He was sure it would help me stand. It sounded good to me; I've never seen an exercise machine I didn't like. I seem to gravitate toward new machines the way some women collect jewelry, and one of my favorite pastimes is browsing through catalogues of athletic equipment. I'd never heard of a machine like the one Buck de-scribed, so we tried to build one ourselves, almost pulling down the roof in the process. Buck then had one made, and we'd like to mar-ket it someday.

I was touched that a man who is an acclaimed screenwriter (*The Graduate*) and satirist would make the effort to help me get up. There was no reason at all for him to help except for his love and his belief in me. This is the kind of friend I have to lean on, and they have made the journey easier and more fun.

During the eighties the days were hectic, full of activity and people and new projects. I raced to different therapies and worked out until sweat soaked the floor around me. Friends came by for dinner and to talk, or I piled into the car to visit them, go to restaurants and to see movies. No one in my family sat still, and that much hadn't changed since I was a girl. In the evenings I sought escape in a glass of champagne, savoring the tingle of bubbles on my tongue and the warmth pulsing through my head. One glass was enough to allow my mind to lift itself out of my body, if only for a few minutes.

I focused all my waking energy on working my body. I moved what I was able to move and tried through sheer force of will to budge any muscle I could. I stared at my little finger, willing it to curl, daring it to disobey my command. I sat for hours on the bike machine, letting the motor carry my legs around and around. I lifted my head up and down off the pillow. I asked whoever was with me to flex my fingers, pump my legs, stretch my arms. I went to the gym and tried whatever exercise machines I could work.

One day I was on the bike machine, doing my usual boring routine, not really thinking of anything in particular and gazing out the window at the glorious ocean. It had become habitual for me to simulate in my mind the flexing and pointing of my feet as they rotated around on the motorized bike. I mentally pushed my legs into the pedals on each revolution. In my mind I pictured my feet: flex, point, flex, point, flex, point. My eyes wandered away from the ocean, and I glanced down at my feet. They were moving! They were flexing and pointing not only in my mind but right here below me. I blinked and looked again. They kept moving. This wasn't an image in my mind; I was moving my feet. I was moving!

I felt another surge of energy and power that propelled me forward, a joyful burst that swelled my already ample stock of confidence. I was sure, once again, that I was on the right track. My studying and my exercise were showing proof of progress. I wasn't sure exactly what it was I had to thank, whether it was one of the therapists or an exercise machine or all the parties. Maybe it was everything and nothing. Maybe it was nearly time to get up.

With my overall body strength increasing daily, I found myself able to use my old standing frame more easily. The frame looks like a very sturdy walker with straps that hug my knees and hips tightly against the metal bars. The frame is good not only for exercise but for circulation and skin tone as well. I had to be lashed to the supports, but I grew strong enough to be able to lean back and forth and to the sides. With music playing on the radio, I put my head down as if I were touching my toes and then leaned all the way back. Then I stretched deeply to the sides and straight again. I could feel the weight on my legs, and I knew the blood was circulating the way it's supposed to. The downward pressure helped strengthen the bones and reminded the joints how they are supposed to work. I was so happy to be standing again!

In the long process of getting up, there was one thing that I'm sure was more important than all my machines and all my therapists: my friends. At the top of the list is Melanie, who never bought into the permanence of my injury. I've always tried to focus on the future instead of on the past, and Melanie has stood shoulder-to-shoulder with me to concentrate on the positive side of recovery rather than the negative side of the injury. I know she's been inspired by my progress, and she says she's been able to apply the lessons to her acting. One of her favorite stories is about the day my name came up during a script meeting for *Working Girl*.

The discussion turned to how her character, Tess, was supposed to triumph over adversity. "I've got a girlfriend named Heidi von Beltz," Melanie told the people sitting around the table in a studio conference room. "She had this terrible accident, and the doctors said she would be paralyzed for life, but she keeps on fighting and is going to get up and walk again. I'm sure of it."

Everyone seemed interested in my story, and a few people said they had read about the crash years before and were curious to hear how I was doing. Only Melanie's costar, Harrison Ford, was silent, a dark cloud passing across his face at the mention of my name. Melanie thought it was kind of a strong reaction, but she didn't think much of it.

Harrison came up to her after the meeting. "I knew Heidi," he said, using the past tense.

"Oh, really," Melanie said, her curiosity aroused.

"I can't believe what happened to her," he said.

"She's my buddess," Melanie said. "She'll be okay."

"I hope so. I really do," he said. He looked her in the eye, then turned away.

Melanie couldn't get over how moved he seemed. How odd, she thought, even for a sensitive guy. She excused herself and grabbed the first telephone she could find. "Buddess," she whispered. "Did you sleep with Harrison?" Her actual words were more graphic.

I laughed.

"Buddess, you're awful!" She mostly was upset that I had discovered him first and hadn't informed her.

I told Melanie that I had seen Harrison so many times before we were formally introduced that I felt like I had known him for years. Before the crash, I was living in my apartment above Universal Studios in a quiet neighborhood filled with other young working actors and semi-starving hopefuls, people like the writer Rita Wilson, who later married Tom Hanks. My place was comfortable and Hollywood stylish, with hardwood floors and decorated in gray, mauve, and pink. One of the great features was the view: I could see right into the backyard of Harrison Ford. Every morning I woke up and watched him puttering around the yard in his robe, checking the grass and watering the flowers. At that time he was separated from his wife and living alone.

I didn't actually speak with him until a party at Candice Bergen's house. I had gone with Buck Henry, who knows everyone in the world, so while Buck went north, I went south, schmoozing and working the room. When I saw Harrison, I had to introduce myself.

"You don't know me, but I know you," I said.

"Oh, really?" he said, surprised and a little curious. "How's that?"

"We wake up every morning together."

He laughed. "Hmmm. Interesting," he said, cocking his head and waiting for more.

"I live up the hill from you, and every morning when I'm still in bed, I can look out my window and see you walking around the garden in your robe. Not to be spying on you or anything, but I can't help it. It's like I'm right there."

"I don't mind you spying on me," he said, moving a little closer. "In fact, if you want to come over and see the rest of the house sometime, I'd be delighted."

Harrison had a real movie star's house with a brick terrace in back and a swimming pool. He had just finished *Star Wars*, and the kitchen was filled with R2D2 cookie jars and other souvenirs from the movie. Our friendship blossomed pleasantly, and we spent languid afternoons by the pool. Many days Harrison would call and ask what I was up to. If I wasn't busy, I'd drop by for a visit and a dip. He's adorable, and we became close friends—and more—without the hassles and hang-ups of a full-blown romance. I enjoyed those moments of romantic escape from the world, just the two of us with no pressure and no hurry. A few months later, Harrison started shooting *Raiders of the Lost Ark*, and his career took off. Then he fell happily in love with the woman who wrote *E.T.*, and they were married. Our poolside afternoons ended as tenderly and quietly as they had begun, with barely a splash.

Melanie was satisfied with this G-rated version of the story, and she pumped me for details about Harrison. I had fond memories of him, but it seemed like that adventure had occurred such a long time ago. The focus of my life has never been on dating, and since high school I've almost always had a steady boyfriend. The sometimes turbulent romance with Ray was the deepest and most rewarding of my loves, and I tucked him away forever in a protected corner of my heart. Now I was far too busy for romance. My dance card remained full, but suitors had been replaced by therapists, business contacts, friends, and family.

After finishing her scenes for *Working Girl*, Melanie went off to Miami to shoot an episode of *Miami Vice* at the request of Donnie. This was a special episode, and Don would be directing her, but more importantly this show turned out to be a catalyst in rekindling their youthful romance, which had ended in divorce. Melanie, who was single again after splitting with Rocky, called me from Florida and told me that she and Don were together and in love, even more so than the first time. This affected me in two ways. One, I wasn't surprised because they seemed to be the definitive soul mates. Two, if they could get back together after a twenty-year hiatus, there might be hope for Ray and me. We talked and laughed on the phone, and Melanie seemed so happy. She didn't know it then, but she was about to embark on the year of her life.

There was a huge premiere at Fox Studios for *Working Girl*. An entire section of the studio was transformed into a New York street scene with hot dog vendors, a skating rink, and all the familiar street life. Our friend David Marconi, an up-and-coming filmmaker, Kathleen, Mom, Brad, and I attended, along with my ninety-year-old Uncle Horton. (Hort has vowed to stick around to have the first dance when I'm able.) After the film, Kathleen, Marconi, and I piled into a limo for a private dinner party Don had arranged at Le Dome on Sunset Strip. Brad and Mom went home, saying they were exhausted from the evening, and dragged along poor Uncle Hort, who complained the entire way about being kidnapped by party poopers.

The movie was a smash. Melanie was critically acclaimed and wooed to host the *Saturday Night Live* Christmas show. That night Don surprised her with a proposal and a four-carat emerald-cut diamond ring with baguettes on each side. She called me immediately and shared her joy. Soon after Christmas I got another late-night call from the happy couple. Melanie giggled, "Guess who's preggers? Yep, yep, yep."

To top off this already wonderful year, Melanie was nominated for an Oscar for best actress for *Working Girl*. On the day of the awards, Donnie took a bungalow at the Bel-Air Hotel, L.A.'s most luxurious. I spent the afternoon with them, enjoying a nice lunch from room service to prepare for the gala ahead, and people came in and out all day. Carly Simon, who was nominated for best song, dropped by to wish Melanie luck, and they were like two giddy schoolgirls. Jeweler Harry Winston sent his people to drop off the gems, and Melanie disappeared to drape on the pearls and diamonds and plenty of 'em, including a choker to go with her white peau de soie Cinderella dress. She was a vision, with her little pregnant tummy squeezed snugly into the teeny bodice.

When the double doors swung open and that gorgeous couple made their appearance in the living room, I was surprised to see a pout on Melanie's lovely face. "I hate these Harry Winston earrings!" she scowled. She brightened as her eyes zeroed in on the fifteen-millimeter pearls I was wearing. "Give me those," she ordered, and greedily snatched them from my ears.

Melanie was on the road constantly in 1989 and called often to keep me posted. One morning I was awakened by her excited voice calling from Donnie's beautiful ranch in Aspen. They were planning their second wedding there and wanted to be sure I would be staying in one of the ranch's guest houses. I happily listened to all of Melanie's plans and projects, but I was noncommittal about whether I would attend.

I couldn't imagine missing the wedding, but I didn't see how I could manage. My main muscle, Brad, was out of town for an important business trip, and although I thought my mom, Reina, and I could make it to Denver, I had serious concerns about the trip from Denver to Aspen. The short hop is notoriously bumpy on a plane that's not exactly a roomy 747. When I reported the call from Miss Melanie, my mom and Reina scoffed at my misgivings. "Whatever happened to *Carpe diem*?" they goaded. "This sounds like fun."

Never able to resist a challenge, I got on the phone to our local travel agent, who promptly informed me that Aspen was booked solid for the annual music festival. By now I had convinced myself that we were going, so I made a few more calls, pulled in some favors, and managed to score a great suite at my favorite hotel in Aspen, the historical Jerome. I didn't say a word to Melanie, but we were on our way.

The day of the flight, the limo arrived late. We threw ourselves in and urged on the driver, making it onto the plane just as the doors closed behind us. A few glasses of champagne later, we landed in Denver to complete the easy leg of the journey. From my skiing days, I was a veteran of those rocky shuttle flights across the mountains, and I smiled at the thought of my mom and Reina seeing the little plane. First we had to run clear across the airport, with Reina pushing me in a wheelchair piled high with luggage and Mom huffing and puffing behind us, bags hanging off each arm, grumbling about being a blankety-blank pack mule.

Breathless, we clattered up to the gate, only to find that the plane was delayed. Just as my mom was settling into a chair, I got her up again. In one of the little shops about twenty gates behind us, I had noticed a fantastic pair of snakeskin cowboy boots that would be perfect for my wedding outfit. It took some persuading, but I convinced her to run back and buy them for me. She returned as the plane was boarding—and at that precise moment I remembered something very important about these flights: There was no fancy jetway to take us on board, just a glorified ladder. We pondered the steep, narrow steps and gulped.

We weren't going to turn around now, so we assumed the position we call a "double," in which Mom grabs me under the arms and Reina puts her arms under my knees. Together we bumped my butt up the stairs, an ignominious but effective entrance, and no thanks to the half dozen people who watched, mouths open, without offering to help. So much for handicap access.

When we arrived at the hotel, I called Melanie. I kept up the charade of not being able to attend the wedding, until the end of the conversation when I asked, "Well, how do I get there?" She was totally, happily surprised and quickly read me in on the secret instructions to circumvent the security network Don had set up to foil the tabloids. We got into the car, left the highway, and headed up a narrow country road. Deputy sheriffs, armed with the official guest list, waived us through checkpoint after checkpoint. The final barricade was at Don and Melanie's street, just in front of Don Henley's house. The last deputy kindly pointed us up a hill to the big, old-fashioned farmhouse.

The grounds are beautiful anyway, but for the wedding they were spectacular. Don had directed a cadre of gardeners to bring in hundreds of plants already in bloom to transform the lush fields into blossoming meadows leading to the verdant glade where they would take their vows, while a wonderful string quartet played wedding music. Huge weather balloons were tethered to keep away the photographers circling overhead in noisy helicopters.

The day was fabulous. Don and their boys, Jesse and Alexander, were dressed in formal white cutaway coats. The radiant Melanie was something to behold in a heavy silk and satin crepe de chine Edwardian gown, with flowing train and the legendary bosom atop a white bridal cascade. She was attended by Patti D'Arbanville (Jesse's mom) and Miss Pamela Des Barres, gowned in summery floral chiffon.

Following the ceremony, guests sipped Dom Perignon and dined al fresco from a sumptuous buffet. Hand in hand, Mr. and Mrs. Johnson joined friends in an area set up for skeet shooting. All eyes were on Melanie, still in her gown, as she hoisted a shotgun and yelled, "Pulllll!" The gun roared BOOM!, simultaneously shattering the clay pigeon and popping her bra strap. Naturally, the tabloids reported that Melanie was trying to shoot down their helicopters.

If anyone ever was cut out to be a movie star, it's Melanie. She moves easily from one high-pressure situation to another with complete poise and assurance. The word *élan* comes to mind, a quality that translates into all situations. It's something in the genes, I guess, because her mother is that way, too. After we all worked together on *Roar*, about endangered African animals, Tippi set up a preserve near the remote village of Acton, California, to protect animals that no one wanted or were being "retired" from circuses. Called Shambhala, which means "a meeting place of peace and harmony for all beings both animal and human," the preserve is home to more than one hundred animals, including lions, tigers, and two African elephants, Timbo and Kurra, living happily in a constantly shifting environment that simulates perfectly their natural habitat. They are safe because of countless dedicated volunteers organized by the tireless Tippi.

Melanie's acclaim for *Working Girl*, Kathleen's success onstage in *Dangerous Liaisons*, and an inspiring trip to see *Phantom of the Opera* awakened my dormant acting bug. I made the decision to jump back into classes. I joined an acting class that met on Point Dume and was directed by Jeff Corey, a famous character actor and one of the best teachers in the business. I loved being back, but I quickly became aware of my limitations when we were asked to prepare a monologue. I usually spent the entire class parked in one spot, which did not make it easy to act out a piece that would be memorable. My face and my voice would have to carry the show.

I considered various possibilities until I remembered the advice of my pal, the agent Michael Black, who said, "Milk it, honey." I decided to read the monologue from *Whose Life Is It Anyway?* in which a quadriplegic Richard Dreyfuss asserts his right to die.

The big night of my reading arrived, and I did my best. I thought it went well, but when I finished speaking, there wasn't a sound in the room; you could have heard a pin drop. Then the entire class leapt to their feet—a standing ovation! I was pleased the ol' girl still had it, but I had to admit that even after more acting classes, the professional parts were few and far between. I did receive an intriguing call from a friend informing me that a TV series was looking for an actress to appear in a wheelchair. "Hey, that's me," I said. "I can do that. I even have my own chair."

Sarah Jessica Parker was starring in a quality drama called *Equal Justice*. I went in to meet the casting people, and they gave me a script and asked me to come back the next day to read. I took it home and memorized the entire part of the defense attorney, who was supposed to be in a wheelchair. To be on the safe side, I also memorized everybody else's part so I wouldn't have to fumble with the script during the reading. They loved me, and I was called back three times. The director loved me, too, and I had the part. Then my bubble burst. The director asked, "Let me see you move around the room while you do the dialogue." I explained that I still didn't have the strength in my arms to push the chair myself. The director tried everything he could to find a solution, but to no avail. Call us when you can walk.

The setback fueled my fire. I was getting up and getting up now. I expressed my renewed urgency to an old school friend, Randie Hassen. I hadn't seen her in years, and she told me that she also had been in an accident. She had hurt her leg so badly that the doctors said she'd be lucky to ever use it again. She ignored the doctors, signed up for aqua-therapy, and fully recovered. This was a regular exercise program but done in the water to make movement easier. I thought it was worth a try for me, that perhaps eliminating gravity from the equation would make it easier to work with the strength I had. Eager to help, Randie sent me to the perfect teacher.

Paul Stader, a veteran stuntman and respected "water guy," did Tarzan's stunts and was the stunt coordinator for the show *Sea Hunt* and doubled for the star, Lloyd Bridges. Paul's beautiful wife, Marilyn, often worked with him and doubled the women. They were enthusiastic about trying to help me and couldn't wait to get me in the water. At first swimming was a bit awkward because the pool at Pepperdine University was kept very cool for the water polo team. The cold water made my muscles contract to the point that I consciously had to relax them, which proved as difficult as flexing them. But as I became acclimated to my new environment, movement grew easier and I enjoyed the feeling of being weightless.

On the first day, Paul held my upper body while Marilyn faced him holding my feet. She backed up to the wall for resistance, and Paul walked toward her, squeezing me like an accordion.

"Now push," Paul commanded, as he released my upper body.

Gritting my teeth, I pushed with all my might. To my amazement, I shot away from Marilyn, propelled by my own muscles.

Brad and I looked at each other and gave a mental high five, while Marilyn and Paul cheered. "You did it! You did it!"

Paul and Marilyn gave me further verification that I was intact. They went on to develop a program that included respiration work under water to build up my lungs. What a pair of mensches they were—two wonderful people who took time out of their lives to help me reach my goal. I'm also grateful to Randie, who had set me up with Paul. This wasn't the first time this talented, creative, and passionate woman had come through for me. Her future husband, Jim Wiatt, proved a valuable friend as well.

Jim, who later became president of the mega-agency ICM, was an agent for many big clients, including Willie Nelson. Willie's harmonica player, Mickey Raphael, lived near me in Malibu and became my friend. Mickey dropped by one day with a mysterious bundle in his hand. He opened the package and pulled out a harmonica.

"I thought this would be good to help you strengthen your diaphragm," he said.

I wasn't sure how I was going to keep the harmonica in my mouth, until Mickey produced one of the holders he wears around his neck. He adjusted it to my head, slipped in the harmonica, and voila!—an instant one-woman band. I was moved to tears. Later, Mickey sent a car for me to see them backstage at the Greek Theater and then to attend a party hosted by Willie. Every time I sing one of my theme songs, "On the Road Again," I think of those two guys and their kindness and sensitivity.

The harmonica also produced a running joke for our family. When someone is going on and on with a bad case of b.s., we repeat the immortal words from the instruction book: "Suck-suck, blow-blow, suck-suck, blow-blow."

Just when things were going so well in our lives, we received some bad news. The woman who owned the house I rented at Cove Colony had decided to sell. Great, I thought, just what I need. I had established a disciplined program of exercise and study (and entertaining), and I wasn't sure what a major move was going to do to my progress. But there was nothing to do but start looking for a new place, so we set out with a list of houses for rent.

My worries vanished the day we pulled off the Pacific Coast Highway and headed up a long winding drive that ends on a bluff. Majestically perched on this magnificent cliff looming over Zuma Beach was my dream house. I had seen the sprawling red ranch house many times since I was a child, and I'd always imagined living there. Situated on twelve glorious acres, it's more Greenwich, Connecticut, than California. The house was built in the forties by a pair of maiden sisters, and since then it's been home to Bonnie Raitt, Lee Grant, and Robbie Robertson—and now me.

On weekends the new house was filled with a stream of family and longtime friends with their kids. Usually we barbecued, everyone taking a turn at the grill, basking in brilliant sunsets that give new meaning to the phrase "Gold Coast." One of the regulars was John Pierre Henreaux, a talented and successful agent and one of the best-looking guys in town. He introduced me to a colleague, Risa Shapero, who started out in the business prettier than most of her clients and soon was representing such stars as Julia Roberts. Risa called to invite me to a housewarming party for Kevin Huevane, another agent who had joined the mass exodus from the William Morris Agency.

The party sounded like fun, but I had mixed feelings about going. One reason that I like to have people to my house is that I have everything I need and I'm able to sit in a regular chair. This is not a vanity thing, but it has to do with the way you are perceived in a wheelchair. My role model, FDR, certainly was aware of this, and he knew that no matter how brilliant he was or how politically skilled, he could never allow himself to be photographed in the chair. He always managed his public appearances carefully so as to appear standing unaided, often braced shoulder-to-shoulder between his two strong sons. I hate to say it, but I doubt he ever would have become the most powerful leader of the free world if he hadn't protected his image this way.

Maybe people don't like wheelchairs because they don't want to confront their own mortality—but I think it's more endemic. Whatever the reason, people in a chair are no longer seen as who they are. Once you're sitting in a wheelchair looking out, you realize it's no big deal. I see a wheelchair as a convenience or, to borrow a phrase from Mary Baker Eddy, "the right use of temporary means." For some strange reason, people choose to see it as a symbol of weakness. I think it represents the absolute opposite. The strongest people I know are on wheels, dealing with adversity each day.

I couldn't let a silly thing like a chair worry me. I had things to do. I immediately made appointments with two of the people who largely are responsible for keeping my act together for all these years. One is Jose Eber, the best friend a person could have and who always can be counted on for a trendy "do" at a moment's notice. The other is Claire Amsal, a tiny French lady, personally trained by Aida Grey in the Beverly Hills salon. Claire is like a sister to me, and she has kept my skin glowing, even right after the crash when my body was functioning at a diminished capacity.

When Jose and Claire had finished with me, I was presentable at least, but I still was anxious about the wheelchair. And although we've distilled it down to a science, the whole process of going somewhere is still awkward. I have to be helped from a chair to the car, back to a chair, legs and arms everywhere. Are there going to be stairs? Are the doors wide enough? Where will they put me so I don't block traffic? It's enough to give a girl a complex.

I asked Jeff to take me. We always have fun together, and he's a great writer, so I knew he'd have a lot in common with the other guests. Ever since I was little and he used to take me riding, Jeff has made everything easy for me, and he came through again for the party. When we arrived at Kevin's beautiful new home, Jeff did a little "recon" of the place to map our strategy. Yes, he reported, there were stairs. Yes, the door was narrow, and yes, the place was mobbed. There also was valet parking, which sounds nice unless you don't want some guy gawking at you while you're being wrestled limb by limb out of the car. We decided on a covert entry.

Jeff parked down the street from the house on Outpost Road, a popular thoroughfare used to cross from Universal Studios to Paramount. He summoned the force of ten to carry me and the chair in his arms, whisk me up the steps and through the front door, gracefully arranging me on a roomy couch before anyone noticed. In a few minutes we were swarmed with old friends and new. Michael Black, Steve Reuther, Rita Wilson and hubby Tom Hanks. I felt like it was old-home week, drinking champagne and catching up on the latest gossip. Friends like these constantly supplied me with strength and support, and I thrived on their feedback. I stopped worrying about the wheelchair or looking "different." It was yet another lesson in slaying that big bad dragon: the fear of the unknown. Every time I tackled the dragon head on, it paid off. Conquering my fear—and taking the party by storm—convinced me to push harder. I was motivated, and the next day I did extra sets of all my exercises, and I stepped up my studies and spiritual work.

I took great pleasure, even joy, in discovering new things. There were times when I read something that verified a hunch or feeling of my own. Other times revelations came out of nowhere, shedding light on something that I never had considered or never had seen from that particular angle. Being strong spiritually, like being strong physically, requires practice. Every day I'm offered new evidence that my thoughts shape my reality, not the other way around. It is the inner reality of my mind that is shaping the outer reality of my body.

Just as I had hoped, I had shifted into another mode in my recovery process. After I sat up on the bed in 1989, supporting my own body, feet on the ground, I was ready for more. It was just another confirmation that I was on-line and jacked in and waiting for further instructions.

I had reached the point where I had the strength to support my upper body and could move my torso easily. My arms and legs were tingling in anticipation of something good happening. I had fought hard to get to this point, and now I was ready for the next and hardest stage—getting up and walking.

GETTING UP

One beautiful day at my house, I was visiting with some of my friends when I overheard Michael Gregory talking about a doctor he was seeing. I could hear bits and pieces about "neuromuscular" treatment, and it sounded interesting. I wasn't eavesdropping—Michael, the original Rick Webber on *General Hospital* and the hottest soap hunk, has a voice like a cathedral organ.

"Major," I called across the room. "Tell me who you're talking about. Did you mention the name Glum? I keep hearing about this guy. Is he really that good?"

Major confirmed that the doctor really was good and gave me his number.

I was excited to meet the man with the rather gloomy-sounding name of Gary Glum, who practiced something called "neuromuscular reeducation." I liked that description, and it seemed close to my own efforts. I saw what I was doing as trying to spark the dormant memory in my nerves and muscles, which is similar to reeducating them. Hearing about Glum's work was another affirmation that I was on the right track, and I was forever running into people who independently had come to the same conclusions I had reached. If only all of us had been able to get together sooner, we would have progressed so much faster.

When Glum first laid eyes on me, he was enthusiastic. I have always looked deceptively healthy, which seems to encourage people to think I'm about to jump out of my chair any second. One time my mother was driving so slowly that a police officer pulled us over. He complained about my mother's low speed, and she said, "I'm driving this way because this girl is paralyzed." The cop peered into the backseat. He looked at me and then back at my mom. "She is not," he said. We convinced him, finally, and he drove off, shaking his head.

In spite of all the doctors' predictions that I would break down and fall apart, wasting away to the bone as my skin collapsed and sagged, I've remained round and curvy, and my skin never has stopped being pink and healthy. I had long since learned how to control my own bowels and bladder. At first I had difficulty breathing and was exhausted by the slightest effort, but now I could go all day without tiring. Improvement was almost daily. I was partially frozen but also partially thawed, depending on how you looked at it. Like me, Glum was a supreme optimist. He enthusiastically explained his technique, and I thought it was worth a try. He examined me, flexed my limbs, and checked my reflexes.

"You can get up," he said with assurance. "You can walk."

"That's what I want to hear," I said. "We're burning daylight. Why don't we go for it today and see what happens."

Glum dug right in, and I mean dug. I thought my old therapist Tom Griner was rough, but he was nothing compared with Glum. He pushed, pulled, and pummeled me. He didn't cajole my muscles into performing; he beat them into submission. He attacked and bent my arms into places they hadn't been in years, if ever. He pulled so hard I really was afraid he was going to snap the bones. I bit my tongue and tried not to yell out in pain.

Let it not be said that my muscles are stupid: They got reeducated. I think my muscles, bless their little hearts, knew Glum wouldn't stop until they got better. Maybe this was nothing more than the physical version of Mrs. S.'s tough love, but I noticed improvement immediately. Deeply encouraged, I visited Glum nearly every day. He was a bit strange, but I enjoyed his company, and whatever he was doing, it was working.

Then he surprised me. His secretary called one day and said that Glum couldn't see me anymore. My heart sank. I assumed that he was leaving town. No, she said, Glum was going out of business because he planned to run for president. Knowing him, this didn't sound all that unusual. If the secretary had said that Glum's work on earth was completed and he was returning to his planet, I would have understood. Still, I was crushed, and I wondered if somehow we couldn't keep going. There was one way Glum could continue seeing me, she said. I would be his only patient, and we would work together all day, every day. When he wasn't campaigning for president, of course. For his services I would pay $250,000 a year.

My jaw dropped open. Not only did that seem like an outrageous amount of money, I felt like Glum was abandoning me. He knew that I was paying him out of my own pocket because the insurance wouldn't cover such unconventional techniques. I didn't mind paying, because I figured that was why the jury had awarded me money: to use it to get better. But Glum's price was out of my reach. I already was paying for round-the-clock care, rent on my house, and a pile of other bills every month. There was no way I could afford Glum, so I said good-bye.

I was devastated by the loss of Glum—for about an hour. Then I realized he was not the only one who could do this technique. I had some good mileage under my belt and was going to keep going. I tried to contact Griner again, since he did basically the same thing. No luck. He was happily retired, but I remembered that he had been training his stepsons, so I tracked them down.

Tom's stepson, Dr. Eliot Griner, remembered me and was thrilled that I was still at it and making such great progress. He wanted to get to work right away, and he pushed his little fingertips into my flesh. "Your body feels good," he said, setting us off on a wonderful relationship. Eliot believed in me all the way. He's adorable and has a terrific sense of humor, and we became great pals. Finding him was just another demonstration that we are guided in the right way, if we'll just let it happen.

I established a regular schedule with Eliot, which meant double treatments three times a week. I would have done even more, but the tissue needs time to heal after each session. I exercised hard between visits to welcome fresh tissue back into the world. The more I exercised, the stronger I felt. This was a perfect combination of breaking down and building up. Now I wanted to do more for myself, instead of just being worked by another person. I wanted to up my program, the part that I controlled, but I wasn't sure how.

My friend Ross Sheldon, Sidney Sheldon's nephew, recommended that I contact a woman named Gayle Olinekova, a world-class marathon runner who had started a second career as a personal trainer. Ross said that Gayle had worked with people as badly injured as I was, and she had gotten them up.

I got in touch with Gayle, who already knew about me through several common friends. When Gayle arrived at the house for the first time, Reina led her into the room where I keep all my exercise equipment. I was sitting on the bike machine, my legs whirring around, and reading an anatomy book with the page-turner between my teeth. Gayle stopped short when she saw me.

"What's wrong with you?" she said, startled. "You look fine."

I just laughed, accustomed to the reaction and proud of myself for keeping fit.

Gayle found a chair and told me that she worked exclusively with professional athletes and others in peak physical condition, like a mechanic who specializes in race cars. I considered that a plus because the more I was pushed, the better the results would be. She explained that the method of treatment depends on the individual and the specific injury, but the common base is a blend of traditional therapies with the latest technical and scientific advances. Gayle asked what I had done to be in such great shape, so I ran down my program and the equipment I had been using. I explained my philosophy concerning the mind and my common-sense approach. Gayle was full of suggestions and information about new resources available. For example, she told me of a machine used in cases of tennis elbow or severely injured knees, such as those of professional football players, that strengthens the damaged tissue. It's called a TENS, or transcutaneous electrical nerve stimulator.

"Do you want to try it?" she asked.

"Definitely," I said.

She went to her car and returned with a portable TENS. She plugged it in, switched on a few knobs and dials, and placed two pads on my arm. She turned up the juice, and my arm jumped. We both laughed.

"Something's working," she said.

I had heard about the TENS several years before from my sister. Christy had gone to a spa that advertised passive muscle workouts, performed without moving. The person being worked lies on a table, and a technician places electrodes on the surface of the skin over major muscle groups. The machine uses electric pulses to cause contractions of the muscle, as if it were being flexed. Obviously, the best type of exercise is to move yourself, but since the machine provides a form of stationary isometrics, Christy got very excited, thinking it could help me. The spa manager refused to work on me, however, citing my "condition" and her insurance. Once again I was categorized as having a "condition," when I wasn't at all sick. I just wanted my body to move.

The pulses of electricity cause involuntary contractions that feel like being grabbed by giant pinching fingers. The higher the voltage, the stronger the contraction. Scientists have shown that applying electrical stimulation several times a week will make a muscle stronger, even if the owner can't move it voluntarily. How come no one put me on this thing in the beginning? It was not new. My mom was using the machine when I was a kid, and Hollywood has used it for years. During the forties and fifties, the studios sent their stars to a woman named Louise Long, who was famous for using this machine to trim fat and lift breasts. I could have been using it since the first day, and maybe my progress would have been swifter. Then again, maybe things are supposed to happen the way they do. I was just happy to be getting my own machine.

I learned that these machines are now standard for relieving pain and rehabilitating weakened muscles after surgery. They also are used to prevent muscle atrophy in arthritics, as well as to treat paralysis from spinal cord injuries. Dr. Roger Glaser, chairman of Rehabilitation Medicine at Wright State University in Dayton, Ohio, has seen dramatic improvement in paralyzed people using these machines. The electrical pulses build muscle mass and help circulation to the extremities, which in turn prevents clotting problems. Dr. Glaser says people often get a psychological boost from the added muscle because they feel stronger and look better.

Gayle likes a challenge, and she agreed to start working with me immediately. She cautioned that the treatment would not consist of merely hooking me up to a machine and leaving me there; far from it. I was going to have to work hard and meet her halfway, at least. Nor was the treatment to be in isolation from the rest of my life, something I could do for a few hours each day and then put aside. Hers was a total approach to the mind and the body. She was not just going to change my exercise routine; she set out to change my lifestyle and my life.

I liked and admired her right away, and I accepted her challenge. She seemed to be offering the next logical step on the path I had taken since the crash. I was fully awake now. I had the scientific knowledge I needed to understand what I needed to do, and the physical and emotional strength to keep me going. I hoped that I also had the spiritual strength to hear the guidance available to me.

Before we started on the actual therapy, Gayle asked me to have X rays and a complete neurological workup, just to see what she was getting into. I was curious myself, so we went to see a specialist who was an orthopedic surgeon and a neurologist. He put me on a table, examined me closely, and took a whole battery of pictures. He left the room to develop the film and came back shortly to show the results to Gayle and me.

They were impressed. My bones were thickly dense, my muscles were rich and firm. "I can't believe these pictures," Gayle said, holding an X-ray image to the light. "I can't believe you've been sitting there for ten years without moving and your body hasn't degenerated at all. It's like you've been in suspended animation."

"I haven't been sitting for ten years," I corrected her. "I kept moving the whole time. I needed help, but I didn't sit still any longer than I absolutely had to."

"One other thing," Gayle said. "I thought you had posts or wires inserted to support your neck."

"Yeah," I said. "This guy Dr. Cloward. He was wonderful. He put a piece of whalebone in there and wired the whole thing together. I saw an X ray of my neck, and it had more metal than the Bay Bridge."

"Well, it's gone now," Gayle said.

"What do you mean, gone?"

"Look."

She held the X ray in front of my face. I saw what appeared to be a normal head and a thick but normal neck. The web of wires that Cloward had woven through my spinal column was gone, vanished. The whalebone was gone, too, apparently dissolved or absorbed by my body. The only evidence I saw that Cloward had been there at all was the fused area where the vertebrae came together. I squinted at the X ray but could find only two tiny wires remaining, knotted into little bow ties.

Gayle wanted to know what I was eating. I was a little embarrassed to tell her. Before the crash I was mostly a vegetarian, but I ate balanced, healthy meals because I was so active. These days I didn't have the same desire to eat, nor the feeling of stoking a powerful engine. Now I ate to stay alive, mostly vegetables and usually only one meal a day.

"I'm going to put you on a diet heavy with complex carbohydrates," Gayle said. "I hope you like pasta. You're gonna eat protein, too. I don't care if you don't eat meat, but you're gonna get protein. We're going to build muscles, not just work them."

Gayle began to educate me on the chemical composition of the cells and atoms of the body, teaching me how to supply building blocks for my muscles. She was full of good practical knowledge and already had a supplement line of her own. I always prided myself on being aware of the ingredients necessary for optimal health, but it wasn't until I dusted off my old chemistry books that I realized how much I didn't know.

The eating process is how we supply the body with the nutrients that are distributed throughout the system. We are laboratories of chemical compositions, and the whole mix is influenced by thought. Complex chemical processes are going on all the time, and there is nothing—not even a nearly fatal car accident—that can stop this life force.

Gayle put me on a tough physical program for the 1990s beginning with long electrical stimulations of entire sections of my body, muscle by muscle. I turned up the juice, and each muscle pulsed . . . pulsed . . . pulsed. Afterward, I felt as if I had spent hours lifting weights. I improved my diet as she directed and found I had more energy. She encouraged me to keep studying and to continue my spiritual quest, wherever it might lead.

The physical results were astounding: I was coming back. It didn't happen in bits and pieces the way I had expected, but all at once and all together. Instead of an arm coming back first and then a leg, there was a general humming and glowing as my entire body started to wake up.

I had no doubt I was improving, but to be able to measure the progress, Gayle connected me again to a biofeedback machine. The first time I had tried one at the Bressler Center, I had managed to focus on a few muscles and get a couple of them to flick the dial. This time, Gayle placed the probe on specific muscles and asked me to squeeze. I concentrated and focused to isolate the thick fibers. Then I ran the light into the red, the highest possible score. I could do it several times, tighten and relax, until the muscle was exhausted and we moved on to another area. Every single major muscle group registered movement: my arms, my legs, my back and shoulders.

Everything was alive again. I couldn't yet put all the pieces together and they weren't strong enough to support me walking, but I was supercharged and pumped full of inspiration.

I always knew I was getting better, and now I was seeing the evidence. Maybe this is what's meant by the passage from Hebrews 11:1, "Faith is the substance of things hoped for, the evidence of things not seen." Maybe the "things not seen" refers to our thinking, which influences the molecular and cellular aspects of life, which in turn become the substance and matter of our existence.

I was on a roll now, and we had a game plan. After several months of consistent muscle stimulation, isolating and pulsing each muscle group in my back and shoulders, the structure of my body was changing. Not only did I look stronger, I felt stronger. I was ready to put these pumped-up muscles to work.

The next goal was to strengthen my upper body and arms enough to use a new piece of equipment. I was so excited the day my new toy arrived. This was an arm bike, technically called a UBE or upper-body ergometer, designed to strengthen the arms and torso. It was my first piece of heavy equipment without a motor, powered by my very own muscles.

Gayle set up the arm bike while I supervised, all the while squirming in my seat and ready to ride. It looks like a miniature stationary bike but with handles instead of pedals. "Just let me at that thing and watch me fly," I said.

"Hold your horses," Gayle said. "I'm going as fast as I can." Gayle got me fitted into special handles that are easy to grip and also put pressure on the hands, which is good for the bones. I braced my brow against the headrest and gathered my energy. Focus. See the motion, visualize the muscle fibers. Go deep inside the arms and hands.

I pulled back on the left arm and pushed forward on the right. The wheel began to turn. I pushed harder, and my right hand rose to the top, then fell forward to complete the first rotation.

"Yes!" we cried out together. "I did it! It's going around!"

I pushed another rotation, gritting my teeth and grinding my forehead into the headrest.

"Yes!" Another rotation fell before me. And another, and another.

"Whoa!" Gayle said. "That's enough for today. I don't want you to get sore."

"One more," I pleaded. "Let me go one more."

"All right. But just one."

The final rotation strained and burned everything I had, and I collapsed, elated but exhausted. My chest heaved, and sweat glistened on my skin. A broad smile broke across my face, and I laughed out loud with the pleasure of motion. My entire body was on fire, and it was delicious.

"We want to work up to it slowly, until your muscles get used to the movement," Gayle said.

"Okay, okay," I said, catching my breath. "This is the greatest."

The arm bike was another breakthrough because I was beginning to run on my own steam. For more than ten years I had been feeding my internal computer with images of movement, and now the messages were coming through. I smiled to myself and thought, "You can't stop the life force." Like any kid with a new bike, I couldn't wait for the next day to take the training wheels off and really put myself through the paces.

In a couple of months, I had built up to pedaling several miles a day with my arms. I used it not only for strength but also for a cardiovascular workout, easily doubling my heart rate and bringing it back down in one minute. The increased oxygen charged my cells and left me feeling absolutely invigorated. I was a lean, mean fighting machine; a born-again exercise junkie.

Seizing on progress that seemed to accelerate the harder I pushed, I designed a program that would have killed a horse. My day began with the electrical pulses over every inch of my body: hamstrings, quadriceps, lats and obliques, stomach and back, spinal erectors and traps. I visualized the working of each muscle as it contracted. Thinking into each fiber, I felt the muscles tightening, relaxing, building and growing. After the passive stimulation, I rode the motorized bike to shake out the tightened muscles. Then I rode the arm bike for upper-body strengthening, followed by a fast five miles for the cardiovascular workout. As I breathed, I focused on the cells being oxygenated and sending electrical charges up and down the spine.

I finished each session on the standing frame to pull everything together, to coordinate my upper body with the lower and to impact the entire skeletal structure. With my legs strapped in, I leaned forward and back, doing bend-overs and back bends. I was working against gravity and also getting sea legs for the day when I would be standing without the frame. This was much different from the standing I had done at first. Early on, I was just going through the motions to keep my bones stimulated and hoping to provide patterning to jog the muscle memory. Now I could feel the muscles voluntarily pushing me up and letting me down.

After less than a year of this intensive new program and working with Gayle, my body responded dramatically. My newly strengthened torso muscles pulled my twisted rib cage back over and above the center of my hips. I was straight again, and my spine no longer had an _S_ curve. My upper body grew so powerful that no one could push me over. By the mid-1990s I could move every part of my body, although I still couldn't walk.

When I told Ross how much I loved Gayle and all the great things we were doing, he asked me if I had tried a remarkable machine that taps into the electromagnetics of the body. The device, invented in 1978 by a Los Angeles biochemist, uses a computer to locate and repair damaged cell tissue. A Y-shaped prong tipped with little metal balls is rubbed on the damaged area, and the computer determines where the body's electrical charge is impaired. Microprocessors detect low conductivity and automatically send in a compensating electrical charge to reestablish normal conditions.

Ross got me some literature about the machines, and I learned that San Francisco 49ers quarterback Joe Montana and Pittsburgh Steeler Terry Bradshaw had used them for elbow injuries. The Professional Golf Association had them. When runner Joan Benoit had arthroscopic surgery on her knee and then pulled a hamstring, she used one of the machines for nine hours daily. Seventeen days after surgery she won the first women's Olympic marathon trial. The machines were being used for everything from migraines to muscle strains and fractures.

As I read more, something clicked in my memory. I went back and reread the technical literature. The manual explained, "After the machines take the readings, they instantaneously calculate and administer a painless stimulation that recharges the bioelectric harmony."

"Wait a minute," I said to myself. "This principle sounds familiar." I realized that this is what Tom Griner had been doing all those years with his deep-tissue work: identifying damaged cells and restoring them. Here was a machine that could help; technology finally had caught up to what the wise Griner knew all along. This focused regeneration is what I was doing with my mental work, too. I didn't have fancy words to explain it, but what I was trying to do was rejuvenate the cells. Maybe we had been right all along. Thank God we hadn't given up.

Gayle supplied me with more textbooks and inspired me to become my own expert. I memorized all of the muscles and nerve routes and all the names of the bones. Once I had mastered "bonehead" physiology, I plunged deeper into molecular structure and subatomic particles, the quarks and neutrinos of quantum physics. The most fascinating thing to me was that the patterns and actions of these tiny particles are influenced by the people measuring them. The very act of observation changes the particles, so scientists must keep their distance through double-blind experiments. That's the power of thought that I had been talking about all along!

The way to harness that thought power to healing became even more clear when I investigated the phenomenon known as multiple personality disorder, or MPD. In these cases, a single person has various personalities, each with its own biochemical makeup; there is a completely different physiology demonstrated with each personality. The case histories are full of instances where one personality has an allergy and another doesn't. One woman needs glasses for her adult personalities but can see perfectly when the child "alter" is in the body.

Researchers also note that some multiples heal faster than other people. Perhaps a personality that doesn't suffer the injury lacks the cellular memory of the wound. A new "memory" or personality automatically reprograms the body into health. At the National Institute of Mental Health, Dr. Frank Putnam studied the brain-wave patterns of ten people with MPD. "They seem to vary as much from one personality to another as from one normal person to another," Putnam said. "Multiples may, in fact, be one of those experiments of nature that will tell us a whole lot more about ourselves." I, for one, am convinced that's true.

The body performs millions of functions every day without any direction from our conscious minds, which implies an underlying intelligence we are just beginning to understand and tap. We participate in the overall picture by supplying the environment in which the functions take place. This is the mind-body connection.

I loved the drawings in Gayle's anatomy books, and I marveled at how the body is infinitely complex and minutely organized. The nerve roots, plugged into the muscles, carry messages from the brain. When you see an object and want to pick it up, the message is sent down the arm to the hand. The neurons that compose the brain and central nervous system "talk" across gaps called synapses. We have billions of these cells, and the possible combinations of signals jumping across them rival the number of atoms in the universe.

In the words of Dr. Deepak Chopra, "The action taking place at the gaps in the nervous system is like that of a cosmic computer reduced to a microscopic scale. This awesome computer operates continuously, handles hundreds of programs at a time, deals in multiple billions of 'bytes' of information every second, and, most miraculous of all, knows how to run itself." If that's not an information superhighway, I don't know what is!

The truly amazing thing about my deep probes into the body is that they led me back to where I started: to the organizing force that keeps us together, the spirit. So my spiritual journey, which led to the study of biology, anatomy, and physics, had come back full circle to the spirit. That's when the fun part of the journey began.

The concept of a spiritual journey is an ancient one. The basic idea hasn't changed, and the journey hasn't gotten any easier. That's why in the Bible it's been likened to a "narrow gate, and few there be that find it." Our notions of one power can be dated from Abraham or King Amenhotep IV of Egypt, who got it from an earlier source in India; or Jesus or the great Hindu mystic Shankara. All taught the oneness of God and man, and that the world of the senses is an illusion. The premise of their teaching is that each of us is born with all the qualities of God—truth, intelligence, love, eternal life, and a oneness with the invisible universe—and this power is the reality of our being.

I believe that the gate to this knowledge is no longer so narrow. We are coming into the age of the spiritual superhighway, and instead of a relative few finding the route to expanded consciousness, many will come on-line. Everyone can become convinced of the truth that is available to all. We need not be victims of any outward circumstance. God or spirit is always with us, but if we don't practice conscious awareness, we are like our ancestors who relied on whale oil and kerosene because they were unaware of electricity. Electricity was always there, but it took one person to harness it and show the way. The same is true for spirit.

Before I start my day, before I get out of bed, I try to focus on this truth. I repeat to myself, "As the wave is one with the ocean, I am one with the power. As the sunbeam is one with the sun, I am one with the power." The spiritual network is there, but if we're not jacked into it, we aren't getting the information. Learning to access this force is our job. It's a full-time endeavor. As human beings, we are waiting to be programmed, and it's up to us to feed in the information. We all start at different places on the spiritual highway. There are plenty of instruction manuals, everything from the Bible to Tony Robbins to the Urantia book and *The Celestine Prophecy*. Find the manual that's right for you.

Press the ENTER key now.

THE BEGINNING

Just the other day, I was listening to Howard Stern's radio program, and who should I hear mentioned? Ray, my sweet Ray.

Howard had received a letter from a woman professing her undying love for Ray. As a gag, Howard had a guy imitate Ray, call the woman on the phone, and invite her on a date. The woman was a true fan, though, and she saw through the scam when "Ray" said he had been married once. The young woman said she knew for a fact that Ray had never married and that his only real romance was with "some girl who was paralyzed."

That got Howard's attention. He was shocked. "I can't believe that he went out with a paralyzed woman," he said. "No kidding. He met a girl who was a paraplegic, a quadriplegic? That doesn't make any sense. Did he meet her before or after? I told my wife if she ever becomes a quadriplegic, I'm leaving."

Howard figured that the only possible explanation was that Ray had fallen in love, and then his beautiful, lithesome girlfriend had suffered a terrible, disfiguring accident. Ray probably waited a decent interval and "dumped" the girl, Howard guessed. There were plenty of jokes about "quadriplegic sex," and everyone got to hear

Howard's vivid imagination at work. I laughed so hard I almost wet my pants.

Howard wanted to meet this mystery girl in a wheelchair. "If you're listening, darling," he said. "Call in."

I couldn't resist. Also, I felt bad that people might get the idea that Ray had "dumped" me or that he was anything less than the greatest, most lovable and loving guy around. I sent Howard a fax explaining that I had indeed met Ray after the crash and that we'd separated to pursue our separate paths: my recovery and his career. I also included a very sexy photograph of myself, which I knew Howard would enjoy.

The next day Howard was ecstatic. He told his listeners about my photograph and gushed, "Do you think she still looks like this? I don't think Ray goes out with any slouches. I would go out with this girl if she were a quad. If that's her picture, roll her in here and I'll do her. She's a knockout."

He insisted on speaking to me on the air, and his producers called me live before 8:00 A.M. in New York, which was before 5:00 A.M. here.

"Is this Heidi?"

"Yes, Howard, it's Heidi."

"So how did this happen? You can't even move your arm, and he falls in love with you? Wow!"

"There's a lot more to me than my body, Howard."

"You must have a special charm, my darling. My wife's uptight about sex, and she can move everything."

I told him about my recovery and how the power of the mind has no limits. Howard actually stopped making jokes to listen, and a sweet person briefly emerged from behind the sarcastic, biting mask he wears as a performer. Only briefly, though, and Howard caught himself before any of his listeners figured out there was a decent person lurking in there. After the show, I received hundreds of letters, all of them kind and supportive and curious about my efforts to recover. The most surprising was from a "mutual friend" of Ray's, a man whom Ray had played in a movie. The letter was signed, "Your favorite Wiseguy & Goodfella, Henry Hill."

Ray continues to be a strong influence in my life, even though I rarely see him. Recently I was contacted by Stephen Fried, a writer who was doing an article about Ray for *GQ* magazine. I told him I didn't see how I could contribute other than to say that Ray's a wonderful guy. Stephen told me that, in fact, Ray had never stopped talking about me and my recovery. Stephen was curious about me and asked a lot of questions about my program and where the process was taking me. He ended our conversation by asking if I would be interested in sharing my story with others. He said it would help a lot of people, and I promised I'd think about it.

I was hesitant. I knew that when people go public they become fair game to be molded by the perceptions of the biographers. Plus, I'd heard plenty of horror stories from friends who had gone into interviews expecting one kind of story only to see something completely different in print. I had been encouraged to write my own story by my friend Mim Eicher, herself a prolific writer, and also by Jess Stearn, but I still had serious reservations. I certainly didn't want to come off like "Poor, Pitiful but Courageous Pearl, the Wheelchair Person."

When Stephen called the next day to say *Vanity Fair* liked the idea of a story about me, I decided to take a chance. Stephen ended up writing a story that got a very strong response. I was astounded by how many people wanted more information. I thought, My God, that article went on for twelve pages. How much more can I say? The answer, I found out, was anything I was willing to share.

One of the people who saw the story was my dear friend Dick Bacalyn, who'd been an actor most of his life. He told me of someone trying to locate me and wondered if he could give out my number. When he told me the name of the person, I almost fell out of my chair.

Bill Shoemaker needed me? I laughed to myself because I had just watched the Kentucky Derby on television, and there had been a piece on Bill. It was a warm, tender tribute, but it seemed like a memorial to a dead man. At the time I thought maybe I should contact him. Now he was trying to send me a message. The great thing was that he didn't even need the phone—we already were in contact, wireless on the spiritual superhighway.

Noreen Sullivan, who works for Bill, called me and asked for help. Since he'd been hurt in a car crash in 1991, Bill hadn't moved or showed the slightest interest in getting better. He was well-off financially and had been approached by all sorts of faith healers, quacks, and therapists offering miracle cures. He hadn't even looked into any treatment or therapy—until he heard about me. Please, she said, just meet with him once.

Bill Shoemaker was my hero; he was my jockey. I used to cut school to see him race at Hollywood Park. This guy's a champion, the most successful jockey in the history of the sport, a fierce competitor. Of course I would see him!

I was so excited the day Bill came to the house for a barbecue. Alvin, Bill's driver, wheeled him out back, and we sat together, just visiting and looking out over the ocean, where sometimes you can see whales spout and dolphins break the surface. The sun was warm, and the air smelled sweetly of eucalyptus. Bill was very shy and quiet. I could see his eyes on me as we ate. I'm completely natural and comfortable with my body, and people tend to forget I'm paralyzed. Bill just watched my every move.

"I've got a present for you," I said, grinning.

"What?" he said shyly.

"This is to help your breathing. It's a harmonica I got from Mickey Raphael, who plays with Willie Nelson. Now it's time for me to pass on the torch to you." I also gave him a book by Joel Goldsmith on the very basic stuff about moods and how the mind affects healing. I got going about life not being static, and how his body really wasn't sitting there doing nothing. There was renewal and regeneration going on all the time, and he could help the process along. I couldn't tell if I was getting through to him. He's not very excitable; he just watched me.

The other guests drifted off. I looked Bill dead in the eye and said, "We are the only ones who know what I'm talking about." He nodded, and for the first time I saw that I was inside.

He spoke softly. "You're doing really good."

"You want to go in and check out what equipment I got? Let's do some stuff!" I said. "You want to try some stuff?"

He smiled and said yes.

My house is old, and the doors are small. There is nothing about it that is wheelchair-accessible. I decided long ago that it was better to spend the money on getting better than on ramps and lifts and giant spatulas to flip me over in bed. Brad and everybody got Bill and me inside.

"How long have you been sitting there?" I asked.

"Two years."

"What was your injury?"

"My neck."

"That's it?"

"Yes."

"Your neck?" I said. "I had my shoulder and my leg and the whole thing. You're healed. It's done. Let's go!"

Bill sat on the bike. The foot straps were pulled tight. We prepared to flip the switch. I remembered so well the first time I got on that thing and let it move my legs around. Watching Bill, I was bursting, so proud to be passing on a glorious feeling to another person. I was giving someone else movement, and it felt so good to me.

"Ready?" Brad said.

Bill nodded.

Brad flipped the switch, and the grinding motor began to turn. Bill's legs flipped and flopped for a minute but then quickly caught the rhythm. The guy hadn't forgotten everything he'd learned from a lifetime on horseback. He looked down, focused on his legs.

"How does that feel?" I asked.

"I can feel it," he said, smiling now. "I can feel it."

"Hey, Brad," I said. "Let's for the heck of it put the skates on, see what he can do with his arms."

Brad put the wooden table in front of Bill and strapped a roller skate on each arm. Brad gave the arms a little shove, and Bill was off to the races. Now he was really smiling.

I saw my mom outside the window. "Hey, Mom!" I shouted. "Check this out!"

"Oh my God!" she said. "He's doing it! He's moving!"

"Looks to me like everything is moving," I said. "You want to try standing?"

"Sure," he said, not really believing he could do it.

Brad had to drop the standing frame as low as it would go before strapping in Bill's hips and legs. As Brad cranked him up, Bill's body started twitching and twisting, trying to stand up by itself. There was all this strength and activity in his supposedly paralyzed body.

"Yeah!" I shouted. "Go for it! You're up. You're standing."

Bill looked at me, grinning from ear to ear, and he promised: "That's what I'm going to be doing myself one of these days— standing!"

"All this equipment is available," I said. "The most important thing to remember is that it starts in the mind."

I sent him off that day with the harmonica and a little boost. Over the next few months, I helped him find the right equipment and tried to coach him as much as I could. We are friends now and keep each other inspired, but Bill's progress is up to Bill. I'm proud to say I helped. If he's the only person in my whole life whom I help, I'll feel like I've done something.

Bill wasn't the only pleasant surprise to come out of the *Vanity Fair* story. The other was Annie Leibovitz. Naturally I was impressed when the very best was sent to photograph me. Even in Hollywood, everyone goes all atwitter when Annie comes to town. In no time she talked her way into my confidence, and before I realized it she was shooting me without makeup or my hair fixed—in my bedroom! We started in the morning with the machine giving electrical pulses to my half-dressed body, and we took it from there.

Several days of shooting later, at the end of a long session, Annie was rubbing her chin and staring at the standing frame. The next thing I knew, the frame was headed down to the beach with all of us in tow. She set up the shot by the shoreline, with the sun going down and the wind getting stronger. The air was chilly, and keeping my muscles relaxed enough to perform was one of my toughest feats. If it hadn't been for Annie, I wouldn't have thought it was possible, but I did it. In fact, I stood without any straps, with my own muscles holding me up. A great new teacher for the same old lesson: If you're afraid you can't do something, do it.

I'll always consider Annie a kindred soul, if only for the unusual bond we share: a love for white V-neck T-shirts. I wear them so regularly with jeans that people call it my uniform. Annie loved my shirts because they're broken in, so I became her official supplier.

An exhibit of Annie's photographs was being held during 1994 at the Los Angeles County Art Museum, and we were invited to the opening reception. This was a glitzy catered affair stocked with many of the noteworthy people Annie had photographed. Annie herself was a work of art that night, a glorious column of black velvet and a beautiful strand of genuine pearls, all atop her trademark boots.

My mom the fashion expert announced, "Annie, I'm so impressed. Donna Karan and pearls."

Annie jokingly snorted back, "Puleeze, Ma. Try Comme des Garçons!"

After the reception, we went back to Annie's hotel for a small dinner party in the penthouse of the famed Château Marmont. The hotel had just been restored, and it was a truly elegant affair. I enjoyed meeting Annie's parents, and after her dad warmly bundled me in conversation, I understood how Annie got to be so special. Annie kneeled down next to me in her Comme des Garçons and told me she was so proud of the exhibit, adding that the following day she was going to lecture and show slides, including six of me. "I wish you would be there," she said.

The next morning we arrived for the lecture to find lines of admirers wrapped around the museum. Annie sent someone to escort us inside and greeted us warmly. I slipped her a roll of T-shirts, tied with a red Chanel bow. She laughed and thanked me, saying that her supply was running low, and hurried backstage. When she came to the podium, to thunderous applause, she was wearing an elegant Armani suit—over one of my T-shirts.

The lecture was enlightening and featured twenty-foot high slides of her work. I didn't know what to expect and couldn't imagine why, with all the history-making images she has made, she would include me. I also was a little nervous about what the pictures might show, because I really had let down my hair and allowed her into my life.

When Annie presented the images of me working out, she told everyone how inspired she was by me. She finished her talk by telling the audience that I was there, to which the crowd broke into applause. How honored I was for such a wonderful tribute from Annie, who inspires me to do more.

My greatest inspiration continues to come from Melanie, who also is learning to take charge of her life. She recently invited me and my parents to a double celebration for her and her beau, Antonio Banderas. It was an intimate gathering at their beautiful new hacienda that began on August 9, which is Melanie's birthday, and continued past midnight into Antonio's birthday on the tenth. Brad made a beautiful turquoise-inlaid knife for Antonio, and I bought Melanie, the girl who has everything, a fryer to make tempura. Antonio is loving and compassionate, articulate and deeply spiritual. Most important to me, he makes Melanie happy. I've never seen her so radiant and relaxed.

My rekindled fame also prompted calls from television programs and talk-show hosts. I turned down most of them, but I decided to try one as a test because I thought my message might be of use to people. My first experiment was with *Entertainment Tonight*, and the response was huge and overwhelmingly positive. The show's producer told me they had never received so many calls after a program. So when I was contacted by my favorite news anchor, Tom Brokaw, I agreed to appear on his newsmagazine show, *Now*.

Tom Brokaw is one of the cutest guys I've ever seen. I know that he's perceived as very serious, but I found the opposite to be true. When Tom breezed into the house with a twinkle in his eyes, we were instantly charmed. No pomp and no circumstance; he drove himself and carried his own bags. He put us at ease right away, commenting on how much we'd done with the house on Broad Beach. He knew it quite well, he said, because when he's in town he often stays just down the beach with another of my favorites, Robert Redford.

Tom and I visited outside while producer Kelly Sutherland and the crew set up the equipment. To check the sound level, I launched into the Gettysburg Address, which I know by heart, and Tom and I discussed a mutual love of Abraham Lincoln. The first part of the interview went well because he's so easy to talk to and I'm not exactly shy. Next, for shots of me working out, Kelly wanted to shoot Tom helping me at the standing frame. I got in position, and Tom faced me holding my hands. I was leaning forward and back as I usually do, straining to grind out a good set. I could see over Tom's shoulder into a large mirror that I use to watch myself exercise. Quiet on the set. Ready, action.

"Heidi," Tom said, holding my hands in front of him. "I can see how hard you're concentrating by the focus and commitment in your eyes."

"Tom," I said, twisting and turning. "I'm actually looking at your butt!"

For a split second, Kelly and the crew held their breath. Then Tom collapsed in laughter, and we joined him.

A few weeks later, I was delighted to receive a copy of *Lincoln at Gettysburg* by Garry Wills—gracefully inscribed: "Here, the power of words to change a world—To a woman who's changing her world as well. Ever, Tom."

Sigh—what a man!

As fate would have it, when the show finally aired, Malibu was burning down around my ears. It was devastating to see my neighbors losing their homes in a firestorm that swept incredibly fast across the hills on either side of me. As sad as it was, we could see by their determination that people would rebuild and get their lives back, proving the adage, "As long as you've got your health . . ."

The losses made me think about the importance of things, that material stuff we work so hard to acquire. I was struck by the realization that in the face of disaster people come together, and those who lose material possessions are given aid immediately, whether by insurance companies or the government. The effort is speedy to make whole those who have suffered loss. Not so with a personal injury; at your weakest, you have to begin to fight harder than you ever could imagine, with the system working against you. Those items that are necessary to my daily life, the equipment and most of the therapies I've tried, are costly and are not covered by insurance. Neither private insurance nor Medicare will pay for treatments that will absolutely prevent long-term illness and hospitalization. I've had a Medicare card for fifteen years and haven't used it once because it doesn't cover anything I need. I also carry private insurance, which I've used only for dental work. Even with dental care, the underlying philosophy is misguided: Medicare won't pay for fillings, but it will pay to pull out all your teeth and install dentures.

Fortunately, except for a few routine checkups, I haven't been to the doctor since 1980. If I feel the sniffles coming on, I take a simple herbal combination of echinacea and goldenseal, or Brad's Vermont folk remedy: two teaspoons of apple cider vinegar and two teaspoons of honey in a glass of water. Sure beats an antibiotic (covered by insurance, naturally).

The bottom line is that in the case of catastrophic illness or injury, the insurance providers will stabilize the patient and then as quickly as possible relegate him to the status of "futile care" or "marginally beneficial care," which translates into a blank check for hospitalization or institutionalization but not a dime for prevention of infection and bedsores and everything else that comes with serious illness. In my case, the insurance companies were willing to pay a huge fee to put me in a convalescent facility for the rest of my life but nothing for home care. If I had lost my house instead of my spine, it would have been easier to get help.

I was concerned that the Brokaw piece wouldn't receive much attention because the big California story was the fire, but boy, was I wrong. The producer called the next day to tell me it was the highest-rated show they had done, and the phones were still ringing. Besides people who wanted more information for themselves or their loved ones, several universities wanted me to lecture or try their facilities. Since I didn't need validation or praise from the "experts," and I didn't want to be their lab rat, I declined. When you enter an academic arena, you become their "noble experiment." This was not my objective. My goal was to speak to the people in my position, and those indirectly affected, about how to recover.

The show affected me, too. Tom had included some old footage of me, and I was shocked to see myself as I had appeared shortly after the accident. I'm so focused on the present that the early images were like a forgotten dream that surfaced to remind me how devastating the experience had been. It also made me realize how far I'd come and where I would have been if I'd bought into the official prognosis.

During the show, two doctors were interviewed. The first, my beloved Dr. Ghanem, recalled how a doctor friend took one look at me and said, "Elias, if you ever find me like this, don't do anything to help me." The second, a noted expert in the field, stated patronizingly, "One of my problems with people like Heidi is that they think what worked before will work again and blah, blah, blah." He said I needed to combine my idealism with "reality and science." That's exactly what I am doing! Thank God his reality is not my reality.

The good news is that the official prognosis for spinal injury has changed: Now doctors assume that recovery is possible. No one would listen to me before, but now when a person suffers a spinal injury, the medical intervention is immediate and massive. No one these days should have to be bolted in bed for sixteen days waiting for something to happen. Steroids are used right away to promote healing and reduce inflammation, and every effort is made to prevent the buildup of scar tissue. Researchers at the University of British Columbia are making giant steps toward curing "permanent" paralysis with enzymes, which are natural substances that act as catalysts to initiate or speed up healing.

This is the new "reality and science," a reality that *must* include the spirit. Throughout history, wise people have known that our thoughts influence our reality. There could be no science for us without a fixed foundation. As long ago as 1641 René Descartes showed the possibility of positive knowledge based on self-consciousness, which he expressed in the phrase "*Cogito ergo sum*"—"I think therefore I exist."

Even the ultimate pragmatist, Charles P. Steinmetz, the renowned mathematician and former director of physical research at the General Electric Laboratories, said, "Someday people will learn that material things will not bring happiness and are of little use in making men and women creative and powerful. Then the scientists of the world will turn their laboratories to the study of God and prayer, and the spiritual forces, which as of yet, have hardly been scratched. When this day comes the world will see more advancement in one generation than it has seen in the past four."

There is a growing acceptance even among doctors that spirituality is a key ingredient in healing. A terrific example is Larry Dossey, a medical doctor who wrote a book called *Healing Words: The Power of Prayer and the Practice of Medicine*. The former chief of staff at Humana Medical City in Dallas, Dossey became so convinced by the scientific evidence linking prayer to health that he now devotes his life to working and lecturing on the subject.

On a recent *Oprah Winfrey Show*, Oprah asked Dossey, "As a doctor, were you surprised at the scientific evidence that prayer works?"

"To tell you the truth," Dr. Dossey replied, "the evidence knocked my socks off!" Dossey said that as a physician he saw too many supposedly hopeless cases that appeared to be cured by prayer. Were these just strange coincidences, or was prayer responsible? What helped convince him was a 1988 study in San Francisco of four hundred heart patients, of whom two hundred were prayed for and two hundred were not. Neither the patients nor the doctors knew who got the prayers, but after one year, the group without prayers had more deaths, and was five times more likely to require antibiotics and three times more likely to develop complications.

"It looked like the prayed-for group had been given some potent miracle drug," Dossey said. "But so far, pharmaceutical companies have not been able to put this in a tablet form and make money off of it."

Asked what he means by prayer, Dossey said: "I think everyone has to define it for themselves. For my part, it's communication with the absolute. You can put any personal spin on it that you want to, on what the 'absolute' might mean."

Oprah asked if certain prayers worked better than others.

"This is where science comes in, I think, beautifully. It shows us clearly in these experiments in the laboratory that no particular religious persuasion has a monopoly on prayer. As a matter of fact, you can take an agnostic into the lab—"

Oprah burst in: "That's why God is so cool!"

Dossey agreed, laughing heartily, and continued, ". . . take an agnostic, have them be the ones who pray in these experiments, and you tell them, 'We want you to develop an empathetic, compassionate, loving attitude for what it is you're praying for,' and the experiment works.

"If you adopt an open-ended way to pray and you don't pray for anything specific, you just say, 'May thy will be done' or 'May the best thing happen in this situation,' if that's your form of prayer, then you have to have faith that that outcome—whatever it might be—is the right thing."

The amazing thing, Dossey says, is that these results are found not only in humans, who might be expected to respond to the positive thinking involved with prayer, but even with bacteria. And not only did prayer help bacteria grow in laboratory experiments, Dossey says, but the more open, Thy-will-be-done-type prayer was two to four times more effective than specific prayers.

I'm with the bacteria on that score. I set a nebulous sort of goal: All I knew was that I wanted to walk. I wasn't going to limit the how or even the when by writing it in stone. That's what's meant by "Thy will be done": You appeal to the intelligence of the system. To use a computer analogy, you use a key to bring up the menu and access the program of choice to help you arrive at the goal.

The program of choice for me today is called PEERS, which stands for Physical and Electrical Engineering Rehabilitation Systems. I learned about PEERS from its cofounder, Dr. Paul Berns, who called me after the Brokaw show. Compared with other people in the rehab business, Dr. Berns is very supportive and positive, and after talking with him and the staff, I felt like I had found my kind of people and wanted to be their spokesperson. The first one I thought of was Bill Shoemaker, and I was so happy to have a ready-made program to send to him instead of him having to develop his own.

At PEERS, they regard paralyzed people as athletes in training. The aggressive program requires daily therapy of three to six hours over the course of two to six months. Exercises, similar to what I had developed on my own, are used to build strength and balance. Then people are fitted with the unique Reciprocating Gait System developed by Dr. Roy Douglas, who was an associate professor in the Orthopedics Department at the LSU School of Medicine. Lightweight braces are used to support the legs. Then pads are placed on the legs to administer mild electric shocks, which contract the muscles to move the legs. Controlling the shocks ambulates the legs. Gradually, the braces are shortened and the shocks are lessened until the person is walking under his own power. I'm getting deeper into the program, and I'm sure I'll be walking soon.

PEERS is for well-motivated people who want to leave their wheelchairs and rejoin the mainstream. It's worked for hundreds challenged by spinal cord injury, spina bifida, and multiple sclerosis as well as muscular dystrophy and cerebral palsy. The PEERS staff believes that anyone who is capable and willing should be able to participate, but the reality is that it's not economically feasible for many people. I'm lucky to have the option to pursue many alternative rehabilitation techniques, and the reason is simple: I pay cash.

I have enough money for my therapies because we made a fortuitous investment with the money from the lawsuit, although it didn't look like much in 1987 when we bought a shabby little beach shack on Malibu's Broad Beach. We thought a house would be a hedge against inflation, but we never dreamed it would become a glamorous beachfront studio for filmmakers and the fashion industry. Brad pulled apart the house and remodeled it in his best 1930s Bauhaus-cum–Frank Lloyd Wright tradition. He capitalized on the fantastic natural light, and now anyone who works with a lens loves to shoot there.

Oliver Stone filmed *The Doors* there, and Clint Eastwood and Carl Reiner have done scenes at the house. The TV shoots are routine: *Columbo, Melrose Place, Baywatch*. Designers, including Chanel and Donna Karan, shoot their collections there, complete with alterations people, steam-press tables, and racks of opulent fashions. The shoots are great fun as well as hard work, especially when glamour photographer Herb Ritts brings in a caterer with delectable goodies to munch on while the models are transformed from giggling and gossiping young girls to hip professionals who know the business end of a camera. My family still gets into the act, too, and photographer Mark Seliger was so impressed with Brad that he was recruited to appear in a Courtney Love rock music video, even though Brad's taste in music runs more toward classic jazz.

Several times each month, limousines, Testarossas, and Land Rovers pull into the courtyard and disgorge such high-profile folks as Elizabeth Taylor, Sharon Stone, Michelle Pfeiffer, Barbra Streisand, Angelica Huston, Kate Moss, Tom Cruise, Tina Turner, Cindy Crawford, Kim Basinger, Elle MacPherson, Claudia Schiffer, Winona Ryder, and k. d. lang, who roared up on her Harley. Everyone is safe there from the prying lenses of the paparazzi—most of the time. Once when Herb Ritts was out on the dunes shooting the beauteous Nicole Kidman, in bikini and negligee, while her little daughter played in the sand with the crew, a sneaky photog with a four-foot lens got off a couple of shots before we spotted him. Sure enough, they turned up on tabloid TV with the banner, "When Tom Cruise is away, Nicole will play."

Most people don't have beach houses to produce income, and they must rely on insurance companies or the government for medical care. They become prisoners of a health-care system that is as costly as it is inefficient. We hand over our lives to faceless corporations, lobbyists, and bureaucracies and allow them to take charge. Something's not right when we spend millions of dollars and years of tests to approve drugs that are getting good results in other countries, or when people in Washington talk about idiotic things like regulating vitamins.

Thank goodness for those hardy souls who fight the system and do what it takes to find the answers, such as the family portrayed in the movie *Lorenzo's Oil*, the true story of a boy stricken with a fatal nerve disease called ALD. Parents Augusto and Michaela Odone, played by Nick Nolte and Susan Sarandon, refused to accept the medical verdict that nothing could be done for their son, Lorenzo. They threw themselves into research and discovered that a certain kind of oil, now called Lorenzo's Oil, could arrest the symptoms. The doctors dismissed their findings as "anecdotal evidence" as opposed to real, scientific evidence, but the Odones stuck with it and so did other parents, leading to a breakthrough in the fight to cure the disease.

Jim and Nancy Abrahams waged a similar battle when their baby son, Charlie, was diagnosed with a rare form of epilepsy. Prognosis: severe retardation by age twenty. Jim, a film director and creator of such wacky comedies as *Airplane*, put his career on hold to research the disorder, and turned up a seventy-five-year-old home remedy called a ketogenic diet or "Millie's Recipe." Despite the objections of the attending physician, they put Charlie on the diet, and within three days the seizures stopped. Jim now is dedicating his time and talent to spreading the word, starting with a documentary film narrated by Meryl Streep.

I nominate all these people, along with my family, for the Anecdotal Evidence Award.

Fortunately, life-threatening challenges like these are rare, but everyone who comes into this world must contend with adversity, and that's why I wanted to share some of the things I have learned on my journey.

We're all exposed to universal concerns and fears: fear of accidents or illness, fear of aging and death, fear of want and poverty, fear we won't have satisfactory relationships, fear our careers aren't happening, fear of world terror and natural disasters. These are examples of how outside pressures dominate our lives and stress us out, always looming in the backs of our minds, even if they aren't there consciously. The fear robs us of the pleasure we could be having and is exacerbated by what we see, hear, and read in the daily bombardment of gloom-and-doom predictions.

This fear works on us by means of suggestion, much like hypnosis. When the suggestion is working on the whole society, on the collective consciousness, the effect is even more powerful. For example, every winter we see a barrage of advertisements warning that flu season is soon to arrive, and every summer we are warned about hay fever. The message is that you better prepare yourself to be sick, and the only remedy is to buy the drugs being pushed. The commercials are doubly effective because when our attention is not focused, we are extremely open to suggestion.

Personally, I tend to look favorably on the way the body handles foreign objects and illness. An elevated temperature is an indication that the immune system is fighting off infection. Sneezing and coughing ease congestion and remove irritants. Why try to suppress this? Even the loathsome D-word is helpful because it removes intestinal toxins. "Better out than in," as Mrs. S. used to say. Of course, carried to extremes any of these things can be dangerous; common sense is always the key.

In my case, I was confronted by the suggestion of total and permanent paralysis, which is what the doctors assumed for me. If I hadn't found this suggestion so absurd and rejected it absolutely and categorically, my life would have been much different. I was forced to choose between being "frozen" forever or taking charge of my organism and living in what was dismissively called "denial." Making the correct choice started me on the most important passage of my life: the study of the science of being.

I've always been fascinated by the inner workings of our physical world, the science of physics. When I was skiing, I used this interest to analyze the mechanics of the sport—the science of it—to help teach others. My injury gave me the opportunity to do firsthand research on a world-shaking science: the role of thought and spirit in healing.

I take it as a given that the building blocks of our individual universes are subject to our thoughts and respond to what we wish for, imagine, and expect. If those building blocks form our reality, then it doesn't take a huge leap in logic to assume that our individual reality is a direct product of our own programming.

In one of my physics textbooks, by Henderson and Woodhull from Columbia University, the authors state that the only evidence we have of matter is the indirect evidence of the senses, which see, hear, feel, taste, and smell. There is no proof that matter has any substantiality apart from consciousness. The authors conclude with the surprising assertion that the "physical sciences are concerned only with observed properties and behavior of the objects of human cognition, but not at all with the ultimate nature of existence."

If perception is the key to our reality, then we need to closely watch our perceptions. When our perceptions are negative and become stereotypes, then we doom ourselves to realizing them. For example, why do people always want to know someone's age? What does this have to do with anything? Dr. Deepak Chopra, who creates a wonderful blend of Indian philosophy and Western medical science, says there are three ways to measure age. The first, chronological age, is how many times the earth has gone around the sun since you were ejected from the birth canal. The second way, biological age, measures the body in cellular terms. Since human cells are totally renewed in eleven months, you have a new body every year, so quit worrying. The third and best way to measure age is psychological: How old do you feel?

We must slay this dragon of aging and death, and maybe we will reach the state that James Redfield illustrates in *The Celestine Prophecy*. He presents a fictionalized theory that accounts for the disappearance of the Mayan civilization. The process has to do with an energy that is produced by increased spiritual understanding. The raising of consciousness literally speeds up the vibrational frequency of the body's atoms so that the individual becomes light and passes from this dimension without death. The Bible refers to a similar process as transition, transformation, or translation.

This makes sense to me, and it seems to be the next logical step in our evolutionary process. Many studies of complex adaptive systems have found that information can be passed on genetically, that when a species knows something, the descendants are born with that knowledge. This conscious evolution is ever increasing to a higher state, the ultimate destination being a shifting from the physical to the mental and finally to a spiritual level of existence. All of history has prepared us to achieve this spiritual consciousness that will transform us. I sometimes feel that exhilaration of energy when meditating or when I read something profound and have a moment of deep understanding.

This exhilaration of energy is common during healing. When the healing process is allowed to happen, something forces an acceleration in the normal mechanism. Some healing appears "routine," such as with broken bones or measles, while other healing is considered extraordinary, such as with cancer, AIDS, or paralysis. Obviously the failures outnumber the healings in these tough cases, and unable to explain the anomalies, medical wisdom goes with the numbers and rejects the rare healings as "anecdotal."

I reject the numbers and go with the exceptions. I think you can ready your body for healing, and we no longer need faith to believe this because now we have science. We know that spontaneous healings occur, but we also know they don't happen to everyone. The difference is attitude. What the mind can conceive, the body can achieve. People who experience spontaneous healings talk about feeling a buzzing or intense heat, as if all the little cells were speeding up to get better. Could this be what the Bible calls the "quickening of the spirit"?

A positive perception doesn't simply mean thinking positive thoughts once in a while. Dr. Chopra says that more than any single thought, it is overall awareness that guides our lives. The reason is that the awareness generates mental impulses that in turn generate new biological information. In his book *Ageless Body, Timeless Mind*, Dr. Chopra writes, "Awareness is a two-edged sword—it can heal and destroy. What makes the difference is how your awareness becomes conditioned, or trained, into various attitudes, assumptions, beliefs, and reactions."

As you know, our minds are capable of working on many different levels at the same time. Driving home from work, for example, you're thinking about what to bring from the store, feeding the kids, what the weekend holds, and much more. All this is going on consciously, while automatically you're driving at breakneck speed and making potentially life-altering decisions.

The trick is to bring everything to a conscious level and retrain your thinking and automatic reactions. In the course of a day, there are endless ways in which our buttons can be punched, prompting us to react negatively. One of the all-time most annoying things is when someone blasts a horn at you, telling you to move it. Now, you can handle this in several different ways. You can a) make a rude gesture; b) get out of your car, grab a golf club, and smash the guy's windshield (my personal favorite); or c) spend the rest of the day grousing about the s.o.b. The answer, of course, is d) none of the above. To win this game, you have to turn the energy back on the jerk, realizing that it's his problem, thereby releasing you of any ill effects. Don't forget that a nine-iron can be "Exhibit A."

You are responsible. If you're not happy with the direction of your life, it's time to get in touch with your own internal power. You are responsible for creating your own reality, so why pick a bummer? If you want better relationships, better health, a better career, or more money, you can have them by making use of these techniques. Nothing's stopping you but you. I know there are some of you who don't want to hear it, but it's true. I know it, I know it, I know it from my own experience. When I was first injured, I couldn't believe that I was giving "consent to my condition," but I found it to be true. As soon as I began to change my perception and focus on the correct information, I immediately saw results.

I knew the result I wanted. I pulled it up on my screen, and through the worldwide web of consciousness, I got the answer. Remember, we are reprogramming our computers, retraining our thinking from years and years of unconscious conditioning. All we have to be concerned about is the now. Not tomorrow, not yesterday, but right now. This very moment is what determines your next thought. Mrs. S. gave me a tough assignment that I'll pass along. Set an alarm clock for fifteen minutes, and try to focus on one idea or thought. You quickly become aware of your random thoughts and how your mind operates. Remember, you're only as good as your last five minutes.

Don't make me say it again: It all starts inside, from the thought to the thing. Hello (tap, tap, tap), is this thing working?

I am happier now than I have ever been in my life because I have come to the understanding and realization that I am in charge of my life and everything that pertains to it. I have become aware that all my experiences are the result of my perceptions and reactions to them. Awareness is the key.

When I speak of awareness, I mean what you are conscious of, or consciousness. As the physicist Sir Arthur Eddington told *The New York Times* in 1931, "Consciousness is fundamental. It is meaningless to speak of anything except as it forms a part of the web of consciousness." Nothing could exist for us that we do not see, feel, taste, smell, and experience consciously, or hold in thought. So the way you see things, your perception, forms your interpretation of the events around you. The British astronomer Sir James Jeans pointed out that "we used to think that we were studying an objective, physical universe which existed independently of our thinking, but we now recognize that the only nature we can study consists not necessarily of what we perceive but necessarily of our own perceptions."

The force that exists around us is so powerful. It is the guiding principle and intelligence that is responsible for life, holding everything in place in the universe. Once you accept this concept, you will be able to work with it. Everything has intelligence on many different levels. Every cell is preprogrammed with intelligence, exactly like a computer. And just as a computer is only as good as the person running it, we are only as good as we want to be. We are given free will to do whatever we wish—we can run our computers the way we want to run them. The creative intelligence that runs the universe is the "manual." When you pick up this manual, you are accessing the spiritual superhighway, turning to the creative intelligence for guidance to find a solution for any problem.

Accessing this force doesn't mean going up on some mountaintop to meditate and eat granola. On the contrary, it means deliberately plugging in to the web of consciousness that links us all across time and space. There are no days or years, there are no towns or nations in this web. Your personal problems, doubts, and fears take on a whole new light when seen from the vantage point of this web of consciousness. They don't go away, but they assume their proper perspective because you have changed your perception.

You were born with everything you need to connect with this force. Your hand is on the switch. The rest is up to you.

ACKNOWLEDGMENTS

Heartfelt thanks are due to:

Harry Evans, who understands that life is about overcoming.

Peter Copeland, who never tried to reinvent me and actually insisted that I have my own voice; and Maru, Isabella, and Lucas, who were so generous with his time.

Those fabulous and meticulous editors Enrica Gadler and Ann Godoff, who humored this novice and included me in all phases of the process, even the design and marketing; Carol Schneider, the best there is; and the rest of the Random House team, truly a class act.

The legendary agent Frank Cooper, who has guided countless neophytes, from young Frank Sinatra to "Dirty Harry"; and Sylvia, who taught him everything he knows.

Melanie and Antonio, who give new meaning to the phrase "Tienen todo."

Betty Powelson-Howard, who led the way with her own "soul purpose."

"Bunny Man" Bob Hoyt, who brought Newport to Malibu and made "Little Christy Happy at Last."

Stanley and Evi, who nagged me to write about my journey, then shamelessly used Dalí's *The Writer* as an incentive.

Uncle Bob, Uncle Ervin, Uncle Bert, Mary, and Bea, who kept the ship afloat.

Uncle Horton, who can show us all a trick or two.

Brockman, who was always there even when he thought he wasn't.

Tina Brown, for the *Vanity Fair* piece and for providing an outstanding prototype for the twenty-first-century woman.

Judy and Michael, who gave me space to achieve my dream.

Bruce Abbott, who is proof that Prince Charming lives; and Kathleen . . . my spiritual partner.

Neil, aka Doogie, who taught me magic.

Mim, Victor, and Tom . . . Sarah Lawrence meets Uni. of Miami meets Taos.

Phil Gerard, Bruce Reid, and Art Metrano, who get the medal for survival against all odds.

Ricky G., who was my first . . . and to Mimi, Pam, Stewart, Betsy, Randie, Kevin, and Margaret, who proved the concept that lifelong friends do exist.

Master Zhou, Bernadette, and Stuart, who helped me to find my *chi*.

Dean Ferrandini, who scaled walls and rode his dirt bike through my house; and Keefe, who spoke my language as well as Costa Gavras's.

Jeff and Carol . . . surf on.

Clive Pinder and Audree Verduin, the definitive creative couple of the nineties.

Opal, Barbara, Betty Bonnie Judy Johnson, and Mort Lindsay, my Malibu Christian Science pals, for their support.

Double H . . . Double A all the way. Airborne!

David Marconi, J.P., Dickie B., Maj., Charlie Guardino, Jana and Neil Bagg, Kathy Green, Cindy Sonjé, Renée, Lennie, Bernie, Elyssa Davalos, Mickey Callan, Z-Man, and Buddy Joe . . . you always made it fun. I love you guys.

Reina, Anna, Emma, Lucrecia, and Jean, for being the hippest staff on Planet Malibu.

CyCy and Robbie Lambert and all who have gone through the PEERS Program, who know that "quad" is a four-letter word.

Michael O'Keefe, whose poetry makes Bonnie's heart sing.

And to the kids . . . Allison, Tiffany, Chelsea, Max, Zack, Elias, Alexa, Drew, Ashley, Alexander, Dakota, Jesse, and Tyler, who made me know the best is yet to come!

And thanks to Bill Hicks, who said it better than anyone:

All matter is energy condensed to a slow vibration
We are all one consciousness experiencing itself subjectively
There is no such thing as death
Life is a dream and we are only the imagination of ourselves.
It's just a ride!

ABOUT THE AUTHORS

HEIDI VON BELTZ lives in Malibu, California.

PETER COPELAND has written two previous books, both of which were chosen as Notable Books of the Year by *The New York Times Book Review*. *She Went to War: The Rhonda Cornum Story* (Presidio, 1992) is the true story of an army doctor who was shot down and captured by the Iraqis during the Gulf War. *The Science of Desire: The Search for the Gay Gene and the Biology of Behavior* (Simon & Schuster, 1994) was written with the molecular geneticist Dean Hamer. As a correspondent for Scripps Howard News Service, Copeland has covered Latin America, the Pentagon, and the Departments of State and Justice. He has reported from dozens of countries and covered wars in Central America and the Persian Gulf, the U.S. invasion of Panama, and the military intervention in Somalia. He lives in Washington, D.C., with his wife, the artist and dancer Maru Montero, and their two children, Isabella, three, and Lucas, nine months.